McGraw-Hill's
Top 50
Math Skills for
GED Success

Master the Essential Skills
Required on the GED Math Test

ROBERT MITCHELL AND DOLORES EMERY

McGraw·Hill

New York   Chicago   San Francisco   Lisbon   London   Madrid   Mexico City
Milan   New Delhi   San Juan   Seoul   Singapore   Sydney   Toronto

1 2 3 4 5 6 7 8 9 0   QPD/QPD   3 2 1 0 9 8 7 6 5 4

ISBN 0-07-144522-6

Interior design by Linda Chandler
Technical art by Tim Piotrowski

McGraw-Hill books are available at special quantity discounts to use as premiums and sales promotions, or for use in corporate training programs. For more information, please write to the Director of Special Sales, Professional Publishing, McGraw-Hill, Two Penn Plaza, New York, NY 10121-2298. Or contact your local bookstore.

This book is printed on acid-free paper.

Table of Contents

Top 50 Skills

Number, Number Sense, and Operations

Measurement and Geometry

Data, Statistics, and Probability

Algebra, Functions, and Patterns

About the GED Math Test

Test Overview

The GED Math Test contains 50 questions and is divided into two parts:

Part 1 45 minutes: 25 questions for which you **may** use a calculator
Part 2 45 minutes: 25 questions for which you **may not** use a calculator

On Part 1 of the test, students are allowed to use only the Casio *fx-260SOLAR* calculator. A discussion of the use of the Casio calculator is provided on pages vii–ix.

Test Content

Questions on the GED are taken from four major content areas:
- Number, Number Sense, and Operations
- Measurement and Geometry
- Data, Statistics, and Probability
- Algebra, Functions, and Patterns

The 50 questions on the test are of three types:
- Conceptual: 15 questions identifying and applying math definitions, facts, and principles
- Procedural: 10 questions using mathematical procedures
- Application: 25 questions applying math in real-life situations

About *Top 50 Math Skills for GED Success*

Top 50 Math Skills for GED Success is a short, test-directed course in GED math preparation. The 50 skills chosen are those most representative of the type and difficulty level of skills tested on the GED. Each of the 50 questions in the Pretest addresses a particular skill. Guided instruction and follow-up questions for each of the 50 skills are provided in the Top 50 Skills instruction section.

Top 50 Math Skills for GED Success **is divided into 4 main sections.**
- Pretest: 50 questions to check your understanding of 50 core GED math skills. These questions will help identify your strengths and weaknesses in math concepts, procedures, and applications across the four content areas chosen by the GED Testing Service.
- Top 50 Skills: Instruction and follow-up practice on the 50 GED math skills addressed in the overview. The follow-up questions show several ways the skill may be asked on the GED test. These questions also are chosen to increase your understanding, extend your knowledge, and make connections with related skills. Each instructional lesson is two pages and is designed to be completed in one study period.
- Posttest: A two-part model GED test to show your readiness to take the GED. Use the test for practice in test taking under test-like conditions.
- Supporting materials for test success: a thorough computation review, an annotated glossary of important math terms, and an extensive answer key with complete solutions.

Students who need a quick review of basic computation skills should begin this book by reviewing the Computation Review, pages 132–148.

How to Use This Book

To the Instructor

Top 50 Math Skills for GED Success is designed to be instructor friendly, organizing for you in 50 lessons a core of math skills identified by the GED Testing Service. Each two-page lesson addresses a single skill and provides follow-up practice. One or more lessons can be completed in a single study period. Each lesson references related skills for both the less and more advanced student.

Top 50 Math Skills for GED Success can be used in a variety of ways:
- student-directed self-study
- one-on-one instruction
- group instruction

To the Student

- Take the Pretest to determine your strengths and weaknesses. The skill numbers are the same as the Pretest numbers. For example, if you have difficulty with Pretest question 27, turn to Skill 27 for a review of how to solve the problem.
- Review the two-page lesson on each skill with which you had difficulty. Answer all follow-up questions. Refer to the computation review and glossary at the back of the book as needed.
- Work through all follow-up questions for those Pretest questions you answered correctly. This will help you become familiar with alternative ways a similar skill may be tested on the GED Math Test.
- Make sure you understand all topics in the Computation Review and Glossary at the back of the book.
- Take the Posttest. For best results, take the test under timed, testlike conditions.

Sample Lesson

Skill Name

Question and Correct Answer

Supporting Skill Area

Guided Instruction

Calculator Solution

Related Skills

Calculator icon indicates use of calculator for this question.

Follow-up questions in the 3 question types:

procedure, concept, application
- reinforces and develops skill
- gives more practice on the kinds of questions that may appear on the GED Math Test.

Reference to Computation Review

Top 50 Math Skills Checklist

Listed below are the 50 Math Skills presented in this book. These skills are represented by the types of questions most likely to appear on the GED Math Test. Check off each skill after you have mastered it in the circle provided.

Number, Number Sense, and Operations

- ○ Skill 1   Make an Appropriate Estimate
- ○ Skill 2   Write Decimals in Order
- ○ Skill 3   Solve Decimal Word Problems (+, −)
- ○ Skill 4   Understand Order of Operations
- ○ Skill 5   Solve Decimal Word Problems (×, ÷)
- ○ Skill 6   Write Fractions in Order
- ○ Skill 7   Solve Problems with Fractions (+, −)
- ○ Skill 8   Solve Problems with Fractions (×, ÷)
- ○ Skill 9   Relate Fractions, Decimals, and Percents
- ○ Skill 10   Understand Discount and Sales Tax
- ○ Skill 11   Understand Ratio
- ○ Skill 12   Work with Proportions
- ○ Skill 13   Calculate Percent Change

Measurement and Geometry

- ○ Skill 14   Understand Units
- ○ Skill 15   Read and Interpret a Scale
- ○ Skill 16   Change Units of Measure
- ○ Skill 17   Understand Rate
- ○ Skill 18   Calculate Simple Interest
- ○ Skill 19   Understand Similar Figures
- ○ Skill 20   Work with a Scale Drawing
- ○ Skill 21   Solve a Problem Involving Measurement
- ○ Skill 22   Understand the Measure of Angles
- ○ Skill 23   Understand Angle Relationships in a Triangle
- ○ Skill 24   Solve for Distance Using the Pythagorean Relationship
- ○ Skill 25   Solve for Area
- ○ Skill 26   Solve for Volume
- ○ Skill 27   Work with a Coordinate Plane
- ○ Skill 28   Understand Slope of a Graphed Line

Data, Statistics, and Probability

- ○ Skill 29   Apply Measures of Central Tendency
- ○ Skill 30   Find a Missing Term When the Mean is Known
- ○ Skill 31   Interpolate and Extrapolate
- ○ Skill 32   Understand Line of Best Fit
- ○ Skill 33   Interpret a Single Line Graph
- ○ Skill 34   Understand a Multiple Line Graph
- ○ Skill 35   Interpret a Bar Graph
- ○ Skill 36   Understand a Circle Graph
- ○ Skill 37   Interpret a Circle Graph
- ○ Skill 38   Use Two Sources of Data
- ○ Skill 39   Understand Probability
- ○ Skill 40   Base Probability on Data

Algebra, Functions, and Patterns

- ○ Skill 41   Evaluate a Formula
- ○ Skill 42   Write an Algebraic Expression
- ○ Skill 43   Write an Equation to Solve a Word Problem
- ○ Skill 44   Work with an Algebraic Expression
- ○ Skill 45   Extend a Numerical Pattern
- ○ Skill 46   Identify Values Represented by an Equation
- ○ Skill 47   Identify an Equation from a Table of Values
- ○ Skill 48   Identify Points on a Linear Equation
- ○ Skill 49   Write an Equivalent Equation
- ○ Skill 50   Predict Change in Values in a Functional Relationship

Calculator Use on the GED

Part 1 of the GED Math Test contains 25 questions for which you may use a calculator. On this part of the test, you are allowed to use only the Casio *fx-260SOLAR* calculator. **No other calculator is allowed.**

> A Casio *fx-260SOLAR* calculator will be provided to each student at the GED testing center for use on the calculator part of the GED Math Test.

Important Points to Remember

- You are **not required** to use a calculator on the calculator part of the test.
- Some questions in Part 1 can be solved just as easily **without using a calculator.**
- Use a calculator only for questions, or parts of questions, for which you find that the calculator is helpful.
- An important skill is to be able to recognize questions for which a calculator is helpful and questions for which it is not.

Top 50 Math Skills for the GED

Top 50 Math Skills for the GED will help you become familiar with the Casio calculator and its use on Part 1 of the GED Math Test.*

Pretest (pages 1–12)
In the Pretest, 50 core math skills are organized in the four content areas identified by the GED Testing Service. Calculator problems are randomly interspersed among the 50 questions.

A calculator icon [icon] identifies each question for which you may find a calculator helpful.

Top 50 Skills (pages 14–113)
This instructional review of the 50 GED core skills provides example calculator solutions for problems for which a calculator may be helpful. Follow-up practice is provided for each skill.

Posttest (pages 116–129)
The Posttest is a full-length, two-part test designed as a model GED Test.

- Part 1 contains 25 questions. You **may** use a calculator on Part 1 of the test.
- Part 2 also contains 25 questions. You **may not** use a calculator on Part 2 of the test.

* For additional practice with the Casio calculator, see Contemporary's *Calculator Essentials for the GED* or Contemporary's *Calculator Power for the GED*.

The Casio *fx-260SOLAR* Calculator

The Casio *fx-260SOLAR* calculator is shown on the left. The calculator on the right shows only those keys you may find helpful for questions on Part 1 of the GED Math Test.

Casio *fx-260SOLAR*

Complete Keyboard

Keys Useful for GED Test

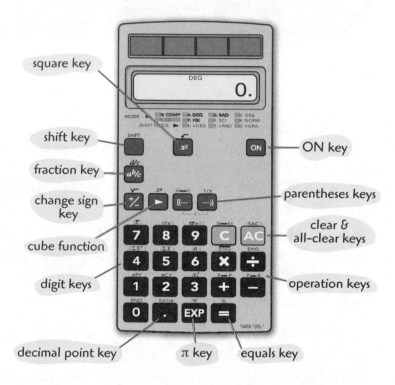

Basic Computation Keys

change sign key `+/−` is used to enter a negative number

fraction key `a b/c` is used to enter a fraction

square key `x²` is used to square a number

parentheses keys `[(− −)]` are used for doing calculations involving parentheses—questions for which order of operations is very important

shift key `SHIFT` is used to access the functions listed above other keys

Correction Keys

ON key `ON` is used to clear the display and to clear all parts of a calculation

Press `ON` each time you . . .

- begin a new question
- make an error entering a number or an operation

Functions

Like many other calculators, the Casio *fx-260SOLAR* has additional functions besides those indicated on the keys. These functions are indicated by symbols placed above individual keys.

To access a function above a key, do the following:

- Press the SHIFT key and then release it.
- Press the key below the identified function.

Calculator Examples

Whole Numbers

Example   Find the value: $19 \times (37 - 29)^2$

 ON 1 9 × [(- 3 7 − 2 9 -)] x² =   1216.

              Parentheses   Square Answer = **1,216**
              $37 - 29 = $ **8** $8^2 = $ **64** 19×64

Fractions

Example   Subtract: $3\frac{1}{8} - \frac{15}{16}$

 ON 3 a b/c 1 a b/c 8 − 1 5 a b/c 1 6 =   2⌐3⌐16.

          Mixed Number   Fraction   Answer = $2\frac{3}{16}$
             $3\frac{1}{8}$ $\frac{15}{16}$

Decimals

Example   Multiply: 13.875×4.5

 ON 1 3 . 8 7 5 × 4 . 5 =   62.4375

        1st Decimal   2nd Decimal   Answer ≈ **62.4**
         13.875   4.5

Percents

Example   What is 7.5% of $250?

 ON 2 5 0 × 7 . 5 SHIFT =   18.75

             7.5%   Answer = **$18.75**

Formulas Involving π

Example   What is the value of $2 \times \pi \times r$ when $r = 5.4$?

 ON 2 × SHIFT EXP × 5 . 4 =   33.92920066

           π 5.4   Answer ≈ **33.9**

The Importance of Estimating

Questions on the GED Math Test vary in difficulty. Forty of the 50 questions are multiple choice. For each of these questions, the correct answer appears in a list of five choices. Your task is to choose the correct answer. Estimation, an important math tool for all problems, is especially useful on many multiple-choice questions. By estimating, you can save valuable time for more difficult problems.

Here's an example:

> Chicken salad is on sale at Kelli's Deli for $1.94 per pound. How much does 4.1 pounds cost?
>
> **(1)** $5.27   **(2)** $6.03   **(3)** $7.95   **(4)** $9.74   **(5)** $11.56

A reasonable estimate can be made by rounding:

- Round $1.94 to $2.
- Round 4.1 pounds to 4 pounds.
- Multiply the rounded numbers.

Estimate: $2 × 4 = **$8**

The estimate enables you to correctly choose (3) $7.95 as the answer.

> For some questions on the GED Math Test, estimation alone will enable you to choose the correct answer.

On some questions, though, answer choices are so close in value that estimation does not help.

Here's an example where estimation is not helpful:

> Shrimp salad is on sale at Kelli's Deli for $2.19 per pound. How much does 2.8 pounds cost?
>
> **(1)** $4.99   **(2)** $5.89   **(3)** $5.94   **(4)** $5.98   **(5)** $6.13

Estimate: $2 × 3 = **$6**

The correct answer, (5) $6.13, cannot be found by estimation. Too many of the answer choices round to the estimated answer.

> Knowing when estimation is <u>not</u> helpful is itself an important math skill.

Estimation and Calculator Use

On Part 1 of the GED Math Test, you are allowed to use a calculator. When you choose to use it, remember this: **A calculator is only as accurate as you are.** Because calculator errors often occur, always ask, "Does the calculator answer make sense?"

You can often use estimation to check a calculator answer. Only if your estimate and the calculator answer are close in value can you be confident that you correctly answered a question.

> Whenever possible, an estimate should be used to check a calculator answer.

Estimating by Using Rounded Numbers

Guidelines for Estimating

Below are some general guidelines for estimating by using rounded numbers.

Whole Numbers

Replace each whole number with a rounded number that contains one or more ending zeros.

Example 1   Divide: $288 \div 48$

Estimate: $300 \div 50 = 6$ Round 288 to the nearest hundred; round 48 to the nearest ten.

[Exact = 6]

Mixed Numbers

Replace each mixed number with the nearest whole number.

The fraction $\frac{1}{2}$ is rounded to the nearest greater whole number.

Example 2   Add: $5\frac{2}{3} + 3\frac{1}{16} + 2\frac{1}{2}$

Estimate: $6 + 3 + 3 = 12$ Round $5\frac{2}{3}$ to 6; $3\frac{1}{16}$ to 3; $2\frac{1}{2}$ to 3.

[Exact = $11\frac{11}{48}$]

Decimals

Replace each decimal with the nearest whole number or nearest 10.

Example 3   Multiply: $\$12.15 \times 6.2$

Estimate: $\$12 \times 6 = \$72$ Round $12.15 to $12, the nearest dollar; round 6.2 to 6.

[Exact = $75.33]

Example 4   Subtract: $56.2 - 38.75$

Estimate: $60 - 40 = 20$ Round 56.2 to 60; round 38.75 to 40.

[Exact = 17.45]

Formulas Involving π

Round whole numbers, mixed numbers, and decimals as discussed above. Round π to 3.

Example 5   Multiply: $\pi \times 6\frac{7}{8} \times 6\frac{7}{8}$

Estimate: $3 \times 7 \times 7 \approx 147$ Round π to 3; round each $6\frac{7}{8}$ to 7.

[Exact ≈ 148.49]

Alternative Answer Formats

On the GED Math Test, 40 questions are multiple choice. The remaining 10 are *alternative answer format* questions. You answer 8 questions by recording answers on a standard grid; you answer 2 questions by recording answers on a coordinate plane grid.

Standard Grid

The standard grid is used to record a numerical answer. You can write your answer in the top row as a guide to filling in the bubbles in the rows below. You are not required to fill in the top row, but the bubbles must be filled in for an answer to be correct.

- Answers can be left justified or right justified. 1-digit or 3-digit answers can also be center justified.
- Fraction or decimal answers can be recorded.
- Mixed numbers cannot be recorded. Thus, no answer on the test in which the standard grid is used will be a mixed number.
- Negative numbers cannot be recorded. Thus, the standard grid will not be used for a negative-number answer.
- Do not fill in unnecessary bubbles or write in unused columns.

Standard Grid

← fraction bar
← decimal point

Example

An answer of $125 can be recorded on the standard grid in three ways:

Left Justified   Center Justified   Right Justified

You are not required to write an answer in the top row. However, seeing the answer serves as a guide for filling in the bubbles below.

Remember: Each digit of an answer must be recorded by filling in a single bubble in the column for that digit. Do **not** fill in more than one bubble in any column.

Example

Because $0.75 = \frac{3}{4}$, an answer of 0.75 can be recorded as the fraction $\frac{3}{4}$. Also, an answer of $\frac{3}{4}$ can be recorded as the decimal 0.75. Here are five ways to correctly record either answer.

As a Decimal   **As a Fraction**

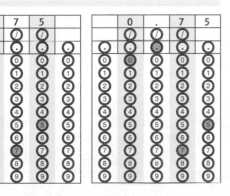
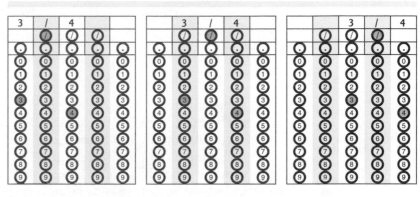

When recording a decimal less than 1, the leading zero need **not** be filled in. Also, you must reduce a fraction to lowest terms before recording it as an answer.

Coordinate Plane Grid

A coordinate plane grid is a grid on which an answer is recorded by filling in one circle that represents a point. Negative numbers are possible, but fractions, mixed numbers, and decimals are not.

Example   Three corners of a square are given by the points ($^-$4,3), (2,3), and (2,$^-$5). What is the fourth corner of the square?

Mark your answer on the coordinate plane grid.

As shown here, you may want to lightly shade the points ($^-$4,3), (2,3), and (2,$^-$5) to help you find the answer. After you fill in the answer ($^-$4,$^-$5), erase these other shaded points.

The answer, ($^-$4,$^-$5), is recorded as **one** filled-in circle (point) on the coordinate plane grid.

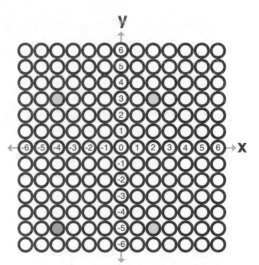

Remember, completely erase all marks except the answer.

About the Pretest

The Pretest is an overview of the 50 skills you are most likely to see addressed on the GED Math Test. The 50 carefully chosen questions are organized by the four content areas tested by the GED Testing Service:

- Number, Number Sense, and Operations
- Measurement and Geometry
- Data, Statistics, and Probability
- Algebra, Functions, and Patterns

The Pretest will help you identify skills in each content area for which you need more work. The Pretest, unlike the actual GED Test, is not a timed test and is not divided into a calculator part and a non-calculator part. In fact, you are encouraged to take as much time as you need to complete each problem and to use a calculator for any problem for which you find it helpful. Problems for which a calculator may be particularly helpful are indicated by a calculator icon ▦. A page of useful formulas is provided for your use on page 115. Included are perimeter, area, volume, and other formulas you will want to become familiar with for GED math study. Refer to the formula page as needed on the Pretest and throughout this book.

Answer every question on the Pretest. If you are not sure of an answer, put a question mark by the problem number to note that you are making a guess. Then make your best guess. On the actual GED Test, an unanswered question is counted as incorrect. So, making a good guess is an important skill to practice. When you are finished, proceed to the instruction section, pages 14–113, for correct answers, detailed instruction, and follow-up practice on every skill.

After working through the instruction section, take the Posttest (GED practice test) on pages 116–129. Your success on the Posttest will indicate your readiness to take the actual GED Math Test.

Pretest

Overview of Core GED Math Skills

This Pretest consists of 50 carefully chosen questions that address the skills most likely to be covered on the GED Math Test. Answer each question to the best of your ability. When you are finished, proceed to pages 14–113 for detailed instruction and follow-up practice.

Number, Number Sense, and Operations

1. Carin is planning to buy a used car that is on sale for $16,249. The dealer is offering 0% financing for a 4-year loan. The salesperson tells Carin that, with a down payment of $1,000, her loan payment will be *about $194 per month for 4 years.* Use your own estimate to decide which phrase best describes the salesperson's estimate of Carin's monthly payment.

   ① very close to the actual value
   ② unreasonably high
   ③ unreasonably low
   ④ exactly correct
   ⑤ Not enough information is given.

2. National Pipe Company stocks copper pipes in the lengths shown in the table. What is the part number of the longest pipe?

   Copper Pipe

Part Number	Length (m)
123C	6.09
013C	6.78
489C	7.09
246C	6.7
182C	7.3
047C	7.28
847C	7.076
237C	5.99

   ① 237C
   ② 182C
   ③ 047C
   ④ 489C
   ⑤ 847C

3. When Trent had the flu, his temperature increased over its normal value of 98.4°F. His temperature rose to the value shown on the thermometer.

   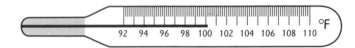

   By how much did Trent's temperature increase over its normal value?

   ① 2.7°F
   ② 2.3°F
   ③ 2.1°F
   ④ 2.0°F
   ⑤ 1.8°F

4. Find the value of the following expression:
   $12 + 5(8 - 6)^3 \div \sqrt{4}$

   ① 8
   ② 22
   ③ 27
   ④ 32
   ⑤ 262

5. On Saturday Lavonne worked 10 hours at Gatsby Department Store. She earns $9.50 per hour for the first 8 hours each day. Lavonne earns time and a half ($9.50 × 1.5) for any hours beyond 8 hours. How much did Lavonne earn on Saturday?

   ① $84.50
   ② $104.50
   ③ $142.50
   ④ $165.00
   ⑤ $180.00

6. Order the following fractions from least to greatest.

$$\frac{5}{6}, \frac{1}{3}, \frac{3}{4}, \frac{1}{2}$$

① $\frac{1}{3}, \frac{1}{2}, \frac{3}{4}, \frac{5}{6}$

② $\frac{1}{2}, \frac{1}{3}, \frac{3}{4}, \frac{5}{6}$

③ $\frac{5}{6}, \frac{3}{4}, \frac{1}{2}, \frac{1}{3}$

④ $\frac{1}{3}, \frac{3}{4}, \frac{1}{2}, \frac{5}{6}$

⑤ $\frac{1}{2}, \frac{3}{4}, \frac{5}{6}, \frac{1}{3}$

7. In June three friends wanted to see how far each could run in 20 minutes. They ran on a track and recorded their distances. After 6 months of training, the friends ran again. Their results are shown in the table.

20-Minute Run Distances in Miles

Name	June	December
Luis	$2\frac{1}{2}$	$2\frac{7}{8}$
Calvin	$2\frac{7}{8}$	$3\frac{1}{4}$
Jake	$1\frac{7}{8}$	$2\frac{3}{8}$

What fraction of a mile farther did Calvin run in December than he ran in June?

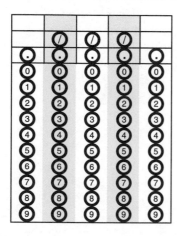

Mark your answer in the circles in the grid.

8. Judy is preparing a Thanksgiving turkey. Her gourmet cookbook gives the following roasting instruction.

Roasting Times (325°F) for Birds 10 to 20 Pounds
- *For the first 10 pounds, bake 15 minutes per pound.*
- *For any additional pound over 10 pounds, bake only 8 minutes per pound.*

According to Judy's cookbook, for how many hours should Judy roast a $17\frac{1}{2}$ pound turkey?

① 5

② $4\frac{3}{4}$

③ $4\frac{1}{4}$

④ 4

⑤ $3\frac{1}{2}$

9. 🖩 Best Furniture Company makes tabletops using 16 tiles as shown. What part of each tabletop is made from white tiles? Write your answer as a fraction, a decimal, and a percent.

① $\frac{1}{2}$, 0.5, 50%

② $\frac{1}{2}$, 0.25, 25%

③ $\frac{1}{4}$, 0.25, 25%

④ $\frac{1}{4}$, 0.4, 40%

⑤ $\frac{1}{4}$, 0.25, 40%

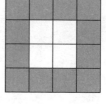

10. 🖩 A set of three music CDs regularly sells for $44.00. The set is on sale at a 25% discount. If the sales tax is 5%, what is the total cost of the CDs?

① $46.20
② $42.60
③ $39.40
④ $34.65
⑤ $30.80

11. Amy Lee made a table of her family's expenses. What is the ratio of the amount spent on February utilities to the amount spent on January utilities?

Lee Family Take-Home Pay Allocation

Expense	January	February
Food	$240	$220
Rent	$720	$720
Medical	$120	$160
Clothing	$60	$180
Utilities	$210	$140
Entertainment	$80	$50
Car Expenses	$260	$240
Child Care	$180	$180
Savings	$200	$200
Other	$330	$310

Mark your answer in the circles in the grid.

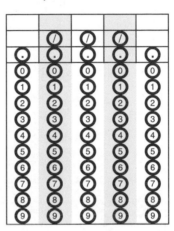

12. About how many calories does an average man use when he bowls for 75 minutes?

Average Calories Used in 30 Minutes

Activity	Calories Men	Calories Women
Biking	350	240
Bowling	120	80
Gardening	220	150
Jogging	300	210
Running	540	370
Walking	150	100

① ✓300   ④ 200
② 275   ⑤ 120
③ 240

13. The sale price of a sweater is $28. The original price was $40. What percent discount is being offered on the sweater?

Mark your answer in the circles in the grid.

Measurement and Geometry

14. Alyce's doctor prescibed a liquid medicine for her cough. Which measure may be one dose of her medicine?

① 5 gm   ④ 5 L
② 5 mL   ⑤ 5 pt
③ 5 oz

15. A thermometer outside Julie's home is shown at right. If the temperature inside Julie's home is 70°F, what is the difference between the inside and outside temperatures?

① 85°F
② 80°F
③ 75°F
④ 70°F
⑤ 55°F

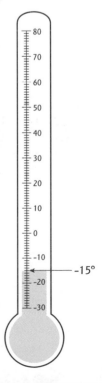

3

16. Jolene made $2\frac{1}{2}$ gallons of chicken soup for a lunch fundraiser.

Capacity	
1 gallon	= 4 quarts
1 quart	= 4 cups
1 cup	= 1 serving

Which expression gives the total number of servings Jolene made?

① $\frac{1}{4} \times \frac{1}{4} \times 4$

② 4×4

③ $4 \times 4 \times 4$

④ $2\frac{1}{2} \times 4$

⑤ $2\frac{1}{2} \times 4 \times 4$

17. Sheena bought 5 pounds of apples for $3.50. If she pays the same price per pound, how much would Sheena pay for 3 pounds?

Mark your answer in the circles in the grid.

18. Keith puts $700 in a savings account that pays 5% simple interest each year. Which expression gives the total Keith will have in 18 months?

① $700 - (\$700 \times \frac{1}{20} \times \frac{3}{2})$

② $700 + (\$700 \times \frac{1}{20} \times \frac{3}{2})$

③ $700 + (\$700 \times \frac{1}{20} \times \frac{2}{3})$

④ $700 + (\$700 \times \frac{1}{5} \times \frac{3}{2})$

⑤ $700 \times \frac{1}{20} \times \frac{3}{2}$

19. Chris is having a poster made from a favorite photo. He asks the printer to make the poster 22 inches wide. What will be the height of the poster?

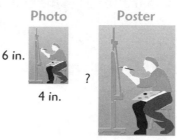

Photo   Poster

6 in.

4 in.   ?

22 in.

① 21 inches   ④ 30 inches
② 24 inches   ⑤ 33 inches
③ 27 inches

20. A scale drawing of an airplane is shown below.

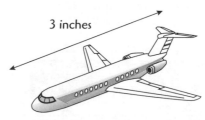

3 inches

Scale: 1 in. = 13 ft 10 in.

What is the length of the actual airplane?

① 16 ft 6 in.   ④ 41 ft 6 in.
② 20 ft 9 in.   ⑤ 45 ft 9 in.
③ 32 ft 8 in.

21. 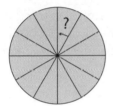 To make shelves for a bookcase, Nate needs 7 pieces of lumber, each 45 inches long. Nate has several 10-foot lengths of lumber in the width and thickness he needs. How many of these 10-foot boards will Nate use?

① 4
② 5
③ 6
④ 7
⑤ Not enough information is given.

22. Zander baked a birthday cake. He cut the cake into 12 equal pieces.

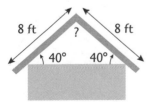

What is the measure of the angle made by the straight sides of each piece?

① 15°   ④ 60°
② 30°   ⑤ 90°
③ 45°

23. Mary is building a backyard storage shed. The dimensions of the roof are shown. Mary will cut a facing piece of plywood to fit the roof line. What is the measure of the roof angle (indicated in the drawing by a question mark) that Mary should cut?

8 ft   ?   8 ft
40°   40°

① 10°   ④ 190°
② 40°   ⑤ 280°
③ 100°

24. Alfonso knows that the distance across the field from his home to Carla's home is 50 meters. A nice place to pick flowers is 40 meters directly east of his home and directly south of Carla's home. How far from Carla's home is the flower-picking spot?

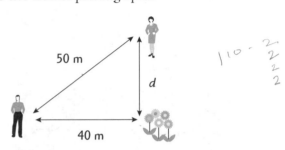

50 m

d

40 m

① 45 m
② 40 m
③ 36 m
④ 33 m
⑤ 30 m

25. Mari plans to decorate a table by covering its top surface with fancy ceramic tiles. The top is 5 feet long and 2 feet wide. If each tile is square in shape and measures 4 inches along each side, about how many tiles will Mari need?

① 90
② 100
③ 120
④ 150
⑤ 200

26. Chester is using paper cones to serve chestnuts at the Fall Festival. Using the dimensions shown, find the volume of the cone Chester is using.

4 in.

7 in.

Use $\pi \approx 3.14$, and round your answer to the nearest cubic inch.

① 18 cubic inches
② 23 cubic inches
③ 29 cubic inches
④ 37 cubic inches
⑤ 42 cubic inches

27. The coordinates of three vertices (corner points) of a rectangle are (⁻4,3), (5,3), and (5,⁻2)

Plot the fourth vertex of the rectangle on the coordinate plane grid.

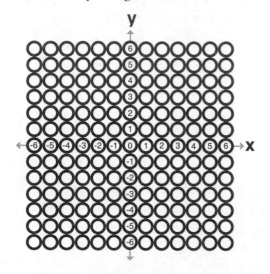

28. Which graphed line has a slope of 1?

①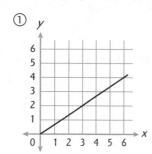

②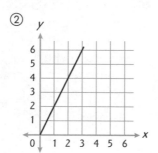

③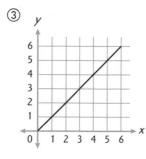

④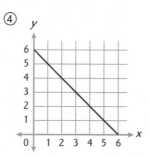

④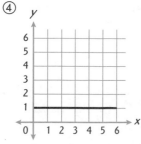

Data, Statistics, and Probability

29. Angela takes a math quiz every Friday. On her first six quizzes, Angela received scores of 95, 92, 87, 96, 87, and 98.

What is the mean, or average, of Angela's six scores?

① 87
② 89.5
③ 91
④ 92.5
⑤ 98

30. Chandra recorded her quarterly sales in a bar graph. Chandra will get a bonus of $5,000 if her average quarterly sales for the year reach $70,000.

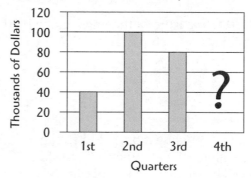

Chandra's Quarterly Sales

What must her sales be for the 4ᵗʰ quarter in order for Chandra to earn the bonus?

① $40,000
② $45,000
③ $50,000
④ $55,000
⑤ $60,000

31. Valley Beverages sells specialty hot chocolate and lemonade drinks at several local outlets. The graph shows how average total sales of each drink depend on the outdoor average temperature.

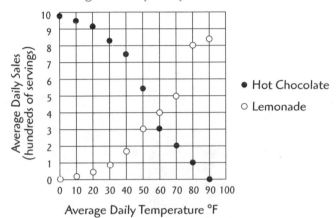

Beverage Sales by Temperature

Estimate the number of lemonades that Valley expects to sell at average daily temperatures of 75°F and 100°F.

① 75°F: 150 servings; 100°F: 0 servings
② 75°F: 650 servings; 100°F: 900 servings
③ 75°F: 40 servings; 100°F: 100 servings
④ 75°F: 450 servings; 100°F: 900 servings
⑤ 75°F: 600 servings; 100°F: 1,000 servings

32. Students in Juanita's GED class were wondering how human height is related to foot length. To find out, each of the 16 students measured his or her height and foot length. A graph of the results is shown below. A *line of best fit* shows the trend in the data.

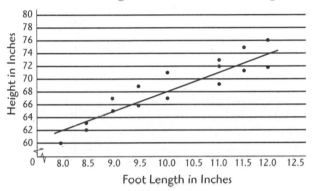

Student Height for Different Foot Lengths

Based on the line of best fit, about how much height increase occurs with each inch increase in foot length?

① about 3 inches   ④ about 0.5 inch
② about 2 inches   ⑤ about 0.25 inch
③ about 1 inch

33. Jocelyn made a line graph to show the distance she traveled during an 8-hour car trip. What was Jocelyn's approximate average speed during the first 5 hours?

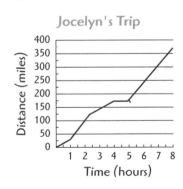

Jocelyn's Trip

① 55 miles per hour   ④ 30 miles per hour
② 45 miles per hour   ⑤ Not enough
③ 35 miles per hour   information is
                             given.

34. To reduce expenses in her store, Karen is considering switching to new energy-efficient light bulbs. The graph shows both purchase price and monthly operating costs using three different bulbs.

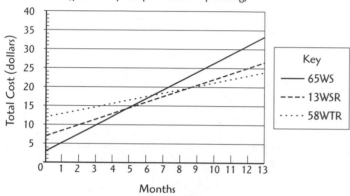

Total Cost of Lighting with Different Bulbs
(purchase price plus cost of operating)

Key

—— 65WS

---- 13WSR

······ 58WTR

What is the purchase price and monthly operating cost of bulb 13WSR?

① $12 purchase price, and $1.50 per month operating cost

② $12 purchase price, and $3.00 per month operating cost

③ $7 purchase price, and $0.75 per month operating cost

④ $7 purchase price, and $1.50 per month operating cost

⑤ $7 purchase price, and $3.00 per month operating cost

35. The bar graph shows the amount of interest paid on a $100,000 mortgage for two different payback periods and for three different yearly interest rates.

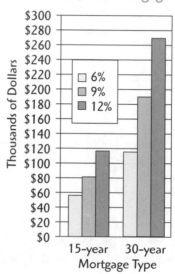

Total Interest Paid on a
$100,000 Mortgage

☐ 6%
☐ 9%
■ 12%

Mortgage Type

Suppose you want to borrow $100,000 to purchase a house, and the interest rate of your loan is 12%.

Estimate the difference in total interest you would pay if you take out a 30-year loan instead of a 15-year loan.

① about $75,000
② about $150,000
③ about $200,000
④ about $250,000
⑤ about $300,000

Problems 36 and 37 refer to the graph of Mayoral Election Results.

Mayoral Election Results
50,200 votes cast

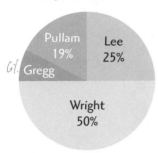

Pullam 19%

Lee 25%

Gregg

Wright 50%

36. Election results for a mayoral race are summarized in the circle graph. What percent of the votes did Gregg receive?

Mark your answer in the circles in the grid.

```
┌───┬───┬───┬───┬───┐
│   │ / │ / │ / │   │
│ · │ · │ · │ · │ · │
│ ⓪ │ ⓪ │ ⓪ │ ⓪ │ ⓪ │
│ ① │ ① │ ① │ ① │ ① │
│ ② │ ② │ ② │ ② │ ② │
│ ③ │ ③ │ ③ │ ③ │ ③ │
│ ④ │ ④ │ ④ │ ④ │ ④ │
│ ⑤ │ ⑤ │ ⑤ │ ⑤ │ ⑤ │
│ ⑥ │ ⑥ │ ⑥ │ ⑥ │ ⑥ │
│ ⑦ │ ⑦ │ ⑦ │ ⑦ │ ⑦ │
│ ⑧ │ ⑧ │ ⑧ │ ⑧ │ ⑧ │
│ ⑨ │ ⑨ │ ⑨ │ ⑨ │ ⑨ │
└───┴───┴───┴───┴───┘
```

37. According to information provided by the graph, what number of votes did Lee receive?

① 2,500
② 6,245
③ 8,050
④ 9,500
⑤ 12,550

Use the following graphs for problem 38.

Mike's Bicycle Store
Profit by Quarter

Mike's Bicycle Store
Percent of Total Profit by Quarter
(Total Profit = $18,000)

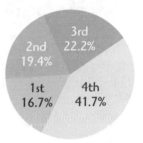

2nd 19.4%

3rd 22.2%

1st 16.7%

4th 41.7%

38. The profit for Mike's Bicycle Store for the four quarters of the year is shown. What is the store's mean (average) profit per quarter?

① $4,500
② $5,600
③ $6,250
④ $6,800
⑤ $7,500

39. Regina is playing a game in which she draws marbles from a bag. If the bag contains 1 white marble, 2 gray marbles, and 3 green marbles, what is the probability that Regina will draw a gray marble on her first try?

Mark your answer in the circles in the grid.

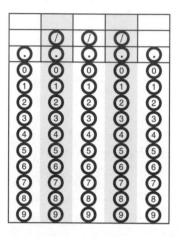

40. To understand parking needs, Michael asks each employee, "How do you get to work?" He records the results of the poll in the table.

Transportation Poll

Method	Number
Bus	10
Car	9
Bike	3
Walk	3

Based on this data, how many of the next 15 employees Michael polls will say they ride a bus to work?

Mark your answer in the circles in the grid.

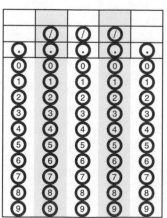

Algebra, Functions, and Patterns

41. Use the temperature formula $°C = \frac{5}{9}(°F - 32°)$ to find the Celsius temperature ($°C$) when the Fahrenheit temperature is 50°F.

Mark your answer in the circles in the grid.

42. Jenni baked a batch of cookies. She kept 6 for herself and divided the rest equally among 4 friends. If Jenni baked a total of n cookies, which expression tells the number of cookies Jenni gave to each friend?

① $\frac{(n-4)}{6}$ ④ $4(n+6)$

② $\frac{(n+6)}{4}$ ⑤ $4(n-6)$

③ $\frac{(n-6)}{4}$

43. Kami, Maria, and Shannelle share living expenses. Kami pays $65 less each month than Maria. Shannelle pays twice as much each month as Kami. If total monthly living expenses are $985, which equation can be used to find Kami's share (k)?

① $4k + \$65 = \$985$
② $4k - \$65 = \$985$
③ $3k + \$65 = \$985$
④ $3k - \$65 = \$985$
⑤ $2k - \$65 = \$985$

44. The dimensions of the rectangle are $12n$ and $4n + 3$.

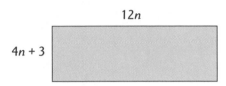

12n

4n + 3

Which expression gives the area of the rectangle?

① $96n^2 + 72n$ ④ $32n + 6$
② $48n^2 + 36n$ ⑤ $16n + 3$
③ $48n + 36$

45. Movie rental prices at Video Circle are shown. Part of the price list is missing. If the price pattern continues, what is the cost of renting 5 movies for 1 week?

Video Circle

Weekly Rental Rates

1 movie	$3.00
2 movies	$5.50
3 movies	$7.50
4 movies	$9.00

Mark your answer in the circles in the grid.

46. Cab fares in Springfield are given by the equation:

$F = \$2.50 + \$1.50n$

where F = total fare
and n = number of miles driven

Which table shows a set of values represented by this equation?

①

n	F
1	$2.50
2	$4.00
3	$5.50
4	$7.00
5	$8.50

②

n	F
1	$1.00
2	$2.50
3	$4.00
4	$5.50
5	$7.00

③

n	F
1	0
2	$1.50
3	$3.00
4	$4.50
5	$6.00

④

n	F
1	$5.50
2	$7.00
3	$8.50
4	$10.00
5	$11.50

⑤

n	F
1	$4.00
2	$5.50
3	$7.00
4	$8.50
5	$10.00

47. Jake, a plumber, charges customers a fixed amount for traveling time and an hourly rate for each hour spent on the job. The table below shows the total cost (C) that Jake charges. The variable n stands for the number of hours Jake works at the job site.

n	0	1	2	3	4	5
C	$25	$60	$95	$130	$165	$200

Which equation tells how the value of C depends on the value of n?

① $C = \$40n$
② $C = \$60n + \$25$
③ $C = \$25n + \$25$
④ $C = \$35n + \$25$
⑤ $C = \$35n - \$25$

11

48. The point (3,2) is a point on the line defined by the equation $y = 2x - 4$. This line is shown on the graph.

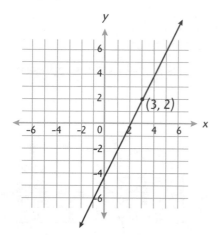

What point on this graphed line has a y-value of 6?

Mark your answer on the coordinate plane grid.

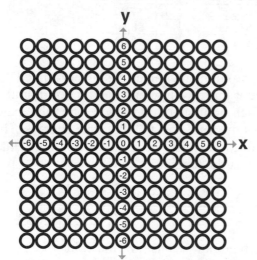

49. Which equation is equivalent to the following equation?

$$y = 3x + 6$$

① $x = y - \frac{6}{3}$

② $x = y + \frac{6}{3}$

③ $x = \frac{1}{3}y - 2$

④ $x = \frac{1}{3}y + 2$

⑤ $x = 3y - 6$

50. Jennifer is preparing to move to a new home. She is packing her clothes in a box shaped like a cube. If Jennifer uses another box the same shape but whose edges are double in length, how does the box volume change?

cube

① The volume becomes 2 times its original amount.
② The volume becomes 4 times its original amount.
③ The volume becomes 6 times its original amount.
④ The volume becomes 8 times its original amount.
⑤ The volume becomes 16 times its original amount.

Top 50 Skills

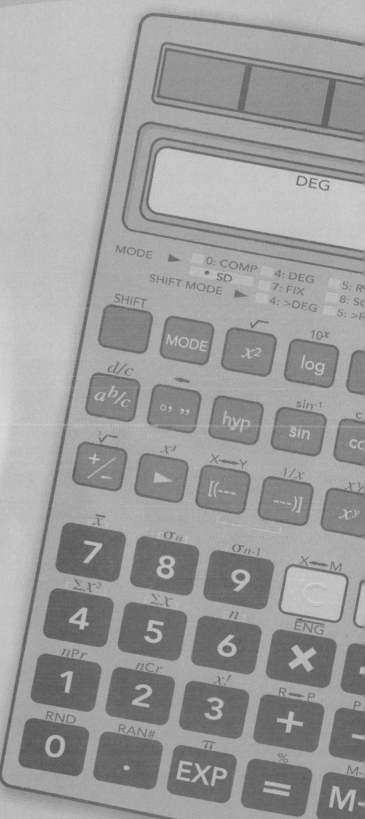

Make an Appropriate Estimate

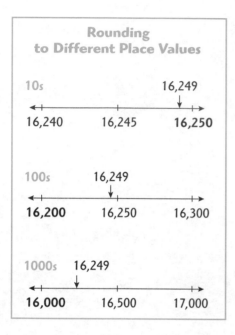

Rounding to Different Place Values

10s

16,240   16,245   **16,250**   16,249 → **16,250**

100s

16,200   16,250   16,300   16,249 → 16,250

1000s

16,000   16,500   17,000   16,249 → 16,000

Estimating

Overestimate: to estimate an amount greater than an actual value

Example: Overestimating the total cost of a purchase to make sure that you will take enough money.

Underestimate: to estimate an amount less than the actual value

Example: Underestimating the amount of gas in your car's tank to make sure you can reach your destination.

Carin is planning to buy a used car that is on sale for $16,249. The dealer is offering 0% financing for a 4-year loan. The salesperson tells Carin that, with a down payment of $1,000, her loan payment will be *about $194 per month for 4 years*. Use your own estimate to decide which phrase best describes the salesperson's estimate of Carin's monthly payment.

  ① very close to the actual value
  ② unreasonably high
  ③ unreasonably low
  ④ exactly correct
  ⑤ not enough information is given

About Estimation

To estimate means to find an approximate answer. One way to estimate is to use rounded numbers that make computations easier.

Numbers can be rounded to different place values.

To the nearest . . .	ten	hundred	thousand
$16,249 rounds to	$16,250	$16,200	$16,000
$194 rounds to	$190	$200	0
48 rounds to	50	0	0

Solution

Step 1

Estimate the amount Carin will owe after making the down payment.

Car price = $16,249 ≈ $16,000 [rounded to the nearest $1,000]

Amount owed after down payment ≈ $16,000 − $1,000 **= $15,000**

Step 2

Estimate the number of payments Carin will make in 4 years.

Number of payments (months) = 12 × 4 = 48 ≈ **50 months**

Step 3

To estimate Carin's monthly payment, divide $15,000 by 50:

$15,000 ÷ 50 months = **$300 per month**

The salesperson's estimate of $195 per month is **unreasonably low**.

A reasonable estimate is $300 per month.

GED Readiness

Concept

1 There were 4,289 fans at today's basketball game. Round 4,289 to the nearest hundred.

  ① 4,000
  ② 4,200
  ③ 4,300
  ④ 4,500
  ⑤ 5,000

2 The price of a new television set has been reduced to $324.99. Round $324.99 to the nearest ten dollars.

  ① $300
  ② $320
  ③ $325
  ④ $330
  ⑤ $350

Procedure

3 For her clothes shop, Kaitlan ordered 19 display stands. Each stand costs $213.50. What is the **best estimate** of the total cost of the display stands?

  ① $10,000
  ② $8,500
  ③ $7,500
  ④ $6,000
  ⑤ $4,000

4 Jamie will make 48 equal payments to pay off a no-interest loan of $2,464.75. What is the **best estimate** of the amount of each payment?

  ① $60
  ② $50
  ③ $40
  ④ $30
  ⑤ $20

Application

5 Estimate the average number of sandwich sales per day for the days shown in the table.

  ① 900
  ② 800
  ③ 700
  ④ 600
  ⑤ 500

Day	Sales
Mon.	619
Tues.	521
Wed.	622
Thurs.	549
Fri.	704
Sat.	683

6 Miguel is planning to buy a new stereo. The stereo costs $539 and is offered with 0% financing for a 2-year loan. After making a down payment of $50, Miguel estimates his monthly payment to be about $20.

Which phrase best describes Miguel's estimate?

  ① very close to the actual amount
  ② much higher than the actual amount
  ③ much lower than the actual amount
  ④ exactly the correct amount
  ⑤ Not enough information is given.

7 Latcisha's car gets 42 miles per gallon. Approximately how far can Lateisha drive on a full tank of 19.5 gallons?

  ① less than 600 miles
  ② between 600 and 750 miles
  ③ between 750 and 850 miles
  ④ between 850 and 1,000 miles
  ⑤ more than 1,000 miles

Write Decimals in Order

National Pipe Company stocks copper pipes in the lengths shown in the table. What is the part number of the longest pipe?

① 237C
② 182C
③ 047C
④ 489C
⑤ 847C

Copper Pipe

Part Number	Length (m)
123C	6.09
013C	6.78
489C	7.09
246C	6.7
182C	7.3
047C	7.28
847C	7.076
237C	5.99

Comparing Whole Numbers

The number with the greatest number of digits is the greatest.

123 is greater than 12.

Comparing Decimals

The number with the greatest number of digits **may** not be the greatest number.

1.23 is **not** greater than 1.3.

Solution

Step 1

Compare lengths in the "Length (m)" column to find the longest length. Compare each length, digit by digit, starting with the greatest place value.

Compare the…

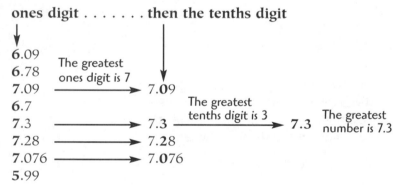

Step 2

Find the part number of the longest pipe.

Comparing Decimals, Another Approach

Write each decimal to the same number of decimal places.

Add zeros as needed.

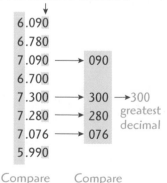

Copper Pipe

Part Number	Length (m)
246C	6.7
(182C)	7.3
047C	7.28
847C	7.076
237C	5.99

Part number of longest pipe is 182C

Longest pipe is 7.3 m

Answer: 182C

GED Readiness

Concept

① According to the bar graph, which is the **best estimate** of the cost of 1 gallon of milk in Dallas?

① $2.00
② $2.10
③ $2.30
④ $2.50
⑤ $3.00

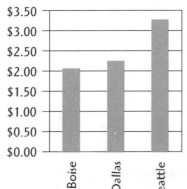

Cost of 1 Gallon of 2% Milk in Selected Cities

Problems 2 to 4 refer to the table on page 16.

② What is the part number of the shortest pipe that is longer than 6 meters?

① 123C   ④ 246C
② 013C   ⑤ 182C
③ 847C

③ How many of the pipes listed in the table are longer than 6.5 meters?

① 7   ④ 4
② 6   ⑤ 3
③ 5

④ How many of the pipes listed in the table are between 6 and 6.5 meters long?

① 0   ④ 3
② 1   ⑤ 4
③ 2

Procedure

⑤ Janet has packages to mail with the following weights: 0.76 lb, 0.6 lb, 0.07 lb, and 0.8 lb. Which of the following lists shows the weights from least to greatest?

① 0.6, 0.8, 0.76, 0.07
② 0.6, 0.8, 0.07, 0.76
③ 0.07, 0.6, 0.8, 0.76
④ 0.07, 0.6, 0.76, 0.8
⑤ 0.07, 0.76, 0.6, 0.8

⑥ The times for the final heat of the girls' 100-meter run at Albany High School were 12.5 sec, 11.8 sec, 11.98 sec, 12.02 sec, and 11.79 sec. Which was the fastest time?

① 12.5 sec
② 11.8 sec
③ 11.98 sec
④ 12.02 sec
⑤ 11.79 sec

Application

⑦ Kendra has several lengths of rope: 9.3 m, 7.6 m, 7.26 m, 6.05 m, and 8.01 m. She will cut one to be exactly 6.4 meters long. Which length of rope should Kendra cut if she wants the least waste?

① 9.3 m
② 7.6 m
③ 7.26 m
④ 6.06 m
⑤ 8.01 m

Computation Review, pages 141, 142, 149

Solve Decimal Word Problems (+, −)

Remember

To add or subtract decimals, always align the decimal points.

$$
\begin{array}{r}
3.1 \\
+\ 1.42 \\
\hline
4.52
\end{array}
$$

When Trent had the flu, his temperature increased over its normal value of 98.4°F. His temperature rose to the value shown on the thermometer.

By how much did Trent's temperature increase over its normal value.

① 2.7°F
② 2.3°F
③ 2.1°F
④ 2.0°F
④ 1.8°F

Clinical Thermometers

A clinical thermometer, like a ruler, has a scale that is a number line. However, unlike a standard ruler, the thermometer scale has 5 equal divisions between each whole number temperature. Each small division is read as two-tenths (0.2).

Reading a Clinical Thermometer

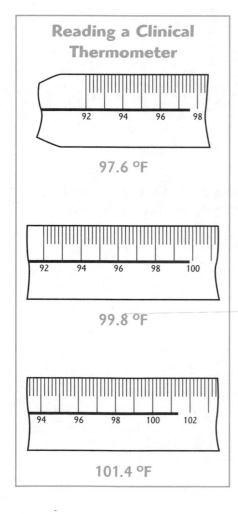

97.6 °F

99.8 °F

101.4 °F

Solution

Approach 1

Read the value that Trent's temperature reached: 100.2°F. Subtract Trent's normal temperature of 98.4°F from 100.2°F.

$$
\begin{array}{r}
100.2°F \\
-\ \ 98.4°F \\
\end{array}
\longrightarrow
\begin{array}{r}
\overset{99\ \ 12}{\cancel{100.2}°F} \\
-\ \ 98.4°F \\
\hline
\mathbf{1.8°F}
\end{array}
$$

Answer: 1.8°F

Approach 2

Identify the point 98.4°F on the thermometer. Count by two-tenths from 98.4°F up to 100.2°F.

98.4 . . . 98.6 . . . 98.8 . . ., etc. . . . 99.8 . . . 100.0 . . . 100.2

Count: 0.2   0.4   1.6   **1.8**

Trent's temperature rose by 1.8°F.

GED Readiness

Concept

1. The bar graph below shows the cost of electricity for selected states. About how much more does 1 kilowatt-hour of electricity cost in Hawaii than in Kentucky?

   ① $15
   ② $10
   ③ $0.15
   ④ $0.10
   ⑤ $0.05

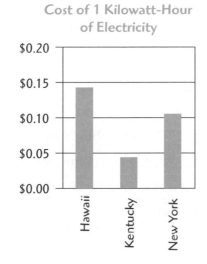

Cost of 1 Kilowatt-Hour of Electricity

2. Alice buys a sandwich for $2.25 and a drink for 75¢. She pays with a $10 bill. Which expression shows how to find the amount of her change?

   ① $2.25 + $75.00 − $10.00
   ② $10.00 − ($2.25 + $75.00)
   ③ ($2.25 + $0.75) − $10.00
   ④ $10.00 − ($2.25 + $0.75)
   ⑤ $10.00 − ($2.25 − $0.75)

3. To save postage, James is mailing several items in one box. Two of the items weigh 13.9 lb and 20.65 lb. The packing material and box weigh 0.3 lb. The maximum package weight the post office accepts is 70 lb. Which expression gives the maximum weight for the remaining items?

   ① 70 − (13.9 + 20.65 + 0.3)
   ② 70 − 13.9 + 20.65 + 0.3
   ③ (13.9 + 20.65 + 0.3) − 70
   ④ 13.9 + 20.65 + 0.3 − 70
   ⑤ 70 − 13.9 − 20.65 + 0.3

Procedure

4. Hailey swam the 50-yard freestyle in exactly 25 seconds. How much slower than the state record time of 23.156 seconds was Hailey?

   Mark your answer in the circles in the grid.

5. The Walkers pay $0.1165 for each kilowatt-hour of electricity they use. Their friends in a neighboring state pay $0.095. How much more do the Walkers pay for each kilowatt-hour than their friends pay?

   ① $0.0215
   ② $0.107
   ③ $0.126
   ④ $0.2115
   ⑤ $1.0665

Application

6. At the beginning of August, Juan's checking account balance was $589.86. He then wrote checks in the amounts of $18.12 and $50.43 and made a deposit of $40.11. What is the balance of Juan's checking account now?

   ① $481.20
   ② $561.42
   ③ $618.30
   ④ $662.28
   ⑤ $698.52

Understand Order of Operations

Find the value of the following expression:

$$12 + 5(8 - 6)^3 \div \sqrt{4}$$

① 8
② 22
③ 27
④ 32
⑤ 262

Order of Operations

$5(8 - 6) = 5 \times (8 - 6)$
$ = 5 \times 2$
$ = \mathbf{10}$

Powers

Squares

$0^2 = 0 \times 0 = \mathbf{0}$
$1^2 = 1 \times 1 = \mathbf{1}$
$2^2 = 2 \times 2 = \mathbf{4}$

base $\longrightarrow 4^2 \overset{\text{exponent}}{\nwarrow}$

Cubes

$0^3 = 0 \times 0 \times 0 = \mathbf{0}$
$1^3 = 1 \times 1 \times 1 = \mathbf{1}$
$2^3 = 2 \times 2 \times 2 = \mathbf{8}$

Roots

Square Roots

$\sqrt{0} = \mathbf{0} \quad (0 \times 0 = 0)$
$\sqrt{1} = \mathbf{1} \quad (1 \times 1 = 1)$
$\sqrt{4} = \mathbf{2} \quad (2 \times 2 = 4)$

Cube Roots

$\sqrt[3]{0} = \mathbf{0} \quad (0 \times 0 \times 0 = 0)$
$\sqrt[3]{1} = \mathbf{1} \quad (1 \times 1 \times 1 = 1)$
$\sqrt[3]{8} = \mathbf{2} \quad (2 \times 2 \times 2 = 8)$

About Order of Operations

To find the value of an expression, follow these rules *in order*.

1. Find the value of the numbers within the parentheses.

2. Find the value of any power and any root.

3. Multiply and divide terms from left to right.

4. Add or subtract terms.

Solution

Follow the order of operations to evaluate the expression.

$12 + 5(8 - 6)^3 \div \sqrt{4}$	Find the value within the parentheses. $\boxed{8 - 6 = 2}$
$12 + \quad 5(2)^3 \quad \div \sqrt{4}$	Find the value of the power and the root. $\boxed{(2)^3 = 2 \times 2 \times 2 = 8 \quad \sqrt{4} = 2}$
$12 + \quad 5(8) \quad \div \quad 2$	Multiply 5 by 8. $\boxed{5 \times 8 = 40}$
$12 + \quad 40 \quad \div \quad 2$	Divide 40 by 2. $\boxed{40 \div 2 = 20}$
$12 + \quad\quad 20$	Add 12 and 20. $\boxed{12 + 20 = 32}$
32	

The value of the expression is 32.

The calculator automatically performs the correct order of operations.

ON 1 2 + 5 × [[(- 8 - 6 -)] SHIFT ▶ x^3 ÷ 4 SHIFT $\sqrt{}$ x^2 = [3 2.]

parentheses   power (2^3) square root $(\sqrt{4})$ display

GED Readiness

Concept

1 Last week Cassie sold 153 raffle tickets. This week she sold 207 tickets. The price of each ticket is $5. Which expression tells the value of the tickets she sold in the two weeks?

① $153 \times 207 \times \$5$
② $153 + 207 + \$5$
③ $\$5(153 + 207)$
④ $(153 \times 207) + \$5$
⑤ $(207 - 153) \times \$5$

2 Cole has two jobs. He works 15 hours each week for $12 an hour at Car Care. Cole also works 20 hours each week for $10 an hour at Auto Depot. Which expression tells how much Cole earns each week?

① $\$11 \times (15 + 20)$
② $(\$10 + \$12) \times (15 + 20)$
③ $(15 \times \$12) - (20 \times \$10)$
④ $\$12 \times (15 + 20)$
⑤ $(15 \times \$12) + (20 \times \$10)$

3 From a catalog, Jim orders 3 denim shirts and 2 sweatshirts. If Jim pays an $11 shipping cost, which expression gives the total cost of his order?

Item	Price
Denim Shirt	$16
Casual Pants	$29
Sweatshirt	$22
Cotton Sweater	$26

① $(3 + 2) \times (\$16 + \$22 + \$11)$
② $(3 + 2) \times (\$16 + \$22 - \$11)$
③ $(3 \times \$16) + (2 \times \$22) \times \$11$
④ $(3 \times \$16) + (2 \times \$22) + \$11$
⑤ $(3 \times \$16) + (2 \times \$22) - \$11$

Procedure

4 The length in centimeters of one side of a machined metal brace is given by the following expression.

$$\sqrt{3^2 + 4^2}$$

What is the length of the brace?

① between 2 cm and 3 cm
② exactly 3 cm
③ between 3 cm and 4 cm
④ exactly 5 cm
⑤ exactly 7 cm

5 An engineer computes the length in inches that a new steel bridge will expand after a 20-degree rise in temperature. She uses the following expression:

$$8 - (7.3 - 2.3)^2 \div \sqrt{25}$$

How many inches will the bridge expand?

① 12
② 9
③ 7
④ 5
⑤ 3

6 🖩 The maximum height, in kilometers, attained by a rocket is given by the expression below. What is this maximum height?

$$5 + \frac{\sqrt{5^2 - 4 \times 2 \times 2}}{3}$$

① 6 km
② 7 km
③ 8 km
④ 9 km
⑤ 10 km

Solve Decimal Word Problems (x, ÷)

On Saturday Lavonne worked 10 hours at Gatsby Department Store. She earns $9.50 per hour for the first 8 hours each day. Lavonne earns time and a half ($9.50 × 1.5) for any hours beyond 8 hours. How much did Lavonne earn on Saturday?

① $84.50   ④ $165.00
❷ $104.50   ⑤ $180.00
③ $142.50

Solution

Step 1

Write an equation for the amount Lavonne earned Saturday. The total Lavonne earned is equal to 8 hours of regular pay plus 2 hours of overtime pay.

The amount earned on Saturday	is	the amount earned for the first 8 hours	and	the amount earned for overtime hours
↓	↓	↓	↓	↓
Total	=	(8 × $9.50)	+	2 × ($9.50 × 1.5)
		(hours × hourly pay)	+	(hours × hourly pay)

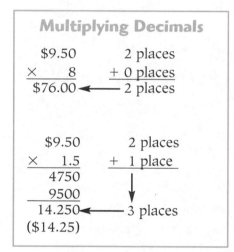

Multiplying Decimals

$9.50   2 places
× 8   + 0 places
$76.00 ←—— 2 places

$9.50   2 places
× 1.5   + 1 place
4750
9500
14.250 ←—— 3 places
($14.25)

Step 2

Perform the operations in your equation.

Total = (8 × $9.50) + 2 × ($9.50 × 1.5)

   = $76.00 + 2 × $14.25

   = $76.00 + $28.50

   =   **$104.50**

On Saturday Lavonne earned $104.50.

The calculator automatically performs the correct order of operations. Each multiplication is performed before the addition is done.

ON 8 × 9 . 5 0 + 2 × 9 . 5 0 × 1 . 5 =   104.5

regular pay   overtime pay   display

GED Readiness

Concept

1 The bar graph shows the taxes on gasoline in selected states. Which answer choice is the **best estimate** of the tax on 10 gallons of gas in Alaska?

① $0.25
② $0.30
③ $2.50
④ $3.00
⑤ $25.00

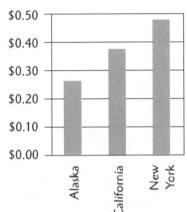

Tax on 1 Gallon of Gasoline

2 A box weighing 11.3 kilograms contains 2 dozen cans of chicken soup. When empty, the box weighs 0.5 kilograms. Which expression gives the weight, in kilograms, of one can of chicken soup?

① $(11.3 + 0.5) \div (2 \times 12)$
② $11.3 \div (2 \times 12) - 0.5$
③ $(11.3 \times 12) \times 2 - 0.5$
④ $11.3 \div (12 \times 2) - 0.5$
⑤ $(11.3 - 0.5) \div (2 \times 12)$

Procedure

3 Malcolm and 3 friends have dinner at The Pizza Palace. Their bill is $22. If they share the cost equally, how much is each person's share?

① $5.00   ④ $18.00
② $5.50   ⑤ $19.00
③ $7.33

Application

4 Carrie runs 4.3 miles Monday, Wednesday, and Friday. She runs 2.5 miles on Tuesday and Thursday. How many miles does Carrie run in 4 weeks?

① 12.9
② 17.9
③ 27.2
④ 71.6
⑤ 93.4

Problems 5 and 6 refer to the table below.

Shipping Charges

Range	Standard	Rush	1-Day
$0.01 to $15	$4.95	$11.95	$22.95
$15.01 to $30	$5.95	$12.95	$24.95
$30.01 to $45	$7.95	$14.95	$26.95
$45.01 to $100	$11.95	$18.95	$34.95
Over $100	$13.95	$20.95	$36.95

5 From a catalog, Kia orders 2 towels for $15.95 each and a pillow for $5.97. What is the total cost for Kia's purchase if she uses standard shipping?

① $15.97
② $27.87
③ $29.92
④ $45.82
⑤ $52.82

6 Yolanda orders 3 pairs of shorts in different colors for $14.50 each. How much more will her order cost if Yolanda chooses 1-day shipping rather than standard shipping?

① $19.00
② $20.00
③ $23.00
④ $43.50
⑤ $51.45

Write Fractions in Order

Equivalent Fractions

$$\frac{5}{6} = \frac{10}{12}$$

5 out of 6

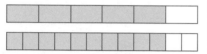

10 out of 12

$$\frac{1}{3} = \frac{4}{12}$$

1 out of 3

4 out of 12

$$\frac{3}{4} = \frac{9}{12}$$

3 out of 4

9 out of 12

$$\frac{1}{2} = \frac{6}{12}$$

1 out of 2

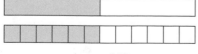

6 out of 12

Order the following fractions from least to greatest.

$$\frac{5}{6}, \frac{1}{3}, \frac{3}{4}, \frac{1}{2}$$

① $\frac{1}{3}, \frac{1}{2}, \frac{3}{4}, \frac{5}{6}$

② $\frac{1}{2}, \frac{1}{3}, \frac{3}{4}, \frac{5}{6}$

③ $\frac{5}{6}, \frac{3}{4}, \frac{1}{2}, \frac{1}{3}$

④ $\frac{1}{3}, \frac{3}{4}, \frac{1}{2}, \frac{5}{6}$

⑤ $\frac{1}{2}, \frac{3}{4}, \frac{5}{6}, \frac{1}{3}$

Solution

Step 1

Compare fractions by finding common denominators. As a first step, write multiples of each denominator.

6: 6 <u>12</u> 18 <u>24</u>

3: 3 6 9 <u>12</u> 15 18 21 <u>24</u>

4: 4 8 <u>12</u> 16 20 <u>24</u>

2: 2 4 6 8 10 <u>12</u> 14 16 18 20 22 <u>24</u>

> 12 and 24 are **common** to all the lists of multiples.
>
> 12 is the **least** (smallest) **common** denominator.

Step 2

Rewrite each fraction using the least common denominator. For each fraction, multiply the numerator and the denominator by the same number, the number that makes the denominator 12.

$$\overset{\times 2}{\underset{\times 2}{\frac{5}{6} = \frac{10}{12}}} \quad \overset{\times 4}{\underset{\times 4}{\frac{1}{3} = \frac{4}{12}}} \quad \overset{\times 3}{\underset{\times 3}{\frac{3}{4} = \frac{9}{12}}} \quad \overset{\times 6}{\underset{\times 6}{\frac{1}{2} = \frac{6}{12}}}$$

Step 3

Order the fractions from least to greatest. Order the fractions according to the numerators of the equivalent fractions.

$$\frac{1}{3} = \frac{4}{12} \quad \frac{1}{2} = \frac{6}{12} \quad \frac{3}{4} = \frac{9}{12} \quad \frac{5}{6} = \frac{10}{12}$$

Step 4

Order the original fractions according to the order in Step 3.

Answer: $\frac{1}{3}, \frac{1}{2}, \frac{3}{4}, \frac{5}{6}$

GED Readiness

Concept

1 At Sam's Coffeehouse, 47 of the 307 coffee beverages served on Monday were decaffeinated. Which fraction is the **best estimate** of the fraction of coffee beverages that were decaffeinated?

① $\frac{1}{3}$ ④ $\frac{1}{6}$

② $\frac{1}{4}$ ⑤ $\frac{1}{8}$

③ $\frac{1}{5}$

2 Lisa's favorite dish is her grandmother's cheese soufflé. Her grandmother says that she must use about $\frac{3}{16}$ cup of flour. Lisa has only $\frac{1}{4}$-cup and $\frac{1}{2}$-cup measuring cups. Which phrase **best describes** the amount of flour Lisa needs for the recipe?

① a little less than $\frac{1}{4}$ cup

② a little more than $\frac{1}{4}$ cup

③ a little less than $\frac{1}{2}$ cup

④ a little more than $\frac{1}{2}$ cup

⑤ much more than $\frac{1}{2}$ cup

3 Nigel is making bags of roasted mixed nuts for a concession stand. So far, he has made bags with the following weights:

$\frac{1}{2}$ lb, $\frac{2}{3}$ lb, $\frac{3}{8}$ lb, $\frac{7}{16}$ lb, $\frac{1}{3}$ lb

Which bags weigh $\frac{1}{2}$ pound or more?

① $\frac{3}{8}$ lb, $\frac{7}{16}$ lb

② $\frac{3}{8}$ lb, $\frac{2}{3}$ lb

③ $\frac{1}{2}$ lb, $\frac{3}{8}$ lb

④ $\frac{1}{2}$ lb, $\frac{2}{3}$ lb

⑤ $\frac{1}{2}$ lb, $\frac{7}{16}$ lb

Procedure

4 The longest dimension on Pamela's quilt piece measures 8 inches long. What fraction of a yard is this length?

① $\frac{1}{3}$ ④ $\frac{3}{8}$

② $\frac{1}{4}$ ⑤ $\frac{2}{9}$

③ $\frac{2}{6}$

5 To the nearest $\frac{1}{16}$ inch, what is the length of the nail below?

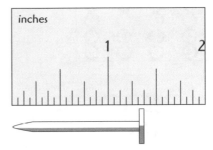

① $1\frac{1}{4}$ inches ④ $1\frac{3}{4}$ inches

② $1\frac{3}{8}$ inches ⑤ $1\frac{7}{8}$ inches

③ $1\frac{7}{10}$ inches

Application

6 As part of a track workout, 5 girls ran as far as they could for 10 minutes. The distance each girl ran is recorded in the table. Who was the fastest runner?

① Amber
② Brianna
③ Lana
④ Nicole
⑤ Tiffany

Name	Distance
Amber	$1\frac{1}{2}$ mi
Brianna	$1\frac{1}{4}$ mi
Lana	$1\frac{5}{8}$ mi
Nicole	$1\frac{3}{4}$ mi
Tiffany	$\frac{7}{8}$ mi

Solve Problems with Fractions (+, –)

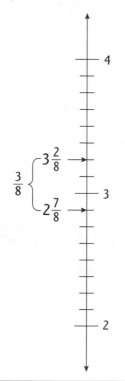

In June three friends wanted to see how far each could run in 20 minutes. They ran on a track and recorded their distances. After 6 months of training, the friends ran again. Their results are shown in the table.

What fraction of a mile farther did Calvin run in December than he ran in June?

The answer $\frac{3}{8}$ is recorded on the grid.

20-Minute Run Distances in Miles

Name	June	December
Luis	$2\frac{1}{2}$	$2\frac{7}{8}$
Calvin	$2\frac{7}{8}$	$3\frac{1}{4}$
Jake	$1\frac{7}{8}$	$2\frac{3}{8}$

Solution

To find the difference between numbers, subtract. When the numbers are far apart, the difference can be estimated. The numbers in the table and in the answer choices are too close to use estimation.

Step 1

Find the distances Calvin ran in June and December.

Calvin ran $2\frac{7}{8}$ miles in June and $3\frac{1}{4}$ miles in December.

Step 2

To subtract, first find a common denominator for the fractions. Then rewrite the mixed numbers using the common denominator. The common denominator is 8. The June distance already has a denominator of 8, so rewrite the December distance.

December: $3\frac{1}{4} = 3\frac{2}{8}$

Step 3

Write each mixed number as an improper fraction. Then subtract.

June: $2\frac{7}{8} = \frac{23}{8}$ December: $3\frac{1}{4} = 3\frac{2}{8} = \frac{26}{8}$ [Note: $3 = \frac{3}{1} = \frac{24}{8}$]

$\frac{26}{8} - \frac{23}{8} = \frac{3}{8}$ **mile**

Alternative Step 3

Show the distances on a number line marked off in eighths. Then count the one-eighth distances.

Number Sense: Conceptual   **Related Skills: 6, 8, and 9**

GED Readiness

Concept

1. Rita walked $\frac{1}{8}$ mile to a neighbor's house. She then walked $2\frac{3}{4}$ miles with friends. Later in the day, Rita walked $2\frac{1}{3}$ miles home. Which is the **best estimate** of the total number of miles Rita walked?

   ① 2   ④ 5
   ② 3   ⑤ 6
   ③ 4

Procedure

2. Before he began working out in the gym, Sammy weighed $147\frac{1}{2}$ pounds. After working out for one week, his weight dropped to $146\frac{3}{4}$ pounds. What fraction of a pound did Sammy lose?

   Mark your answer in the circles in the grid.

3. The average height of a 16-year-old girl is 65 inches. The average height of a 16-year-old boy is $68\frac{3}{8}$ inches. How much taller is an average 16-year-old boy than an average 16-year-old girl?

   ① $3\frac{1}{3}$ in.   ④ $2\frac{3}{8}$ in.
   ② $3\frac{3}{8}$ in.   ⑤ $1\frac{5}{8}$ in.
   ③ $2\frac{5}{16}$ in.

Application

4. Instructions for sewing a Crazy Jacket say to buy at least 3 yards of fabric remnants. So far, Janice has picked out remnants measuring $\frac{5}{8}$ yard, $\frac{1}{2}$ yard, and $\frac{3}{4}$ yard. How much more fabric does Janice need?

   ① $\frac{1}{8}$ yard

   ② $\frac{1}{4}$ yard

   ③ $\frac{5}{8}$ yard

   ④ $1\frac{1}{16}$ yards

   ⑤ $1\frac{1}{8}$ yards

Use the table on page 26 for problem 5.

5. Which of the following statements are true given the data in the table?

   A. Jake was the fastest runner both in June and December.
   B. Comparing their June distances to their December distances, both Calvin and Luis improved by the same amount.
   C. The difference in the distances run by the fastest and slowest runners was greater in June than in December.

   ① None are true.
   ② Only A is true.
   ③ Only A and C are true.
   ④ Only B and C are true.
   ⑤ All are true.

Solve Problems with Fractions (x , ÷)

Judy is preparing a Thanksgiving turkey. Her gourmet cookbook gives the following roasting instruction.

Roasting Times (325°F) for Birds 10 to 20 Pounds

- *For the first 10 pounds, bake 15 minutes per pound.*

- *For any additional pound over 10 pounds, bake only 8 minutes per pound.*

According to Judy's cookbook, for how many hours should Judy roast a $17\frac{1}{2}$ pound turkey?

① 5   ④ 4

② $4\frac{3}{4}$ ❺ $3\frac{1}{2}$

③ $4\frac{1}{4}$

Solution

The number of minutes required to cook the turkey will be the time needed for the first 10 pounds plus the time needed for the weight greater than 10 pounds.

Total time = time for 1st 10 pounds + time for amount over 10 pounds

$$= \quad (10 \times 15) \quad + \quad (17\frac{1}{2} - 10) \times 8$$

$$= \quad\quad 150 \quad\quad + \quad\quad 7\frac{1}{2} \times 8$$

Now simplify $7\frac{1}{2} \times 8$ using one of the approaches below.

Approach 1

Multiply the mixed number.

$$7\frac{1}{2} \times 8 = (7 \times 8) + (\frac{1}{2} \times 8)$$

$$= 56 + \frac{8}{2} = \mathbf{60}$$

Approach 2

Write the mixed number as a decimal and then multiply.

$$7\frac{1}{2} \times 8 = 7.5 \times 8 = \mathbf{60}$$

Complete the addition: $150 + (7\frac{1}{2} \times 8) = 150 + 60 = \mathbf{210\ minutes}$

The answer choices are in hours. So change 210 minutes to hours.

$$210 \div 60 = 3\frac{1}{2}\ \mathbf{hours}$$

Writing a Mixed Number As a Decimal

A mixed number is the sum of a whole number and a fraction:

$$7\frac{1}{2} = 7 + \frac{1}{2}$$

but also can be written as a decimal.

To change the fraction to a decimal, divide the numerator by the denominator.

$\frac{1}{2}$ ⟵ numerator
⟵ denominator

$$\begin{array}{r} 0.5 \\ 2\overline{)1.0} \\ -1\ 0 \\ \hline 0 \end{array}$$

$7\frac{1}{2}$ can be written as **7.5**.

GED Readiness

Concept

1 A $13\frac{1}{4}$-ton railroad car is loaded with 19 pickup trucks, each weighing $2\frac{1}{8}$ tons. Which expression gives the best estimate of the combined weight in tons of the railroad car and the pickup trucks?

  ① $(13 + 20) \times 2$
  ② $20 \times 2 - 13$
  ③ $13 + 20 \times 2$
  ④ $20 \times (13 - 2)$
  ⑤ $13 \times 2 + 20$

Procedure

2 Lucy bought 3 pounds of hamburger on sale. She plans to freeze the meat in individual patties. How many $\frac{1}{4}$-pound hamburger patties can Lucy make?

Mark your answer in the circles in the grid.

3 Justin worked 20 days last month. His total daily commute time is $\frac{3}{4}$ hour. How many hours did Justin spend commuting to work last month?

  ① 30 hr
  ② 20 hr
  ③ 15 hr
  ④ 10 hr
  ⑤ Not enough information is given.

4 The Walter family budgets $\frac{1}{10}$ of their monthly income on entertainment. Last month, the Walters spent $\frac{1}{2}$ of their entertainment budget on concerts. What fraction of their total income did the Walters spend on concerts last month?

  ① $\frac{1}{20}$ ④ $\frac{1}{2}$
  ② $\frac{1}{10}$ ⑤ $\frac{2}{3}$
  ③ $\frac{1}{6}$

Application

Problems 5 and 6 refer to the following information and table.

The boards that Keith will use to make shelves are available in 3 lengths. He needs 6 boards that are each $3\frac{1}{4}$ feet long.

Board Length	Price
6 feet	$5.49
8 feet	$6.93
10 feet	$9.25

5 How much will it cost Keith to make the shelves from boards that are each 6 feet long?

  ① $5.49
  ② $10.98
  ③ $21.96
  ④ $32.94
  ⑤ Not enough information is given.

6 What is the least amount Keith can spend on lumber to make the shelves?

  ① $5.49
  ② $8.49
  ③ $18.50
  ④ $20.79
  ⑤ $32.94

Relate Fractions, Decimals, and Percents

Best Furniture Company makes tabletops using 16 tiles as shown. What part of each tabletop is made from white tiles? Write your answer as a fraction, a decimal, and a percent.

① $\frac{1}{2}$, 0.5, 50%   ④ $\frac{1}{4}$, 0.4, 40%

② $\frac{1}{2}$, 0.25, 25%   ⑤ $\frac{1}{4}$, 0.25, 40%

③ $\frac{1}{4}$, 0.25, 25%

Three Forms of a Number Less Than 1

$$\frac{1}{4}$$

Fraction

Decimal   Percent
0.25   25%

Writing a Fraction

$$\frac{\text{number of identified parts}}{\text{total number of parts}}$$

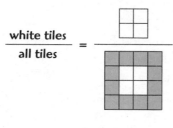

$\dfrac{\text{white tiles}}{\text{all tiles}} =$

$$= \frac{4}{16} = \frac{1}{4}$$

Solution

Fraction

Write the fraction of the tabletop that is made from white tiles. Reduce this fraction by dividing both numerator and denominator by the number 4, the greatest common factor.

$$\frac{\text{numerator}}{\text{denominator}} = \frac{\text{white tiles}}{\text{total tiles}} = \frac{4}{16} = \frac{4 \div 4}{16 \div 4} = \frac{1}{4}$$

Decimal

Change the fraction $\frac{1}{4}$ to a decimal. Divide the numerator (1) by the denominator (4).

$1 \div 4 = \mathbf{0.25}$

$$\begin{array}{r} 0.25 \\ 4\overline{)1.00} \\ -8 \\ \hline 20 \\ -20 \\ \hline 0 \end{array}$$

Percent

To convert a fraction to a percent, multiply by 100%.

$$\frac{1}{4} \times 100\% = \frac{100\%}{4} = \mathbf{25\%}$$

Answer: $\frac{1}{4}$, 0.25, 25%

Fraction

| ON | 4 | a^b/c | 1 | 6 | = | 1 ⌐4. |

Decimal

| ON | 4 | ÷ | 1 | 6 | = | 0.25 |

Percent

| ON | 4 | ÷ | 1 | 6 | SHIFT | =^% | 25. |

On the Casio *fx-260SOLAR*, the percent function is used by pressing the shift key followed by the equals key.

GED Readiness

Concept

① After being on sale for only 2 weeks, 63% of the raffle tickets were sold. Which fraction is the best estimate of the fraction of the total tickets sold?

① $\frac{1}{4}$ ② $\frac{1}{2}$ ③ $\frac{3}{8}$ ④ $\frac{2}{3}$ ⑤ $\frac{5}{16}$

Procedure

② All blankets at Home Plus are on sale for $\frac{1}{4}$ off. What percent discount does this fraction represent?

① 4%
② 14%
③ 25%
④ 30%
⑤ 40%

③ The parking lot at Myrna's Market is shown in the diagram below. What percent of the spaces are taken?

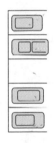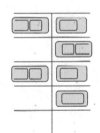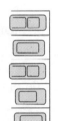

① 15%
② 25%
③ 60%
④ 70%
⑤ 75%

④ In a catalog, the width of a carving chisel is specified as 0.8 inch. How is the width of the chisel written as a fraction of an inch?

① $\frac{1}{8}$ in.

② $\frac{1}{4}$ in.

③ $\frac{5}{16}$ in.

④ $\frac{4}{5}$ in.

⑤ $\frac{8}{12}$ in.

Application

⑤ The Workers' Credit Union charges a 4.32% annual interest rate for new car loans up to 60 months. For 72-month loans, an additional $\frac{3}{4}$% is charged. What annual interest rate is charged on the longer loan?

① 5.07%
② 4.66%
③ 4.58%
④ 4.375%
⑤ 4.125%

⑥ Within two hours after the polls opened, $\frac{3}{8}$ of the registered voters voted on the school bond issue. A television news announcer stated 80% of the registered voters were expected to vote. What percent of voters are still expected to vote?

Mark your answer in the circles in the grid.

Understand Discount and Sales Tax

A set of three music CDs regularly sells for $44.00. The set is on sale at a 25% discount. If the sales tax is 5%, what is the total cost of the CDs?

① $46.20   ④ $34.65
② $42.60   ⑤ $30.80
③ $39.40

Solution

Write a sentence that describes the solution.

Total cost *equals* **sale price** *plus* **sales tax**.

To find the total cost, find the sum of . . .

• the sale price and

• the sales tax

Step 1

sale price	equals	regular price	minus	discount
sale price	=	$44.00	−	(25% of $44.00)
	=	$44.00	−	($44.00 × 0.25)
	=	$44.00	−	$11.00
sale price	=	**$33.00**		

Step 2

total cost	equals	sale price	plus	sales tax
total cost	=	$33.00	+	(5% of $33.00)
	=	$33.00	+	($33.00 × 0.05)
	=	$33.00	+	$1.65
total cost	=	**$34.65**		

Alternate Solution

Step 1

Notice that the sale price is 75% of the original price:

75% = 100% − 25%

Sale price = 75% of $44.00

= $44.00 × 0.75

= $33.00

Step 2

One way of adding 5% of a number to itself is to multiply the number by 1.05.

1 + 5% = 1 + 0.05 = 1.05

Total cost = 1.05 × $33.00

= $34.65

First, use the calculator to find the sale price.

 ON 4 4 × 2 5 SHIFT = − [33.]

Now, use the calculator to add the sales tax to the sale price.

 ON 3 3 × 5 SHIFT = + [34.65]

The Casio *fx-260*SOLAR has a short-cut for computing sale price (percent discount) and for adding sales tax (percent increase).

GED Readiness

Concept

1 The sale price of a set of dishes is $39.99. If the sales tax rate is 8.5%, which expression gives the total cost of the dishes?

(1) $39.99 × 8.5
(2) $39.99 × 0.15
(3) $39.99 × 0.085
(4) $39.99 × 9.5
(5) $39.99 × 1.085

2 A camera regularly priced at $399.99 is on sale for 10% off. Disregarding sales tax, which is the **best estimate** of the camera's sale price?

(1) $40
(2) $60
(3) $300
(4) $360
(5) $390

3 Which expressions show how to find the sale price of a $250 stereo that is being offered at a 25% discount?

A. 0.25 × $250
B. 0.75 × $250
C. (1 + 0.25) × $250
D. (1 − 0.25) × $250

(1) A and C
(2) A and D
(3) B and C
(4) B and D
(5) C and D

Procedure

4 At Music City, music CDs are on sale for $14.50. What is the total cost of a CD if the sales tax is 5%?

(1) $15.23
(2) $15.15
(3) $14.90
(4) $14.55
(5) $13.92

Application

5 A clock radio that regularly sells for $18 is on sale for 30% off. If the sales tax rate is 5%, what is the total cost of the clock radio?

Mark your answer in the circles in the grid.

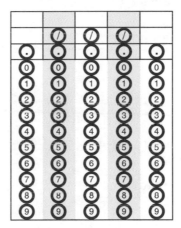

6 Evelyn is buying a new kitchen table and a set of chairs. The original price of $860 is being discounted 20%. What total will Evelyn pay if the sales tax is 6.5%?

(1) $589.84
(2) $605.46
(3) $646.72
(4) $712.84
(5) $732.72

11 Understand Ratio

Amy Lee made a table of her family's expenses. What is the ratio of the amount spent on February utilities to the amount spent on January utilities?

The answer $\frac{2}{3}$ is recorded on the grid.

Lee Family Take-Home Pay Allocation

Expense	January	February
Food	$240	$220
Rent	$720	$720
Medical	$120	$160
Clothing	$60	$180
Utilities	$210	$140
Entertainment	$80	$50
Car Expenses	$260	$240
Child Care	$180	$180
Savings	$200	$200
Other	$330	$310

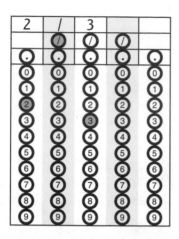

Solution

A ratio is a comparison of two numbers, most often written as a fraction. In the question you are asked to use a ratio to compare February and January utility expenses.

Step 1

Find the utility expenses for January and February.

Expense	January	February
Food	$240	$220

Utilities	$210	$140

Step 2

Write the ratio as a fraction. The order of the numbers is important.

- The numerator is the first number in the question: February utility expense.

- The denominator is the number following the word *to* in the question: January utility expense.

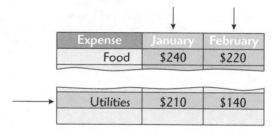

ratio of … February utilities ⟶ $\frac{140}{210}$
to … January utilities ⟶

Reduce the ratio fraction to lowest terms: $\frac{140}{210} = \frac{140 \div 70}{210 \div 70} = \frac{2}{3}$

The ratio of February utilities to January utilities is $\frac{2}{3}$.

A ratio can be written three different ways:

- in words, 2 to 3

- with a colon, 2:3

- as a fraction, $\frac{2}{3}$

When writing a ratio:

- Reduce the fraction to lowest terms

Example

Write 6 to 8 as $\frac{6}{8} = \frac{3}{4}$

- A ratio greater than 1 is written as an improper fraction, not as a mixed number

Example

Write 10 to 4 as $\frac{10}{4} = \frac{5}{2}$

- A whole number ratio is written with a denominator of 1

Example

Write 6 to 2 as $\frac{6}{2} = \frac{3}{1}$

GED Readiness

Concept

① Of the 15 adults who joined the Army Reserves yesterday, 11 are men. What is the ratio of women to men?

Mark in your answer in the circles in the grid.

Procedure

Problems 2 and 3 refer to the table on page 34.

② What is the ratio of the amount spent on clothing in January to the amount spent on clothing in February?

① $\frac{1}{3}$

② $\frac{1}{4}$

③ $\frac{2}{3}$

④ $\frac{3}{1}$

⑤ $\frac{3}{2}$

③ For January, what is the ratio of the amount spent on utilities to the amount spent on child care?

① $\frac{7}{2}$ ④ $\frac{2}{7}$

② $\frac{7}{6}$ ⑤ $\frac{3}{5}$

③ $\frac{3}{7}$

Application

④ A summary of Isaac's paycheck is shown in the table below. What percent of Isaac's gross earnings go to paying taxes? Round your answer to the nearest percent.

Isaac's Paycheck

Gross Earnings	$2,000
Federal Tax	$300
State Tax	$100
Social Security Tax	$124
Medical Insurance	$150
Net Earnings	$1,356

① 34%

② 26%

③ 20%

④ 15%

⑤ 11%

⑤ When estimating a bid for remodeling a kitchen, a contractor uses the allocation shown in the graph below. What is the ratio of the cost for materials to the cost for labor?

Costs of Kitchen Remodeling

Materials 25%

Labor 75%

① $\frac{1}{3}$

② $\frac{1}{4}$

③ $\frac{2}{3}$

④ $\frac{3}{2}$

⑤ Not enough information is given.

Work with Proportions

About how many calories does an average man use when he bowls for 75 minutes?

① 300
② 275
③ 240
④ 200
⑤ 120

Average Calories Used in 30 Minutes

Activity	Calories Men	Calories Women
Biking	350	240
Bowling	120	80
Gardening	220	150
Jogging	300	210
Running	540	370
Walking	150	100

Solution

Step 1

Using data from the table, write a ratio comparing calories with minutes. Notice: An average man uses 120 calories bowling for 30 minutes.

$$\frac{\text{calories}}{\text{minutes}} = \frac{120}{30}$$

Average Calories Used in 30 Minutes

Activity	Calories Men	Calories Women
Biking	350	240
Bowling	120	80
Gardening	220	150

Remember

A proportion is formed by two equal ratios.

Take care when writing the ratios of a proportion. The ratios must be in the same order.

$$\frac{c}{75} \longleftrightarrow \frac{\text{calories}}{\text{minutes}} \longleftrightarrow \frac{120}{30}$$

Step 2

Write a proportion. In the second ratio, write the letter c to represent the number of calories used by an average man in 75 minutes.

$$\frac{\text{calories}}{\text{minutes}} = \frac{c}{75} = \frac{120}{30}$$

Step 3

To solve for c, write equal cross products: $\frac{c}{75} \diagdown\kern-0.8em\diagup \frac{120}{30}$

or, $30 \times c = 120 \times 75$

To solve for c, divide each side by 30: $c = \frac{120 \times 75}{30} = \textbf{300}$

An average man bowling for 75 minutes uses about 300 calories.

GED Readiness

Concept

Problem 1 refers to the table on page 36.

1 Which proportion shows the number of calories, *c*, an average woman uses while gardening for 45 minutes?

1. $\dfrac{c}{45} = \dfrac{30}{150}$

2. $\dfrac{c}{45} = \dfrac{150}{30}$

3. $\dfrac{c}{45} = \dfrac{150}{60}$

4. $\dfrac{45}{c} = \dfrac{150}{30}$

5. $\dfrac{30}{c} = \dfrac{45}{150}$

2 A survey of the employees at Star Electronics reported that 4 out of 5 people preferred Amy's Catering to Valley Catering. If Star Electronics has 240 employees, which expression gives the number of employees who preferred Amy's Catering?

1. $\dfrac{240}{5} \times (245 - 4)$

2. $\dfrac{5}{4} \times 240$

3. $\dfrac{240}{5} \times 5$

4. $\dfrac{4}{5} \times 240$

5. Not enough information is given.

Procedure

3 In Jefferson County, 2 out of every 5 people surveyed walk to work. Out of a population of 200,000 people, how many walk to work?

1. 4,000
2. 8,000
3. 40,000
4. 80,000
5. 100,000

Application

4 The manufacturing job distribution in a rural Oregon county is shown in the graph below. About how many people are employed in the food production business?

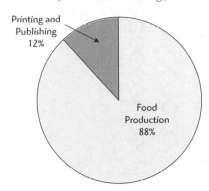

Malheur County
1,395 Manufacturing Jobs

Printing and Publishing 12%

Food Production 88%

1. 1,228
2. 1,130
3. 1,018
4. 167
5. Not enough information is given.

Calculate Percent Change

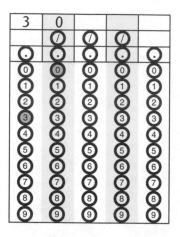

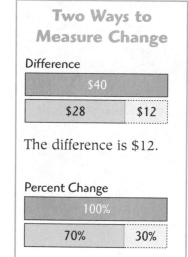

Two Ways to Measure Change

Difference

$40

$28	$12

The difference is $12.

Percent Change

100%

70%	30%

The percent change is 30%.

The sale price of a sweater is $28. The original price was $40. What percent discount is being offered on the sweater?

The answer 30% is recorded on the grid.

Solution

There are two ways to measure change between 2 values:

- Difference — The numerical difference in the two values: Subtract the sale price from the original price.

  difference = original price − sale price

- Percent Change — The ratio of the difference in the two values and the original value, written as a percent. Divide *difference in price* by *original price*.

$$\text{percent change} = \frac{\text{difference in price}}{\text{original price}} \times 100\%$$

Step 1
Find the difference in price.

$40 − $28 = $12

Step 2
Write the percent change as a fraction. Reduce the fraction.

$$\frac{\text{difference in price}}{\text{original price}} = \frac{\$12}{\$40} = \frac{\$12 \div \$4}{\$40 \div \$4} = \frac{3}{10}$$

Step 3
Write $\frac{3}{10}$ as a percent.

$$\frac{3}{10} = \frac{3}{10} \times 100\% = \frac{300\%}{10} = \textbf{30\%}$$

A 30% discount is being offered on the sweater.

Pressing ▭ completes the subtraction and readies the calculator to do the division.

dollar change   original price   write as percent   display

GED Readiness

Problems 1 through 3 are based on the following table.

Sale Item	Original Price	Sale Price
Shirt	$20.00	$15.00
Sweater	$36.00	$31.50
Jacket	$60.00	$49.00
Shoes	$50.00	$35.00
Gloves	$24.00	$12.00

Concept

1 Which expression shows how to determine the percent discount being offered on shirts?

(1) $\dfrac{\$20 - \$15}{\$5} \times 100\%$

(2) $\dfrac{\$20 - \$15}{\$100} \times 100\%$

(3) $\dfrac{\$20 - \$15}{\$35} \times 100\%$

(4) $\dfrac{\$20 - \$15}{\$15} \times 100\%$

(5) $\dfrac{\$20 - \$15}{\$20} \times 100\%$

Application

2 What percent discount is being offered on sweaters?

(1) 1.14%
(2) 1.43%
(3) 1.25%
(4) 12.5%
(5) 14.3%

3 For which listed item is the greatest percent discount being offered?

(1) shirts
(2) sweaters
(3) jackets
(4) shoes
(5) gloves

4 Tino's Pizza recently raised the price of the large combination pizza from $14.00 to $15.50. To the nearest percent, by what percent has the price increased?

(1) 11%
(2) 14%
(3) 15%
(4) 18%
(5) 21%

5 Mariano sees ads for a camera he wants to buy. A summary of the ads is shown in the following table.

Store	Original Price	Discount
Great Photo	$599.99	15%
Photo Snap	$479.99	20%
Shutter Time	$419.00	25%
Dave's Camera	$347.00	10%

Which of the following statements is (are) true about the sale price of the camera at the four stores?

A. The greatest percent discount occurs for the camera with the greatest price reduction.

B. The greatest percent discount results in the lowest camera price.

C. The greatest dollar discount is given for the camera with the greatest cost.

(1) Only A is true.
(2) Only C is true.
(3) Both A and C are true, but not B.
(4) A, B, and C are all true.
(5) None of the statements is true.

Understand Units

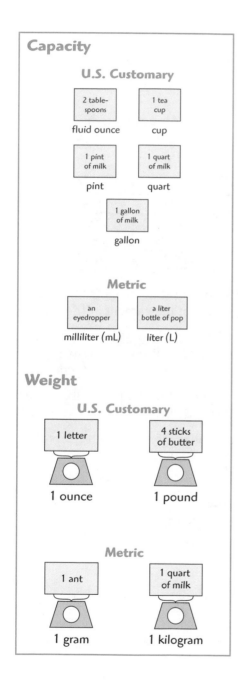

Capacity

U.S. Customary

| 2 table-spoons | 1 tea cup |
| fluid ounce | cup |

| 1 pint of milk | 1 quart of milk |
| pint | quart |

1 gallon of milk

gallon

Metric

| an eyedropper | a liter bottle of pop |
| milliliter (mL) | liter (L) |

Weight

U.S. Customary

| 1 letter | 4 sticks of butter |
| 1 ounce | 1 pound |

Metric

| 1 ant | 1 quart of milk |
| 1 gram | 1 kilogram |

Alyce's doctor prescibed a liquid medicine for her cough. Which measure may be one dose of her medicine?

① 5 gm   ④ 5 L
❷ 5 mL   ⑤ 5 pt
③ 5 oz

About Units

Units tell two things about the object being measured:

• What is being measured: capacity, weight, length, temperature, etc.

• Size: how big, how heavy, how long, how hot, etc.

The unit of measure should be appropriate for the measurement. For example, suppose you are asked to buy 1 gallon of milk. You know that a gallon is a measure of liquid volume (capacity) and you have a good idea of the size of a 1-gallon container.

Now instead, suppose you are asked to buy 128 fluid ounces of milk. You may know that a fluid ounce is also a unit of capacity. But you may not know that 128 fluid ounces equal 1 gallon. Fluid ounces is not the appropriate unit for a large quantity of milk.

There are two major systems of measurement in use today:

• U.S. Customary: the familiar measurement system used in every-day life in the United States

• Metric: the system of measurement used in most other industrialized countries throughout the world and used by doctors and scientists in the United States

Solution

Consider each answer choice:

① 5 gm   Gram is a unit of weight. Alyce would not weigh her liquid cough medicine.

② 5 mL   Milliliter is a unit of capacity and 5 mL is about the amount of a teaspoon.

③ 5 oz   Ounce is a unit of weight. Alyce would not weigh her cough medicine.

④ 5 L   Liter is a measure of capacity. However, a liter is about the same size as a quart, far too much!

⑤ 5 pt   Pint is a measure of capacity, but 5 pints is more than 2 quarts. Again, it is far too much.

5 mL is the most reasonable answer.

GED Readiness

Concept

1 Connie wants to weigh a letter to see if it needs a single stamp or two stamps. Which unit will Connie most likely use?

① milliliter
② pint
③ foot
④ kilogram
⑤ ounce

2 Choose the appropriate measure for *h*.

① 2.1 feet
② 2.1 meters
③ 2.1 millimeters
④ 2.1 centimeters
⑤ 2.1 kilometers

3 What is the approximate distance from Berlin to Paris?

① 677 centimeters
② 677 meters
③ 677 millimeters
④ 677 kilometers
⑤ 677 liters

4 In Japan, which amount would be used to tell the capacity of a large bottle?

① 500 liters
② 500 meters
③ 500 fluid ounces
④ 500 milliliters
⑤ 500 kiloliters

5 What is the approximate length of a ladybug?

① 1 meter
② 1 centimeter
③ 10 centimeters
④ 1 millimeter
⑤ 1 liter

6 What is the approximate weight of a pin?

① 1 gram
② 1 pound
③ 1 kilogram
④ 1 ounce
⑤ 1 liter

7 Joyce is making a cake. What amount of milk is she likely to use?

① 0.75 gram
② 0.75 gallon
③ 7.5 liters
④ 0.75 cup
⑤ 7.5 pints

8 Jim is ordering a custom replacement window. Which height is the most reasonable to order?

① 0.125 m
② 1.25 m
③ 12.5 m
④ 125 m
⑤ 1250 m

Read and Interpret a Scale

Think of a Thermometer as a Number Line

The difference between two points on a number line is equal to the distance between the points.

A thermometer outside Julie's home is shown at right. If the temperature inside Julie's home is 70°F, what is the difference between the inside and outside temperatures?

① 85°F
② 80°F
③ 75°F
④ 70°F
⑤ 55°F

Thermometers

A thermometer shows temperature measurements as points on a scale, drawn as a number line:

• Positive temperatures are shown as numbers greater than 0.

• Negative temperatures are shown as numbers less than 0.

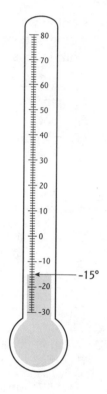

−15°

Solution

The difference between two temperatures is found by subtracting the lower temperature from the higher temperature. On a thermometer (and on any other number line), this difference is represented by the distance between the two temperature values.

Difference = 70°F − (⁻15°F)   Subtracting a negative number is
         = 70°F + 15°F   equivalent to adding a positive
         = 85°F   number.

Answer: 85°F

The Casio *fx-260SOLAR* calculator easily works with negative numbers. To enter a negative number, press the change sign key after you enter the number.

      85.

GED Readiness

Concept

① Approximately how much milk is in the measuring cup?

① 7 fl oz
② 6 fl oz
③ 5 fl oz
④ 4 fl oz
⑤ 2 fl oz

Procedure

Problem 2 refers to the thermometer on page 42.

② The freezing point of water is 32°F. What phrase below describes the temperature that is shown on the outside thermometer?

① 57°F below freezing
② 47°F below freezing
③ 25°F below freezing
④ 17°F below freezing
⑤ 15°F below freezing

③ Diane arrived at the ice skating rink on Saturday at 10:45 A.M. She left at the time shown. How long was Diane at the rink?

① 2 hours 45 minutes
② 2 hours 30 minutes
③ 2 hours 15 minutes
④ 1 hour 45 minutes
⑤ 1 hour 30 minutes

Application

④ On Saturday, Luis gives half-hour trumpet lessons from 9:30 AM to 4:30 PM. He takes a half-hour lunch break at noon. If Luis is paid $20 for each lesson, what is the total amount he makes on Saturday?

① $260   ④ $140
② $190   ⑤ $110
③ $170

⑤ Apples are on sale at 2 pounds for $1. The scale shows the weight of apples Marleena will purchase. Which is the **best estimate** of the total cost of the apples?

① $3.00
② $3.50
③ $6.00
④ $6.50
⑤ $7.00

⑥ A woodworker is laminating several types of wood for a decorative cutting board. What is the width of the walnut strip?

Maple	Walnut	Maple	Cherry

① $\frac{1}{2}$ in.   ④ $\frac{7}{8}$ in.

② $\frac{9}{16}$ in.   ⑤ $\frac{15}{16}$ in.

③ $\frac{3}{4}$ in.

Change Units of Measure

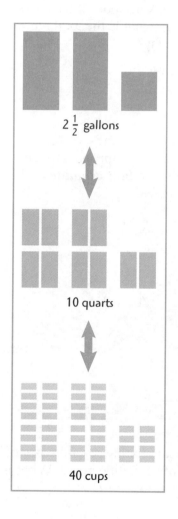

2 ½ gallons

↕

10 quarts

↕

40 cups

Jolene made $2\frac{1}{2}$ gallons of chicken soup for a lunch fundraiser.

Which expression gives the total number of servings Jolene made?

Capacity		
1 gallon	=	4 quarts
1 quart	=	4 cups
1 cup	=	1 serving

① $\frac{1}{4} \times \frac{1}{4} \times 4$

② 4×4

③ $4 \times 4 \times 4$

④ $2\frac{1}{2} \times 4$

⑤ $2\frac{1}{2} \times 4 \times 4$

Changing from One Unit to Another Unit

Each row of the table shows the same amount in different units.

Example 1 gallon is the same amount as 4 quarts.

To change from one unit to another, first decide whether more or fewer of the new units are needed:

- **If more are needed, multiply:** 2 gallons = 2 × 4 = 8 quarts

- **If fewer are needed, divide:** 8 quarts = 8 ÷ 4 = 2 gallons

. **more** but smaller ✕

Capacity		
1 gallon ☐	=	4 quarts ▯▯▯▯
1 quart ▯	=	4 cups ▯▯▯▯
1 cup ▯	=	1 serving ▯

÷ **fewer** but larger

Solution

Using the table, change $2\frac{1}{2}$ gallons to cups (same as servings).

Capacity		
1 gallon	=	4 quarts
1 quart	=	4 cups
1 cup	=	1 serving

❶ Write the number of gallons: $2\frac{1}{2}$ gallons

❷ Change gallons to quarts: $2\frac{1}{2}$ gallons = $2\frac{1}{2} \times 4$ quarts

❸ Change quarts to cups: $(2\frac{1}{2} \times 4)$ quarts = $(2\frac{1}{2} \times 4) \times 4$ cups

Answer: $2\frac{1}{2} \times 4 \times 4$ cups
[= 10 × 4 cups = 40 cups = 40 servings]

GED Readiness

Concept

Problem 1 refers to the table on page 44.

1. Jamal expects 100 people will attend the school barbeque. If he allows 2 cups of punch for each person, which expression tells the number of gallons of punch he should prepare?

   1. $2 \times 4 \times 100$
   2. $2 \times 4 \times 4 \times 100$
   3. $(100 \div 4) \times 2$
   4. $(100 \times 2) \div 4$
   5. $(100 \times 2) \div (4 \times 4)$

Problems 2 and 3 refer to the table below.

Length (Metric)		
1 m	=	100 cm
1 m	=	1,000 mm
1 km	=	1,000 m

2. Darryl's model sailboat is 31.5 centimeters (cm) long. Which is the **best estimate** of the length of his model sailboat in meters (m)?

   1. 0.03 m
   2. 0.3 m
   3. 3 m
   4. 30 m
   5. 300 m

3. On Saturday, Lisa ran in a 5-kilometer race. Which expression tells the number of meters she ran?

   1. 5×10^4
   2. 5×10^3
   3. 5×10^2
   4. 5×10^1
   5. $5 \times 10^{1,000}$

Problems 4 through 6 refer to the table below.

Length (U.S. Customary)		
1 foot	=	12 inches
1 yard	=	3 feet
1 mile	=	5,280 feet

Procedure

4. Wendy bought 2 feet of ribbon for a costume. The price of the ribbon is 80¢ per yard. What fraction of a yard did Wendy purchase?

   1. $\frac{3}{2}$
   2. $\frac{2}{3}$
   3. $\frac{2}{5}$
   4. $\frac{5}{2}$
   5. $\frac{1}{2}$

Application

5. Michael ran the 100-yard dash in 10.11 seconds. To the nearest hundredth of a mile, how far did Michael run?

   1. 0.02 mi
   2. 0.05 mi
   3. 0.06 mi
   4. 0.19 mi
   5. 0.57 mi

6. Ace Paving Company charges $33.25 per linear foot to pave a gravel road. How much will Ace Paving Company charge to pave a gravel road that is 1.3 miles long?

   1. $206.44
   2. $6,864.00
   3. $135,046.15
   4. $175,560.00
   5. $228,228.00

Understand Rate

Sheena bought 5 pounds of apples for $3.50. If she pays the same price per pound, how much would Sheena pay for 3 pounds?

The answer 2.10 dollars is recorded on the grid.

About Rates

A rate is a ratio that compares two units of measure.

• A rate is usually written as a fraction with a denominator of 1.

• The word **per** is used to indicate a rate. *Per* means *for each* (for 1).

Example As a fraction, a rate of **$0.95 per pound** is written $\frac{\$0.95}{1\,\text{pound}}$.

Notice that the units of this rate are dollars and pounds.

Solution

Step 1

Find the price per pound. Write the ratio of price to pounds. Reduce the ratio.

$$\text{Price per pound} = \frac{\text{price}}{\text{pound}} = \frac{\$3.50}{5\,\text{pounds}} = \frac{\$0.70}{1\,\text{pound}}$$

Step 2

Use the rate, price per pound, to find the price for 3 pounds.

$$\text{Price for 3 pounds} = \frac{\$0.70}{1\,\text{pound}} \times 3\,\text{pounds}$$
$$= \$2.10$$

Sheena would pay $2.10 for 3 pounds of apples.

Solving a Rate Problem as a Proportion

Rate problems can also be solved by writing a proportion. In the problem above, each ratio in the proportion is *price* to *pounds*:

$$\frac{\text{price}}{\text{pound}} : \frac{\$3.50}{5\,\text{pounds}} = \frac{c}{3\,\text{pounds}}$$ where c is the price of 3 pounds of apples.

The first step in solving for c is to cross multiply.

$$5 \times c = \$3.50 \times 3$$

The second step is to divide each side of the equation by 5.

$$c = \frac{\$3.50 \times 3}{5} = \frac{\$10.50}{5} = \mathbf{\$2.10}$$

Common Rates

miles per gallon

miles per hour

calories per serving

words per minute

heartbeats per minute

dollars per pound

cents per pound

feet per mile

feet per yard

inches per foot

dollars per hour

dollars per year (interest)

Price per pound can be written 2 ways:

$$\frac{\$0.70}{1\,\text{pound}} \qquad \frac{70¢}{1\,\text{pound}}$$

Use the units that you prefer as you solve this problem.

GED Readiness

Concept

1 During the first 3 hours of his 500-mile trip, Kevin traveled 165 miles. He hopes to complete the trip in 5 more hours. Which expression can be used to find his rate of travel (in miles per hour) for the first 3 hours of the trip?

(1) $\frac{165}{5}$ (4) $\frac{500}{3}$

(2) $\frac{335}{5}$ (5) $\frac{500}{8}$

(3) $\frac{165}{3}$

2 Megan earned $48 working 5 hours Friday afternoon. She plans to work 3 more hours Saturday morning. If she is paid at the same rate, which proportion can be used to find the amount (t) Megan will earn Saturday?

(1) $\frac{t}{3} = \frac{\$48}{5}$ (4) $\frac{t}{3} = \frac{\$48}{8}$

(2) $\frac{t}{5} = \frac{\$48}{3}$ (5) $\frac{t}{8} = \frac{\$48}{5}$

(3) $\frac{t}{3} = \frac{5}{\$48}$

Procedure

3 If Leng walks at a rate of 4.5 miles per hour, how many miles can she walk in 5 hours?

Mark your answer in the circles in the grid.

Application

4 A brand of vitamin tablets comes in three different sizes.

A. 60 tablets for $5.40

B. 100 tablets for $7.80

C. 150 tablets for $11.70

Which size is the best buy?

(1) A

(2) B

(3) C

(4) either A or C

(5) either B or C

5 A 1.2 ounce piece of almond candy contains about 230 calories. About how many calories does a 4-ounce piece contain?

(1) 610

(2) 650

(3) 710

(4) 770

(5) 840

6 Wendy read 38 pages of a novel in 1 hour. At this rate, how many pages can Wendy read in 2 hours 30 minutes?

(1) 70

(2) 78

(3) 86

(4) 95

(5) 112

Calculate Simple Interest

Keith puts $700 in a savings account that pays 5% simple interest each year. Which expression gives the total Keith will have in 18 months?

① $700 − ($700 × $\frac{1}{20}$ × $\frac{3}{2}$)

② $700 + ($700 × $\frac{1}{20}$ × $\frac{3}{2}$)

③ $700 + ($700 × $\frac{1}{20}$ × $\frac{2}{3}$)

④ $700 + ($700 × $\frac{1}{5}$ × $\frac{3}{2}$)

⑤ $700 × $\frac{1}{20}$ × $\frac{3}{2}$

Solution

Write a sentence that describes the solution.

Keith's **total** *is* the **original $700** *plus* **interest** earned in **18 months**.

Now use the **interest formula** to find the amount of interest Keith will earn.

$$\text{interest} = \text{principal} \times \text{rate} \times \text{time}$$

Step 1

Write an expression for the amount of interest earned.

Identify each amount in the interest formula:

- The rate can be written as a fraction (or as a decimal).

- Because the rate is a yearly rate, write 18 months as a number of years.

- Because fractions appear in all answer choices, write the rate and the time as fractions. Reduce each fraction to lowest terms.

principal = **$700**, the amount Keith puts in savings

rate = 5% = $\frac{5}{100}$ which reduces to $\frac{1}{20}$

time = 18 months = $\frac{18}{12}$ years which reduces to $\frac{3}{2}$ years

Step 2

Substitute the values into the interest formula:

interest = principal × rate × time = $700 × $\frac{1}{20}$ × $\frac{3}{2}$

Step 3

Use the expression for the interest to find the total:

total = $700 + interest = **$700 + ($700 × $\frac{1}{20}$ × $\frac{3}{2}$)**

Interest

Interest is an amount of money that is paid for using someone else's money.

- A bank pays you interest for money placed in a savings account.

- You pay a bank interest for money that you borrow.

Reducing Fractions

To reduce a fraction, divide both numerator and denominator by the same number.

$$\frac{18}{12} = \frac{18 \div 6}{12 \div 6} = \frac{3}{2}$$

$$\frac{5}{100} = \frac{5 \div 5}{100 \div 5} = \frac{1}{20}$$

GED Readiness

Concept

1 Amanda read that home mortgage rates are now about 6%. In what other ways can 6% be written?

A. $\frac{6}{100}$

B. $\frac{6}{10}$

C. 0.6

D. 0.06

① A only
② B only
③ A and C
④ A and D
⑤ B and C

2 Takako deposits $400 in a savings account. Which expression gives the total interest Takako will earn after 2 years 6 months if she earns 4% simple interest?

① $\$400 \times \frac{1}{20} \times \frac{5}{2}$

② $\$400 \times \frac{1}{25} \times \frac{5}{2}$

③ $\$400 \times \frac{1}{4} \times \frac{5}{2}$

④ $\$400 \times \frac{1}{20} \times \frac{3}{2}$

⑤ $\$400 \times \frac{1}{25} \times \frac{3}{2}$

Procedure

3 How much interest is earned in 3 years in a savings account that pays 5% simple interest?

① $6
② $12
③ $18
④ $24
⑤ Not enough information is given.

4 Suppose you take out a loan of $2,000 at 12% simple interest. If you make no payments for 18 months, how much interest will you owe?

① $24.00
② $36.00
③ $240.00
④ $360.00
⑤ $720.00

$I = prt$
$2000 \times 0.12 \times 18$

Application

Problems 5 and 6 refer to the chart below.

Central States Bank

Savings Rate*		Car Loan Rate*	
Type of Account		Type of Car	
Regular Savings	3.5%	New	5%
Savings Plus	4.5%	Used	8%

*All rates are computed as simple interest.

5 A customer of Central States Bank places $3,500 in a Savings Plus account for 9 months. What total amount is in the account at the end of this time?

① $362.63
② $3,573.27
③ $3,618.13
④ $3,860.50
⑤ Not enough information is given.

6 Suppose you borrow $7,000 from Central States Bank to buy a new car. You agree to pay the entire amount owed as 1 payment at the end of 15 months. About how much must you pay the bank at that time?

① $7,842.25
② $7,437.50
③ $7,180.94
④ $7,120.30
⑤ $7,074.75

Understand Similar Figures

Similar Rectangles

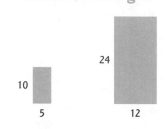

Angles have equal measure.

• All angles are 90°.

Sides are proportional.

$$\frac{10}{24} = \frac{5}{12}$$

Similar Triangles

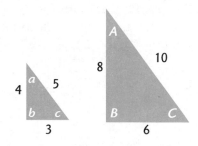

Corresponding angles have equal measure.

$\angle a = \angle A$ $\angle b = \angle B$
$\angle c = \angle C$

Sides are proportional.

$$\frac{4}{8} = \frac{5}{10} = \frac{3}{6}$$

Chris is having a poster made from a favorite photo. He asks the printer to make the poster 22 inches wide. What will be the height of the poster?

Photo   Poster

6 in.
4 in.
?
22 in.

① 21 inches
② 24 inches
③ 27 inches
④ 30 inches
⑤ 33 inches

Solution

Similar figures are the same shape but may be different sizes.

• Corresponding (matching) angles have equal measure.

• Corresponding sides are proportional (form equal ratios). Example: If a picture is enlarged to twice its original width, the new height will also be twice the original height.

Solving a Similar Figures Problem as a Proportion

Step 1

Because the poster is an enlargement of the photo, the photo and the poster are similar figures. The ratios of corresponding sides are equal.

Write a proportion. Each fraction is a ratio of corresponding sides.

$$\frac{\text{width of photo (4)}}{\text{width of poster (22)}} = \frac{\text{height of photo (6)}}{\text{height of poster (}h\text{)}} \quad \text{or,} \quad \frac{4}{22} = \frac{6}{h}$$

Step 2

To simplify, cross multiply:

$$\frac{4}{22} \bowtie \frac{6}{h}$$

$$4 \times h = 22 \times 6$$

Step 3

To find h, divide each side by 4.

$$h = \frac{22 \times 6}{4} = \frac{132}{4} = \mathbf{33}$$

The height of the poster is 33 inches.

You can use the calculator to do the computation in Step 3.

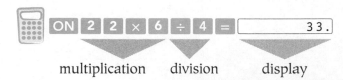

multiplication   division   display

GED Readiness

Concept

1. To find the distance (*d*) across Heron Lake, Lacey marked off distances and drew the picture shown at the right. Which proportion can you use to find this distance?

   (1) $\dfrac{d}{9} = \dfrac{34}{15}$

   (2) $\dfrac{d}{34} = \dfrac{9}{15}$

   (3) $\dfrac{d}{15} = \dfrac{34}{9}$

   (4) $\dfrac{d}{43} = \dfrac{15}{43}$

   (5) $\dfrac{d}{24} = \dfrac{15}{43}$

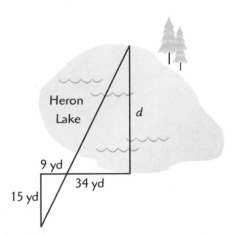

Application

2. Farhat wants to reduce a photograph to wallet size. At most, the copy can be 4 inches high. At this height, what will be the width of the copy?

   (1) 2.4 inches
   (2) 2.8 inches
   (3) 3.1 inches
   (4) 3.2 inches
   (5) 3.7 inches

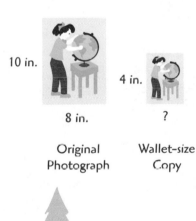

Original Photograph   Wallet-size Copy

3. Two trees stand side by side. The smaller tree is 8 feet high and casts a shadow that is 20 feet long. At the same time, the larger tree casts a shadow that is 48 feet long. To the nearest foot, how tall is the larger tree?

   (1) 19 feet
   (2) 22 feet
   (3) 25 feet
   (4) 28 feet
   (5) 31 feet

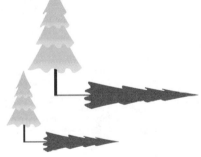

Work with a Scale Drawing

A scale drawing of an airplane is shown below. What is the length of the actual airplane?

① 16 ft 6 in.
② 20 ft 9 in.
③ 32 ft 8 in.
④ 41 ft 6 in.
⑤ 45 ft 9 in.

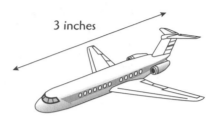

3 inches

Scale: 1 in. = 13 ft 10 in.

Scale Drawings

A scale drawing and the object it pictures are similar figures. The drawing is the same shape but not the same size as the object. Because they are similar figures, the dimensions of the scale drawing and the actual object are **proportional**.

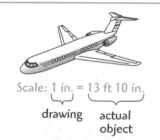

Scale: 1 in. = 13 ft 10 in.

drawing   actual object

1 inch on the drawing is equal to a length of 13 feet 10 inches on the actual airplane.

Solution

Measured on the drawing, the total length of the airplane is 3 inches. To find the actual length of the airplane, multiply 13 ft 10 in. by 3.

$$
\begin{array}{r}
13 \text{ ft } 10 \text{ in.} \\
\times 3 \\
\hline
39 \text{ ft } 30 \text{ in.}
\end{array}
$$

Multiply each unit (ft and in.) separately.

To simplify 39 ft 30 in., write 30 in. as a number of feet and inches. To do this, divide 30 in. by 12.

30 in. ÷ 12 = 2 R6 =
2 ft 6 in.

30 in.

1 ft.   1 ft.   6 in.

Answer: 39 ft 30 in. = 39 ft + 2 ft 6 in. = **41 ft 6 in.**

Solving a Scale Drawing Problem as a Proportion

A scale drawing problem can also be solved as a proportion. In this problem, each ratio in the proportion is *actual size* to *drawing size*.

$\dfrac{\text{actual size}}{\text{drawing size}} : \dfrac{13 \text{ ft } 10 \text{ in.}}{1 \text{ in.}} = \dfrac{l}{3 \text{ in.}}$ where l is the plane's actual length

$l = (13 \text{ ft } 10 \text{ in.}) \times 3 = 39 \text{ ft } 30 \text{ in.} = 39 \text{ ft} + 2 \text{ ft } 6 \text{ in.} = $ **41 ft 6 in.**

GED Readiness

Concept

1. A scale map of Texas has the following scale: 0.5 in. = 15 miles. Which expression tells the actual distance, d, if the distance on the map is 5.25 inches?

   ① $\frac{0.5}{15} = \frac{5.25}{d}$

   ② $\frac{15}{0.5} = \frac{5.25}{d}$

   ③ $\frac{0.5}{d} = \frac{15}{5.25}$

   ④ $\frac{d}{2.5} = \frac{0.5}{15}$

   ⑤ $\frac{d}{15} = \frac{0.5}{5.25}$

Procedure

2. On a blueprint for a house, the scale reads 1 inch = 24 inches. What is the actual length of a window that measures $1\frac{3}{4}$ inches on the blueprint?

   ① 2 feet 10 inches
   ② 3 feet 2 inches
   ③ 3 feet 4 inches
   ④ 3 feet 6 inches
   ⑤ 3 feet 9 inches

3. To find the distance between two nearby cities, Shaan looks at a state map. He measures the map distance between the cities to be almost exactly $2\frac{1}{2}$ inches. If the map scale reads 1 inch = 15 miles, what is the distance between the cities?

   ① between 25 and 30 miles
   ② between 31 and 35 miles
   ③ between 36 and 40 miles
   ④ between 41 and 45 miles
   ⑤ between 46 and 50 miles

Application

4. José made a scale drawing of a sailboat. The length of the sailboat in José's drawing is 8 inches. The actual length of the sailboat is 40 feet. Which of the following scales should José write below his drawing?

   ① 1 inch = 2 feet
   ② 1 inch = 5 feet
   ③ 1 inch = 8 feet
   ④ 1 inch = 20 feet
   ⑤ 1 inch = 40 feet

Problems 5 and 6 refer to the drawing below.

Corner Deck Plans

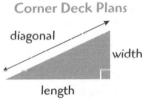

Scale: 1 inch = 8 feet

5. If the width of the scale drawing is 2.25 inches, what is the actual width of the deck?

   ① 9.25 feet
   ② 16.25 feet
   ③ 18 feet
   ④ 20.25 feet
   ⑤ 28 feet

6. If the width of the scale drawing is 2.25 inches and the length of the drawing is 4 inches, what is the actual length of the deck's diagonal?

   ① about 27 feet
   ② about 31 feet
   ③ about 34 feet
   ④ about 37 feet
   ⑤ about 42 feet

Solve a Problem Involving Measurement

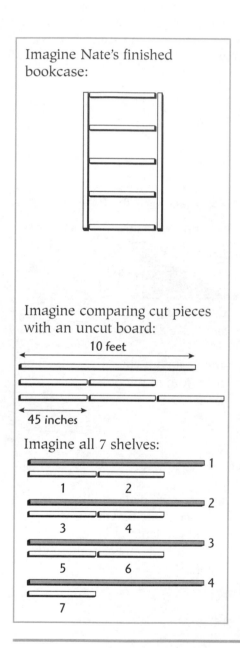

Imagine Nate's finished bookcase:

Imagine comparing cut pieces with an uncut board:

10 feet

45 inches

Imagine all 7 shelves:

1
1   2   2
3   4   3
5   6   4
7

To make shelves for a bookcase, Nate needs 7 pieces of lumber, each 45 inches long. Nate has several 10-foot lengths of lumber in the width and thickness he needs. How many of these 10-foot boards will Nate use?

① 4   ④ 7
② 5   ⑤ Not enough information is given.
③ 6

Solution

Nate will cut each 10-foot board into as many shelves as possible.

Step 1

Notice that the length of each shelf is given in inches and the length of each board is in feet. The first step is to change all lengths to the same unit: feet. You could also change all units to inches.

shelf length = 45 ÷ 12 = 3.75 feet   [12 inches = 1 foot]

Step 2

Find the number of shelves that can be cut from each 10-foot board.

3.75 × 2 = 7.5 feet   2 pieces are shorter than 10 feet.

3.75 × 3 = 11.25 feet   3 pieces are longer than 10 feet.

So, Nate can cut only 2 shelves per board.

Step 3

Ask, "Cutting 2 shelves per board, how many boards will Nate need for all 7 shelves?"

1 board is needed for 1 or 2 shelves.

2 boards are needed for 3 or 4 shelves.

3 boards are needed for 5 or 6 shelves.

4 boards are needed for 7 or 8 shelves. ◄— Nate will need 4 boards for 7 shelves.

Answer: 4

The calculator may help with part of the calculations, but the solution lies in understanding the problem.

ON 4 5 ÷ 1 2 × 2 =   7.5 ◄— 2 shelves are 7.5 feet long.

length of   length in   display
each shelf   feet of
in feet   2 shelves

GED Readiness

Concept

1 A compact disc plays 75 minutes of music. Which expression can be used to find the maximum number of songs, n, that can be recorded on one CD if the average length of a recorded song is 2 minutes 20 seconds?

- ① $n = 75 \div 2.2$
- ② $n = 75 \times 2.2$
- ③ $n = 75 \div 2\frac{1}{5}$
- ④ $n = 75 \times 2\frac{1}{3}$
- ⑤ $n = 75 \div 2\frac{1}{3}$

Procedure

2 For a craft sale, Jessica is making necklaces out of silver chain. She uses 60 cm of chain for each necklace. How many necklaces can Jessica make if she has a total of 8 m of silver chain?

- ① 13 ④ 7
- ② 11 ⑤ 5
- ③ 9

3 To repair a roof, Aaron uses packages of roof shingles that each cover an area of 80 square feet. If the area Aaron has to cover is 3,140 square feet, how many packages will he need to purchase?

Mark your answer in the circles in the grid.

Application

4 Heather is wrapping 10 gifts. For each gift, she needs a single sheet of wrapping paper 26 inches long. If gift wrap comes in rolls 7 feet long, how many rolls of paper must Heather buy?

- ① 3
- ② 4
- ③ 5
- ④ 6
- ⑤ 7

5 Alicia's phone plan includes 10 hours of long-distance calls each month. For each minute more than 10 hours, Alicia must pay an extra 8 cents. Last month, Alicia talked for $2\frac{1}{4}$ hours more than her allowed 10 hours. How much extra will Alicia be charged?

- ① $9.60
- ② $10.80
- ③ $11.40
- ④ $12.10
- ⑤ $12.90

6 Jared drinks 8 fluid ounces of orange juice each day. On his diet, Jared allows himself only 1,500 calories each day. If one quart of orange juice has 420 calories, what percent of Jared's daily calorie intake comes from orange juice?
[1 quart = 32 fluid ounces]

- ① $\frac{7}{100}$
- ② $\frac{2}{25}$
- ③ $\frac{4}{15}$
- ④ $\frac{3}{10}$
- ⑤ $\frac{4}{9}$

Understand the Measure of Angles

Zander baked a birthday cake. He cut the cake into 12 equal pieces. What is the measure of the angle made by the straight sides of each piece?

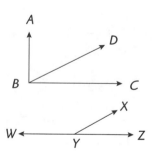

① 15°
② 30°
③ 45°
④ 60°
⑤ 90°

About Angles

An angle is measured in units called degrees. Degrees can be thought of as parts of a circle. A whole circle is divided into 360 degrees. So one degree (1°) is $\frac{1}{360}$ of a circle.

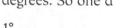

1°

Angles are named in two ways:

- by three letters: $\angle ABC$ or $\angle CBA$

- by the vertex letter only: $\angle B$

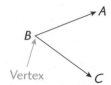

Some angle relationships have special names.

Two angles are called **complementary** if the sum of their measures is 90°.

Example $\angle ABD + \angle DBC = 90°$

Two angles are called **supplementary** if the sum of their measures is 180°.

Example $\angle WYX + \angle XYZ = 180°$

Solution

The cake has the shape of a circle. There are 12 equal pieces. To find the measure of the angle of each slice, divide 360° by 12.

Measure of angle of each piece = 360° ÷ 12 = **30°**

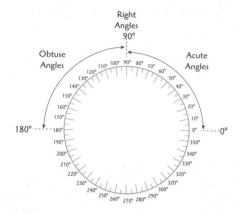

Acute Angles

Angles that measure greater than 0° and less than 90°.

Obtuse Angles

Angles that measure greater than 90° and less than 180°.

Right Angles

Angles that measure exactly 90°. A right angle is shaped like a corner and often indicated by a small square.

Straight Angles

Angles that measure exactly 180°.

GED Readiness

Concept

1 Which is the **best estimate** of the measure of the angle shown below?

① 5°
② 45°
③ 80°
④ 135°
⑤ 185°

Problems 2 and 3 refer to the diagram below.

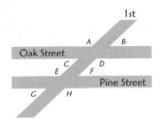

2 Oak and Pine Streets intersect 1st Street making several angles. What is the relationship between ∠A and ∠C?

① supplementary
② complementary
③ acute
④ corresponding
⑤ parallel

3 If the measure of ∠B is equal to the measure of ∠F, which angles have measures equal to ∠A?

① none of the angles
② only ∠D
③ ∠D and ∠E
④ ∠D, ∠E, and ∠H
⑤ ∠D, ∠E, ∠G, and ∠H

Procedure

Problem 4 refers to the diagram below.

4 The measure of ∠ABC is 55.3°. What is the measure, in degrees, of an angle that is the complement to ∠ABC?

Mark your answer in the circles in the grid.

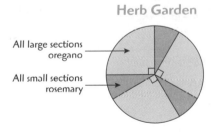

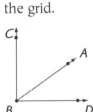

Application

5 Shaquita designed the herb garden shown below. All the large sections (light shaded) will be planted in oregano. All the small sections (dark shaded) will be planted in rosemary. What fraction of her garden will Shaquita plant in rosemary?

Herb Garden

All large sections oregano →
All small sections rosemary →

① $\frac{1}{2}$ ④ $\frac{1}{5}$

② $\frac{1}{3}$ ⑤ $\frac{3}{10}$

③ $\frac{1}{4}$

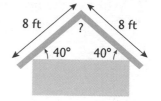

Angles in Triangles

For **all** triangles, the sum of the measures of all three angles is 180°.

$$\angle a + \angle b + \angle c = 180°$$

Isosceles Triangle

2 equal sides

2 equal angles

$$\angle b = 180° - 2\angle a$$

Equilateral Triangle

3 equal sides

3 equal angles

$$\angle a = 180° \div 3$$
$$= 60°$$

Mary is buiding a backyard storage shed. The dimensions of the roof are shown. Mary will cut a facing piece of plywood to fit the roof line. What is the measure of the roof angle (indicated in the drawing by a question mark) that Mary should cut?

① 10°   ④ 190°
② 40°   ⑤ 280°
❸ 100°

Solution

More information is given in the problem than you need. The important point to remember about angles in a triangle is:

The sum of the measures of the three angles in a triangle is always equal to 180°.

Approach 1

Step 1
Add the measures of the two known angles.

$$40° + 40° = 80°$$

Step 2
Subtract the sum of the measures from 180°.

$$180° - 80° = \mathbf{100°}$$

Approach 2

Subtract each of the known angles from 180°.

Measure of the missing angle $= 180° - 40° - 40°$
$$= 140° - 40°$$
$$= \mathbf{100°}$$

Approach 1:

 ON 1 8 0 − [(-- 4 0 + 4 0 --)] = ⎡ 100. ⎤

Approach 2:

 ON 1 8 0 − 4 0 − 4 0 = ⎡ 100. ⎤

GED Readiness

Concept

1 Which is the **best estimate** of the measure of ∠A?

① 15°
② 45°
③ 90°
④ 135°
⑤ 185°

2 Kareem is making braces to support the shelves he is building in his garage. One of the braces is shown. Which expression tells how to find the measure of ∠A?

① 360° − 20°
② 180° − 20°
③ 90° + 20°
④ 180° − (90° − 20°)
⑤ 180° − (90° + 20°)

3 One of the quilt pieces Carla is using in her quilt is shown below. Which expression tells how to find the measure in degrees of ∠x?

① $\frac{3 \times 4}{360}$

② $\frac{3 \times 4}{3}$

③ $\frac{180}{3}$

④ $\frac{180}{3 \times 4}$

⑤ $\frac{180}{4}$

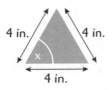

4 in. 4 in.
4 in.

Procedure

Problems 4 and 5 refer to the diagram below.

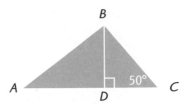

4 What is the measure of ∠DBC?

① 20°
② 30°
③ 35°
④ 40°
⑤ 50°

5 What is the measure of ∠BAC?

① 20°
② 30°
③ 40°
④ 50°
⑤ Not enough information is given.

Application

6 A surveyor is plotting the position of a triangular piece of property between several homes. So far he has made the measurements shown in the diagram. What is the measure of ∠BAC?

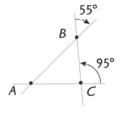

① 20° ② 30° ③ 40° ④ 50°
⑤ Not enough information is given.

Solve for Distance Using the Pythagorean Relationship

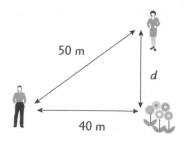 Alfonso knows that the distance across the field from his home to Carla's home is 50 meters. A nice place to pick flowers is 40 meters directly east of his home and directly south of Carla's home. How far from Carla's home is the flower-picking spot?

① 45 m   ④ 33 m
② 40 m   ⑤ 30 m
③ 36 m

The Pythagorean Relationship

The sum of the squares of the sides of a right triangle is equal to the square of the hypotenuse.

$$a^2 + b^2 = c^2$$

$$8^2 + 6^2 = 10^2$$

$$64 + 36 = 100$$

Solution

The key to solving this problem is recognizing that it is a right-triangle problem where the lengths of two sides are known. The Pythagorean relationship tells you how to find the length of the missing side.

Step 1

Write an equation that represents the relationships of the distances. First, name the unknown distance d. Then use the Pythagorean relationship to write an equation for d:

$$d^2 + 40^2 = 50^2$$

Step 2

To solve the equation for d, you must get d standing alone on one side of the equation. First subtract 40^2 from both sides of the equation.

$d^2 = 50^2 - 40^2$ Now take the square root of each side.

$d = \sqrt{(50^2 - 40^2)}$ Next, find the values of the squares.

$\quad = \sqrt{(2{,}500 - 1{,}600)}$ Subtract 1,600 from 2,500.

$\quad = \sqrt{900}$ Finally, find the square root of 900.

$\quad = \mathbf{30\ m}$

Carla's home is 30 meters from the flower-picking spot.

The calculator can be used to find d in the equation: $d = \sqrt{(50^2 - 40^2)}$

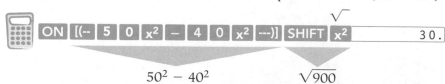

GED Readiness

Concept

1 Which is the **best estimate** of the length of side *AB*? Assume that the diagram may not be drawn to scale.

① less than 3 meters
② equal to 3 meters
③ between 3 and 6 meters
④ equal to 6 meters
⑤ greater than 6 meters

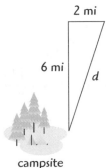

B

? 6 m

70°
A 3 m C

2 Georgia hiked 6 miles north and 2 miles east from the campsite. Which expression can be used to find *d*, the straight-line distance in miles that Georgia is from the campsite?

① $d = 6^2 + 2^2$

② $d = 6^2 - 2^2$

③ $d = \sqrt{6^2 + 2^2}$

④ $d = \sqrt{6^2 - 2^2}$

⑤ $d = \sqrt{(6 + 2)^2}$

2 mi

6 mi   d

campsite

Application

3 To frame a picture, Pegasus Framing Gallery has a labor charge of $3.50 per inch of the picture's diagonal. Materials are an additional charge. What would be the labor charge to frame the picture?

① $10.00   ④ $40.00
② $14.00   ⑤ $49.50
③ $35.00

8 in.

6 in.

4 A 13-foot ramp is attached to a 5-foot-high loading dock.

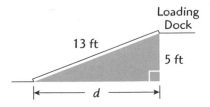

Loading
Dock

13 ft   5 ft

d

What is the distance (*d*) of the bottom of the ramp?

① 8 feet
② 9 feet
③ 10 feet
④ 11 feet
⑤ 12 feet

5 🖩 Mrs. Jones built a deck behind her house.

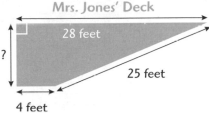

Mrs. Jones' Deck

28 feet

?   25 feet

4 feet

What is the length of the unlabeled side of this deck?

① 7 feet
② 10 feet
③ 12 feet
④ 14 feet
⑤ 16 feet

Solve for Area

Mari plans to decorate a table by covering its top surface with fancy ceramic tiles. The top is 5 feet long and 2 feet wide. If each tile is square in shape and measures 4 inches along each side, about how many tiles will Mari need?

1. 90
2. 100
3. 120
4. 150
5. 200

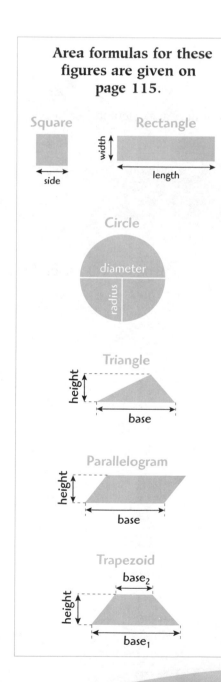

Area formulas for these figures are given on page 115.

Square — side

Rectangle — width, length

Circle — diameter, radius

Triangle — height, base

Parallelogram — height, base

Trapezoid — base₂, height, base₁

Solution

Approach 1

One way to find the number of tiles is to divide the area of the tabletop by the area of a single tile. Both areas must be in the same unit. Write the dimensions of the tile as a fraction of a foot.

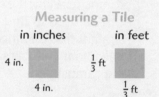

Measuring a Tile

in inches: 4 in., 4 in.

in feet: $\frac{1}{3}$ ft, $\frac{1}{3}$ ft

Area of tabletop = *length* × *width* = 5 ft × 2 ft = **10 ft²**

Area of individual tile = 4 in. × 4 in. = $\frac{1}{3}$ ft × $\frac{1}{3}$ ft = **$\frac{1}{9}$ ft²**

Number of tiles needed = 10 ft² ÷ $\frac{1}{9}$ ft² = $10 \times \frac{9}{1} = \frac{90}{1} =$ **90**

90 tiles are needed to cover the tabletop.

Approach 2

Another way to find the number of tiles is to imagine the tabletop covered by the tiles.

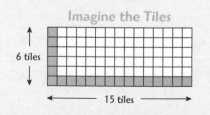

Imagine the Tiles

6 tiles

15 tiles

- 3 tiles placed side-by-side span 1 foot. So the 5-foot-long row of tiles (the length of the table) will contain 15 tiles (5 × 3).

- The 2-foot-long row of tiles (the width of the table) is spanned by 6 tiles (2 × 3).

As the drawing shows, the tabletop will be covered by 6 rows of tiles. Each row will contain 15 tiles. The total number of tiles is equal to the *number of tiles in each row* times the *number of rows*:

15 × 6 = **90**

90 tiles are needed to cover the tabletop.

GED Readiness

Concept

1. Derek is using square tiles, measuring 8 inches on each side, to cover the floor of an entryway. Which expression tells the number of tiles needed if the entryway is 6 feet long and 4 feet wide?

   (1) $(6 \times 4) \times (\frac{2}{3} \div \frac{2}{3})$

   (2) $(6 + 4) \div (\frac{2}{3})$

   (3) $(6 + 4) \div (\frac{2}{3} \times \frac{2}{3})$

   (4) $(6 \times 4) \div (\frac{2}{3})$

   (5) $(6 \times 4) \div (\frac{2}{3} \times \frac{2}{3})$

2. Taylor wants to measure the area of the deck sketched below. Which expression gives the total area in square feet of this deck?

   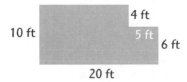

   (1) $(20 \times 10) + (6 \times 5)$
   (2) $(20 \times 10) - (6 \times 5)$
   (3) $(20 \times 10) + (5 \times 4)$
   (4) $(20 \times 10) - (5 \times 4)$
   (5) $(20 \times 10) + (6 \times 4)$

Procedure

3. What is the area in square yards of the triangular garden space shown at right?

   (1) 120 sq yd
   (2) 110 sq yd
   (3) 100 sq yd
   (4) 80 sq yd
   (5) 60 sq yd

Application

4. New tile is being laid on a floor that is 12 feet long and 9 feet wide. Each square tile measures 9 inches on each side. How many tiles will be needed?

   (1) 84
   (2) 136
   (3) 192
   (4) 228
   (5) 246

5. Katarina is having a circular mirror made. The mirror will be 2 feet in diameter. If Katarina is charged 14¢ per square inch of glass, about how much will the mirror cost?

   (1) $65.00
   (2) $60.00
   (3) $45.00
   (4) $30.00
   (5) $15.00

6. A swimming pool, 50 feet long and 30 feet wide, is surrounded by a 5-foot-wide walkway. What is the area of this walkway?

   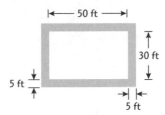

   (1) 90 square feet
   (2) 350 square feet
   (3) 450 square feet
   (4) 900 square feet
   (5) Not enough information is given.

Solve for Volume

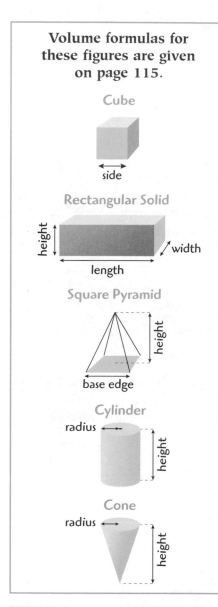

Volume formulas for these figures are given on page 115.

Cube

Rectangular Solid

height | width | length

Square Pyramid

height | base edge

Cylinder

radius | height

Cone

radius | height

Chester is using paper cones to serve chestnuts at the Fall Festival. Using the dimensions shown, find the volume of the cone Chester is using. Use $\pi \approx 3.14$, and round your answer to the nearest cubic inch.

① 18 cubic inches
② 23 cubic inches
③ 29 cubic inches
④ 37 cubic inches
⑤ 42 cubic inches

4 in.

7 in.

Solution

Step 1

Write the formula that tells the relationship between the volume of a cone and the dimensions of the cone.

Volume $= \frac{1}{3} \times \pi \times radius^2 \times height$

Step 2

Identify the values for the formula.

• $r = 2$ inches (half of the diameter)

• $h = 7$ inches

• $\pi \approx 3.14$

Volume of cone $= \frac{1}{3} \times 3.14 \times 2 \times 2 \times 7 \approx$ **29 cubic inches**

Estimating When Using π

A quick estimate can be made with formulas containing π by replacing π with the value 3. In the problem on this page, the volume of the cone is easily estimated.

volume $\approx \underbrace{\frac{1}{3} \times 3}_{1} \times 2 \times 2 \times 7 = 28$ cubic inches

This estimate enables you to correctly pick **29 cubic inches** as the correct answer.

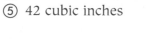

ON 1 aᵇ/c 3 × SHIFT EXP × 2 x² × 7 = 29.32153143

display

GED Readiness

Concept

1 Three tennis balls fit snugly in a cylindrical can. The radius of each tennis ball is *r*. Which expression gives the **best estimate** of the volume of the can?

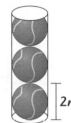

① $(\pi \times r^2) \times 3$
② $(\pi \times r^2) \times 6$
③ $(2 \times \pi \times r) \times 6$
④ $(\pi \times r^2) \times (6 \times r)$
⑤ $(2 \times \pi \times r) \times (6 \times r)$

2 Tyrone is making a driveway out of concrete. The driveway is in the shape of a rectangular solid that is 25 feet long, 16 feet wide, and 6 inches thick. Which expression gives the number of cubic feet of concrete Tyrone will need?

① $25 \times 16 \times 0.5$
② $25 \times 16 \times 0.6$
③ $25 \times 16 \times 0.12$
④ $25 \times 16 \times 2$
⑤ $25 \times 16 \times 6$

Procedure

3 A pile of sand is in the shape of a cone. If the height of the pile is 4 feet and the diameter of the pile is 8 feet, what is the approximate volume of the pile?

① 70 cubic feet
② 110 cubic feet
③ 160 cubic feet
④ 200 cubic feet
⑤ Not enough information is given.

Application

4 A waterbed measures 6 feet long, 5 feet wide, and 8 inches high. What is the approximate weight of the bed when it is full of water? Note: 1 cubic foot of water weighs about 62 pounds.

① about 400 pounds
② about 600 pounds
③ about 800 pounds
④ about 1,000 pounds
⑤ about 1,200 pounds

5 Quan is packing toy blocks that measure 2 inches on each side. She puts them into a box that is 8 inches long, 6 inches wide, and 4 inches high. How many blocks can Quan pack in each box?

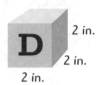

① 12
② 16
③ 24
④ 36
⑤ 48

6 An oil drum in the shape of a cylinder has a diameter of 2 feet and a height of 4 feet. If 1 cubic foot of volume can hold about 7.5 gallons of oil, what is the total capacity of the drum?

① about 120 gallons
② about 90 gallons
③ about 60 gallons
④ about 30 gallons
⑤ Not enough information is given.

Work with a Coordinate Plane

The coordinates of three vertices (corner points) of a rectangle are (⁻4,3), (5,3), and (5,⁻2)

Plot the fourth vertex of the rectangle on the coordinate plane grid.

The answer (⁻4,⁻2) is plotted on the grid.

x-coordinate ─┘ └─ y-coordinate

The Coordinate Plane

Suppose you hang a picture in your room. You might describe the point for the hook as "3 feet to the left of the door and 6 feet above the floor."

In math, a **coordinate plane** is used to describe the location of a point. A **coordinate plane** is formed by two number lines that cross at a point called the **origin**.

- a horizontal line called the **x-axis**

- a vertical line called the **y-axis**

Two numbers, called **coordinates**, tell the location of a point on the coordinate plane. The two numbers are written within parentheses: (x, y) and are often referred to as an **ordered pair**.

- The first number, the **x-coordinate**, tells the distance of a point from the origin along the x-axis: (x,). The sign of the number tells whether the point is right (+) or left (−) of the origin.

- The second number, the **y-coordinate**, tells the distance of a point from the origin along the y-axis: (, y). The sign of the number tells whether the point is above (+) or below (−) the origin.

- The origin has coordinates (0, 0).

Solution

Plot the points (⁻4,3), (5,3), and (5,⁻2) lightly on the coordinate grid. The 4th point is 4 units to the left of the origin (⁻4,) and 2 units below the origin (,⁻2). Fill in the circle on the answer grid at the point (⁻4,⁻2). Erase the first three points.

The coordinates of the fourth point are **(⁻4,⁻2)**.

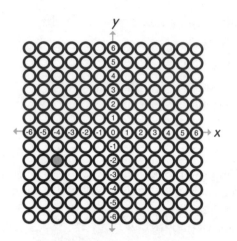

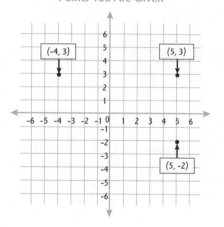

Points You Are Given

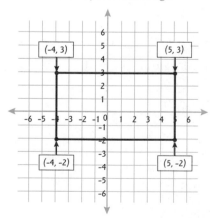

The Completed Rectangle

GED Readiness

Concept

Problems 1 through 3 refer to the coordinate plane below.

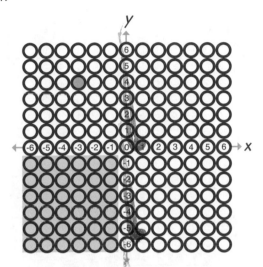

1. What are the signs of the coordinates of points that lie in the shaded part of the coordinate plane shown above?

   ① *x*-value negative; *y*-value positive
   ② *x*-value positive; *y*-value positive
   ③ *x*-value negative; *y*-value negative
   ④ *x*-value positive; *y*-value negative
   ⑤ Not enough information is given.

2. What point is identified by the filled-in circle?

   ① (⁻4,⁻3)
   ② (⁻4,3)
   ③ (⁻3,⁻4)
   ④ (3,⁻4)
   ⑤ (⁻3,4)

3. What point is 5 points to the right and 3 points below the point identified by the filled-in circle?

   ① (2,1)
   ② (3,1)
   ③ (5,2)
   ④ (⁻1,2)
   ⑤ (1,2)

Procedure

4. Suppose △ABC is moved so that the new coordinates of point A become (⁻3,4). In the triangle's new position, what will be the new coordinates of point C?

   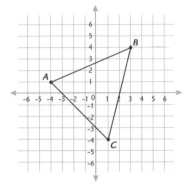

   Mark your answer on the coordinate plane grid below.

   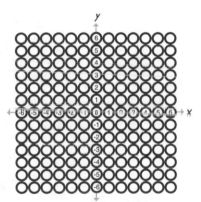

5. The coordinates of three vertices of a parallelogram are (⁻3,⁻2), (⁻1,2), and (3,2). Plot the fourth vertex on the coordinate plane grid below.

   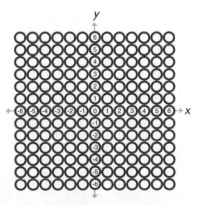

Understand Slope of a Graphed Line

Which graphed line has a slope of 1?

①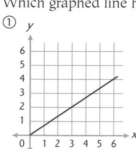

②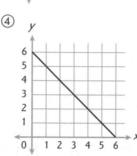

3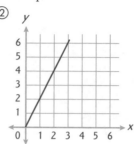

④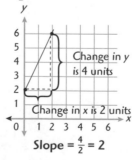

④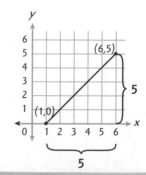

Thinking about Slope

When you walk uphill, you walk up a slope. When you walk downhill, you walk down a slope. A graphed line, like a hill, has a slope.

Positive Slope ↗

Negative Slope ↘

Two Special Lines

A *horizontal line* has a slope of 0.

←——————→

Slope = 0

A *vertical line* has an undefined slope. The concept of a slope does not apply to a vertical line.

↑

Undefined Slope

↓

Slope of a Graphed Line

The slope of a graphed line is given as a number. When you move between two points on a line, the slope is found by dividing the change in *y*-value by the corresponding change in *x*-value.

- A line that goes up from left to right has a *positive slope*.
- A line that goes down from left to right has a *negative slope*.

$$\text{Slope of a graphed line} = \frac{\text{change in } y\text{-value}}{\text{change in } x\text{-value}}$$

Examples

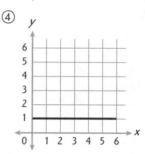

Slope $= \frac{4}{2} = 2$

Slope $= -\frac{6}{2} = -3$

Solution

To see that choice 3 is correct, choose two points on the graphed line.

Example (1,0) and (6,5).

Slope $= \dfrac{\text{change in } y\text{-value}}{\text{change in } x\text{-value}} = \dfrac{5-0}{6-1} = \dfrac{5}{5} = 1$

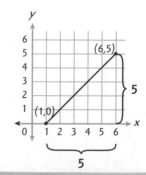

GED Readiness

Concept

1 How would you describe the slope of the line on the graph below?

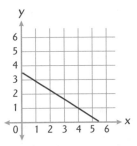

① positive
② negative
③ zero
④ undefined
⑤ None of the above.

2 Two points, (5,1) and (2,0), are on a graphed line. Which expression gives the slope of this line?

① $\frac{5-1}{2-0}$

② $\frac{2-1}{5-0}$

③ $\frac{5-2}{1-2}$

④ $\frac{1-0}{5-2}$

⑤ None of the above.

Procedure

3 What is the slope of a graphed line that passes through the points (1,2) and (6,4)?

① 3   ④ $\frac{2}{5}$

② $\frac{5}{2}$ ⑤ $\frac{1}{4}$

③ 2

Application

Problems 4 and 5 refer to the graph below.

The line graph shows a summary of health insurance costs of employees at Laserton Electronics.

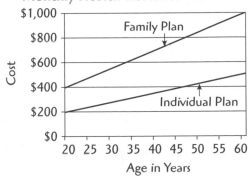

4 After the age of 20, what is the **best estimate** of the yearly increase in cost of monthly health insurance for a family covered by the Family Plan?

① $5.00
② $7.50
③ $15.00
④ $50.00
⑤ Not enough information is given.

5 After the age of 20, what is the **best estimate** of the yearly increase in cost of monthly health insurance for an individual covered by the Individual Plan?

① $6.25
② $7.50
③ $15.00
④ $50.00
⑤ Not enough information is given.

29 Apply Measure of Central Tendency

Angela takes a math quiz every Friday. On her first six quizzes, Angela received scores of 95, 92, 87, 96, 87, and 98.

What is the mean, or average, of Angela's six scores?

① 87 ④ **92.5**
② 89.5 ⑤ 98
③ 91

Measures of Central Tendency

A typical value is often used to summarize a set of numbers. In math, a typical value is given as one of three numbers: **mean**, **median**, or **mode**. These values are called **measures of central tendency**.

- **Mean**, or *average*, is the sum of a set of numbers (data) divided by the number of numbers in the set.

- **Median** is the value closest to the middle of the numbers in the set. To find the median, list the numbers from least to greatest.

  For an odd number of numbers, the median is the middle number.

  For an even number of numbers, the median is the mean (average) of the *two* middle numbers.

- **Mode** is the number that occurs most often in the set. If no number occurs more often than any other, there is no mode.

The **range** of a set of numbers is the difference between the greatest and least values. The range is a measure of the spread of data values.

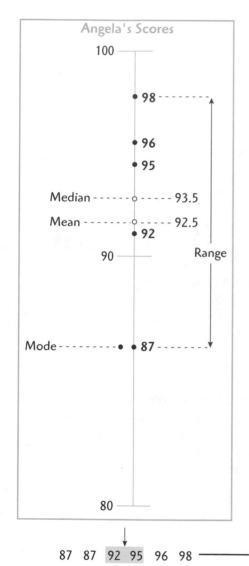

Angela's Scores

Solution

Mean =

$$\frac{\text{sum of Angela's scores}}{\text{number of scores}} = \frac{(95 + 92 + 87 + 96 + 87 + 98)}{6} = \frac{555}{6} = \mathbf{92.5}$$

Angela's mean test score is 92.5.

87 87 **92 95** 96 98 ⟶ The **median** of Angela's scores is 93.5, the mean of 92 and 95.

87 87 92 95 96 98 ⟶ The **mode** of Angela's scores is 87, the only score that occurs twice.

87 87 92 95 96 98 ⟶ The **range** of Angela's scores is 11 (98 − 87 = 11).

On the calculator, the parentheses keys are used to group the sum of scores to be added.

ON [(-- 9 5 + 9 2 + 8 7 + 9 6 + 8 7 + 9 8 --)] ÷ 6 =   9 2 . 5

add the scores   divide by 6   display

GED Readiness

Concept

1 Which of the statements below are true about a set of numbers?

   A. The mean of any set of numbers is always a whole number.

   B. The mean of any set of numbers is always a number in the set.

   C. The median of any set of numbers is always a number in the set.

   ① None of the statements.
   ② A only
   ③ B only
   ④ C only
   ⑤ A and C

2 Out of a possible 100 points, Riley scored 80 and 100 points on his first two math exams. If he scores 90 points on his next exam, which of the following data measures would change: mean, median, mode, or range?

   ① mean only
   ② median only
   ③ mode only
   ④ range only
   ⑤ None will change.

3 In her first four basketball games, Chelsea scored 15, 5, 0, and 20. Which expression tells her average (mean) score in these four games?

   ① $\dfrac{15 + 5 + 20}{3}$

   ② $\dfrac{15 + 5 + 0 + 20}{4}$

   ③ $\dfrac{15 + 5 + 20}{2}$

   ④ $\dfrac{15 + 20}{2}$

   ⑤ $\dfrac{5 + 15}{2}$

Procedure

Problems 4 and 5 refer to the table below.

Garcia Family Budget

Expense	January	February	March
Housing	$700	$700	$700
Utilities	$134	$218	$95
Food	$256	$214	$301
Medical	$210	$40	$64
Clothing	$141	$89	$56
Entertainment	$102	$145	$80

4 What is the median cost of entertainment for the months on the table?

   ① $145   ④ $102
   ② $248   ⑤ $80
   ③ $209

5 What is the average (mean) food cost for the months on the table?

   ① $301   ④ $230
   ② $276   ⑤ $124
   ③ $257

Application

6 Mario keeps a record of his mileage and gas expenses while on a business trip. His summary is shown on the table below.

May Business Trip

Miles Driven	Gas (gal)	Cost
287	17.5	$32.85
310	16.8	$32.60
298	15.7	$29.89

What is the average (mean) miles per gallon that Mario gets on his business trip?

   ① 17.94 mpg
   ② 17.9 mpg
   ③ 17.1 mpg
   ④ 16.67 mpg
   ⑤ 16.5 mpg

Find a Missing Term When the Mean is Known

Chandra recorded her quarterly sales in a bar graph. Chandra will get a bonus of $5,000 if her average quarterly sales for the year reach $70,000.

What must her sales be for the 4th quarter in order for Chandra to earn the bonus?

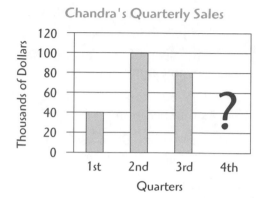

Chandra's Quarterly Sales

① $40,000
② $45,000
③ $50,000
④ $55,000
❺ $60,000

Alternate Solution

Write an equation for the average quarterly sales. Let each amount represent the number of $1,000s.

$$\text{Average} = \frac{\$40 + \$100 + \$80 + n}{4}$$

Replace "average" with $70.

$$\$70 = \frac{\$40 + \$100 + \$80 + n}{4}$$
$$= \frac{\$220 + n}{4}$$

Solve the equation for n:

• Multiply each side by 4:

$\$70 \times 4 = \$220 + n$

or, $\$280 = \$220 + n$

• Subtract $220 from each side:

$\$280 - \$220 = n$

or, $\$60 = n$

Because n is the number of $1,000s, the **answer is $60,000**.

Solution

This "average" problem is unlike most you have seen before. Here you are told what the average is; your task is to find a missing term.

Step 1

Write two different expressions for total sales for the year. Represent the unknown 4th-quarterly sales amount by the letter n.

1) total sales for the year = the sum of the four quarterly sales

$$= \$40,000 + \$100,000 + \$80,000 + n$$

$$= \mathbf{\$220,000 + n}$$

2) total sales for the year = 4 × (average quarterly sales)

$$= 4 \times \$70,000 = \mathbf{\$280,000}$$

Step 2

Set the two expressions for *total sales for the year* equal to each other.

$\$220,000 + n = \$280,000$

To find the value of n, ask, "What do you add to $220,000 to get a sum of $280,000?"

Answer = $60,000

Chandra's sales for the 4th quarter must be $60,000 (or greater).

GED Readiness

Concept

1 Holly, a coworker of Chandra's, also wants her average quarterly sales for the year to be $70,000. Which information could Holly use to compute what her 4th quarter sales must be?

A. her average sales for the first 3 quarters

B. the sum of her sales for the first 3 quarters

C. her sales amount for each of the first 3 quarters

① A only
② B only
③ C only
④ A or C only
⑤ A, B, or C

Application

Problems 2 and 3 refer to the graph on page 72.

2 Chandra has been offered a bonus of $10,000 if her average quarterly sales for the year reach $80,000. What must her sales position for the 4th quarter be in order for Chandra to earn this larger bonus?

① $100,000
② $90,000
③ $80,000
④ $70,000
⑤ $60,000

3 An additional bonus of a Caribbean cruise is offered if the average quarterly sales for just the 3rd and 4th quarters is $120,000. What must Chandra's sales for the 4th quarter be to earn the cruise?

① $50,000
② $100,000
③ $120,000
④ $140,000
⑤ $160,000

Problems 4 through 6 refer to the information and graph below.

Josh's final math grade is based on his scores on 4 math quizzes. To get an A, Josh needs an average quiz score of 88 or higher. His scores for the first 3 quizzes are shown on the graph.

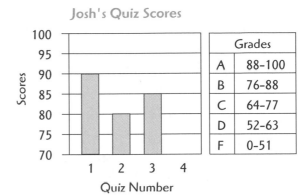

Josh's Quiz Scores

	Grades
A	88–100
B	76–88
C	64–77
D	52–63
F	0–51

Procedure

4 What is Josh's average score on the first 3 quizzes?

① 92   ④ 85
② 90   ⑤ 80
③ 88

Application

5 If the highest score Josh can get on the 4th quiz is 100, what is the highest average score Josh can possibly get on the 4 quizzes?

① 93.5   ④ 89.25
② 92.25   ⑤ 88.75
③ 90.5

6 What is the lowest score Josh can get on the 4th quiz and still earn an A grade?

① 99   ④ 93
② 97   ⑤ 91
③ 95

31 Interpolate and Extrapolate

Valley Beverages sells specialty hot chocolate and lemonade drinks at several local outlets. The graph shows how average total sales of each drink depend on the outdoor average temperature.

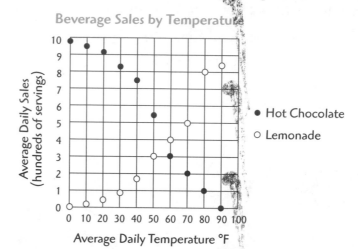

Beverage Sales by Temperature

Average Daily Sales (hundreds of servings)

Average Daily Temperature °F

● Hot Chocolate
○ Lemonade

Another Way to Interpolate

Another way to interpolate is to find the average of two data points:

Let s_{70} = servings at 70°F

s_{75} = servings at 75°F

s_{80} = servings at 80°F

Then $s_{75} \approx \dfrac{s_{70} + s_{80}}{2}$

$\approx \dfrac{500 + 800}{2}$

$\approx$ **650 servings**

Estimate the number of lemonades that Valley expects to sell at average daily temperatures of 75°F and 100°F.

① 75°F: 150 servings; 100°F: 0 servings
② 75°F: 650 servings; 100°F: 900 servings
③ 75°F: 40 servings; 100°F: 100 servings
④ 75°F: 450 servings; 100°F: 900 servings
⑤ 75°F: 600 servings; 100°F: 1,000 servings

Solution

Estimate the number of servings at 75°F:

Draw a line connecting the data points for 70°F and 80°F.

Place a dot at the point on your line halfway between 70°F

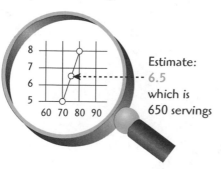

Estimate: 6.5 which is 650 servings

and 80°F. This point is close to 6.5 on the vertical axis: 6.5 stands for 650 servings.

Estimate: 650 servings

Estimate the number of servings at 100°F:

Draw a line connecting the data points for 80°F and 90°F. Extend this line to 100°F and draw a dot.

This dot is close to the 900-servings line.

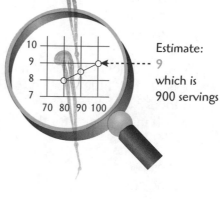

Estimate: 9 which is 900 servings

Estimate: 900 servings

GED Readiness

Problems 1 through 4 refer to the graph on page 74.

Concept

1. Which is the **best estimate** of hot chocolate sales at a temperature of 45°F?

   ① about 3 servings
   ② about 3.5 servings
   ③ about 6.5 servings
   ④ about 65 servings
   ⑤ about 650 servings

Application

2. At approximately what temperature are the sales of lemonade and hot chocolate equal?

   ① 30°F
   ② 40°F
   ③ 50°F
   ④ 55°F
   ⑤ 60°F

3. At approximately what temperature is the number of lemonade sales about 50% of the maximum value shown?

   ① 75°F
   ② 63°F
   ③ 50°F
   ④ 38°F
   ⑤ 30°F

4. At approximately what temperature is the number of hot chocolate sales about $\frac{2}{3}$ of the maximum value shown?

   ① 45°F
   ② 56°F
   ③ 66°F
   ④ 78°F
   ⑤ 90°F

Problems 5 and 6 refer to the information and graph below.

On a drive from Salem to Bend, Lupita records the elevation of Highway 20 every 5 miles in a logbook. Her data points are plotted on the graph below.

Elevation of Highway 20

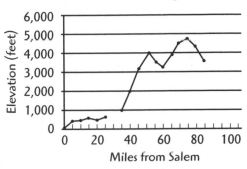

Procedure

5. Using interpolation, which is the best prediction of the missing elevation at the 30-mile point?

   ① 200 feet
   ② 400 feet
   ③ 600 feet
   ④ 800 feet
   ⑤ 1,000 feet

6. What is a reasonable estimate of the elevation at the 100-mile point?

   ① 1,000 feet
   ② 2,900 feet
   ③ 4,800 feet
   ④ 6,000 feet
   ⑤ Not enough information is given.

32

Understand Line of Best Fit

Students in Juanita's GED class were wondering how human height is related to foot length. To find out, each of the 16 students measured his or her height and foot length. A graph of the results is shown below. A *line of best fit* shows the trend in the data.

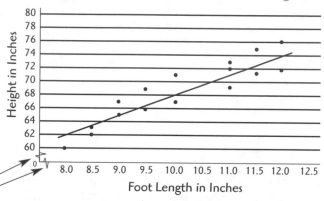

Student Height for Different Foot Lengths

> ### Note on Graph
> The wiggly lines on the graph tell you that the axes do not meet at the origin—the 0 point of each axis.

Based on the line of best fit, about how much height increase occurs with each inch increase in foot length?

① about 3 inches   ④ about 0.5 inch

② about 2 inches   ⑤ about 0.25 inch

③ about 1 inch

Line of Best Fit

A *line of best fit* shows an average trend of data points. This line is a visual guide and may not actually pass through any specific data points.

• A line of best fit makes it easier for you to both *interpolate* and *extrapolate*—estimate additional data values.

• The slope of the line gives the average rate of change of data values.

> ### A Quick Way to Estimate Slope
> Choose any inch length on the foot-length axis. Now see how much the height changes over that inch.
>
> **Example:** Between 8 and 9 inches of foot length, the height changes about **3 inches** (from 62 inches to 65 inches).

Solution

The average height increase for each inch of foot-length increase is given by the slope of the line of best fit. This slope can most accurately be found by choosing any two easily read points on the line.

Example A foot length of 8 inches corresponds to a height of 62 inches. A foot length of 10 inches corresponds to a height of 68 inches.

Slope $= \dfrac{68-62}{10-8} = \dfrac{6}{2} \approx$ **3 inches of height per 1 inch of foot length**

GED Readiness

Problems 1 through 4 refer to the graph on page 76.

Concept

1. Use the line of best fit to estimate the average height of a student who has a foot length of 10.5 inches.

   ① about 62 inches
   ② about 64 inches
   ③ about 66 inches
   ④ about 67 inches
   ⑤ about 69 inches

2. Use the line of best fit to estimate the foot length of a person who has a height of 62 inches.

   ① about 8 inches
   ② about 8.5 inches
   ③ about 9 inches
   ④ about 60 inches
   ⑤ about 62 inches

Procedure

3. What is the median foot length of students in Juanita's class?

   ① 8 inches   ④ 11 inches
   ② 9 inches   ⑤ 12 inches
   ③ 10 inches

Application

4. Two students in Juanita's class have a foot length of 10 inches. How much greater is the average height of these two students than the height shown by the line of best fit?

   ① about 1 inch
   ② about 2 inches
   ③ about 3 inches
   ④ about 5 inches
   ⑤ about 6 inches

Problems 5 and 6 refer to the information and graph below.

Students in Judy's class were given a list of 100 vocabulary words. At the end of the week, they took a quiz. Each point on the graph shows a student's score and the number of hours that student studied for the quiz. A line of best fit is drawn for the data points.

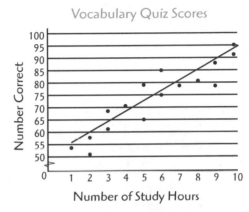

Vocabulary Quiz Scores

Concept

5. Based on the line of best fit, how many words is a student most likely to get correct after studying for 5 hours?

   ① 56
   ② 72
   ③ 80
   ④ 90
   ⑤ 100

Application

6. Based on the line of best fit, how many more words is a student likely to learn for each additional hour of study? Round your answer to the nearest whole number.

   ① 1
   ② 2
   ③ 4
   ④ 6
   ⑤ 7

33 Interpret a Single Line Graph

Understanding Slope

You can understand a lot about a graph just by looking at a changing slope.

For example, look at the distance/time graph in this problem:

- The steepest slope represents the greatest speed. Jocelyn's greatest speed was during the final 3 hours of her trip.

- During the 5th hour of the trip (between 4 and 5 on the time axis), the slope of the graph is 0. A 0 slope means that the speed is 0. During this hour the car is stopped. Perhaps Jocelyn stopped for lunch.

- Other than the time Jocelyn stopped, her slowest speed was between 2.5 hours and 4 hours.

Jocelyn made a line graph to show the distance she traveled during an 8-hour car trip. What was Jocelyn's approximate average speed during the first 5 hours?

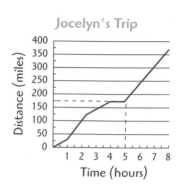
Jocelyn's Trip

① 55 miles per hour
② 45 miles per hour
③ 35 miles per hour
④ 30 miles per hour
⑤ Not enough information is given.

Understanding the Graph

On this distance/time graph, the vertical (y) axis shows miles traveled. The horizontal (x) axis shows hours of travel.

- The difference between two points on the horizontal axis tells the change in hours—the time of travel.

- The difference between two points on the vertical axis tells the change in miles—the distance traveled.

On this graph, the graphed line is made up of four straight-line parts. Each part has its own slope and represents a different speed—measured as the slope of the line segment. [The slope tells the change in distance divided by the change in time (miles per hour).]

The average speed during a period of time is the total distance traveled during that time divided by the time of travel.

Solution

To determine the average speed, divide the miles traveled during the first 5 hours (175 miles) by the time of travel (5 hours).

To find the distance traveled, identify the 5-hour point on the time axis. Locate the point on the graphed line above the 5-hour point. Scan directly to the left, to the distance axis. [See the dotted lines on the graph.]

$$\text{average speed during first 5 hours} = \frac{\text{distance traveled during first 5 hours}}{\text{time of travel}}$$

$$= \frac{175 \text{ miles}}{5 \text{ hours}}$$

$$= \textbf{35 miles per hour}$$

GED Readiness

Problems 1 through 4 refer to the graph on page 78.

Concept

1. How far did Jocelyn travel during the 1st hour of her trip?

   ① about 10 miles
   ② about 25 miles
   ③ about 50 miles
   ④ about 65 miles
   ⑤ about 85 miles

2. During which of the following hours was Jocelyn's speed the greatest?

   ① 1st hour
   ② 4th hour
   ③ 5th hour
   ④ 7th hour
   ⑤ Not enough information is given.

Application

3. What was Jocelyn's average speed during the final 3 hours of her trip?

   ① about 45 miles per hour
   ② about 50 miles per hour
   ③ about 55 miles per hour
   ④ about 65 miles per hour
   ⑤ Not enough information is given.

4. Not counting the hour she stopped, what was Jocelyn's approximate average speed for the trip—the average speed during the time she was actually driving?

   ① 57 miles per hour
   ② 54 miles per hour
   ③ 51 miles per hour
   ④ 48 miles per hour
   ⑤ 45 miles per hour

Problems 5 and 6 refer to the following information and graph.

The graph shows data recorded for an adult patient during a step exercise as part of a physical examination.

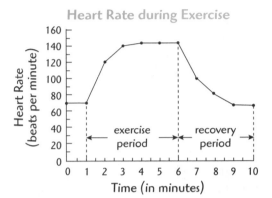

Concept

5. What is the patient's resting heart rate (normal heart rate when not exercising)?

   ① 60 beats per minute
   ② 70 beats per minute
   ③ 80 beats per minute
   ④ 100 beats per minute
   ⑤ 150 beats per minute

Application

6. During the first 3 minutes of the recovery period, how many beats per minute, on the average, did the patient's heart rate decrease?

   ① about 80
   ② about 50
   ③ about 38
   ④ about 33
   ⑤ about 23

Understand a Multiple Line Graph

To reduce expenses in her store, Karen is considering switching to new energy-efficient light bulbs. The graph shows both purchase price and monthly operating costs using three different bulbs.

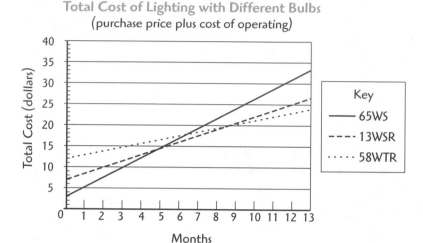

Total Cost of Lighting with Different Bulbs
(purchase price plus cost of operating)

Key
—— 65WS
---- 13WSR
······ 58WTR

Multiple Line Graphs

A graph with multiple lines will have a **key** that identifies each graphed line.

Often, several lines are graphed on a single graph so that data can be easily compared.

What is the purchase price and monthly operating cost of bulb 13WSR?

① $12 purchase price, and $1.50 per month operating cost
② $12 purchase price, and $3.00 per month operating cost
③ $7 purchase price, and $0.75 per month operating cost
④ $7 purchase price, and $1.50 per month operating cost
⑤ $7 purchase price, and $3.00 per month operating cost

Solution

As a first step, take time to understand the graph.

• The starting point of each data line (the *y*-intercept) shows the purchase price of each bulb—the cost at 0 months of use.

• The slope of a data line tells the operating cost (usage rate)—dollars spent per month of use. A steeper slope shows a greater monthly cost.

The data line for bulb 13WSR intersects the *Total Cost* axis at the $7 point.

The purchase price of bulb 13WSR is $7.00.

The monthly operating cost of bulb 13WSR line can be found as follows:

Monthly operating cost of bulb 13WSR

$$= \frac{12 \text{ months' operating cost}}{12} = \frac{\$25 - \$7}{12} = \frac{\$18}{12} = \mathbf{\$1.50}$$

Remember

To find operating cost, you must subtract the purchase price from the total cost.

The 12-month operating cost of bulb 13WSR is found by subtracting $7 from $25.

GED Readiness

Problems 1 through 4 refer to the graph on page 80.

Problems 5 through 7 refer to the graph below.

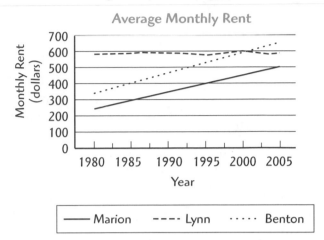

Concept

1 What is the purchase price of the 58WTR bulb?

① $6.00
② $8.00
③ $10.00
④ $12.00
⑤ Not enough information is given.

2 What is the total cost of purchasing and operating the 65WS bulb for 1 year?

① about $25
② about $28
③ about $31
④ about $38
⑤ about $41

Procedure

3 If Karen chooses bulb 13WSR, about how many months of use will she get for $14, not counting purchase price?

① about 1 month
② about 3 months
③ about 5 months
④ about 7 months
⑤ about 9 months

4 What is the monthly operating cost of the 58WTR bulb?

① about $1.00
② about $1.50
③ about $2.00
④ about $2.50
⑤ about $3.00

Procedure

5 In about what year did rent costs become equal in Benton and Lynn?

① 1985 ④ 2000
② 1993 ⑤ 2004
③ 1995

Application

6 For the year 2000, which is the best estimate of the ratio of average rent costs in Lynn to those in Marion?

① about $\frac{12}{5}$ ④ about $\frac{2}{3}$

② about $\frac{2}{1}$ ⑤ about $\frac{5}{12}$

③ about $\frac{4}{3}$

7 By about what percent did the rent in Marion increase between 1980 and 2000?

① 10% ④ 65%
② 25% ⑤ 80%
③ 40%

Interpret a Bar Graph

Bar Graph Basics

The Graph Key

The key tells you that each dark green bar represents 12%.

Reading a Bar

What total interest is paid on a 30-year $100,000 mortgage with an interest rate of 12%?

Answer: About 270 thousand dollars

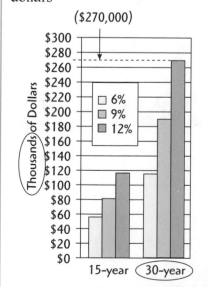

The bar graph shows the amount of interest paid on a $100,000 mortgage for two different payback periods and for three different yearly interest rates.

Suppose you want to borrow $100,000 to purchase a house, and the interest rate of your loan is 12%. Estimate the difference in total interest you would pay if you take out a 30-year loan instead of a 15-year loan.

① about $75,000
② about $150,000
③ about $200,000
④ about $250,000
⑤ about $300,000

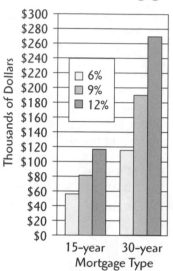

Total Interest Paid on a $100,000 Mortgage

Solution

A loan taken to buy a house is called a mortgage. The title of the bar graph tells you that the bars represent the total interest paid on a $100,000 mortgage. The graph key tells you that 12% mortgages are represented by dark green bars.

Step 1

Estimate the values represented by the dark green bars for a 30-year mortgage and a 15-year mortgage.

- The total interest paid on the 30-year mortgage is about $270 thousand, about halfway between $260,000 and $280,000.

- The total interest paid on a 15-year mortgage is about $120,000.

Step 2

To find the difference in total interest, subtract $120,000 from $270,000.

$270,000 − $120,00 = **$150,000**

The difference in total interest paid is about $150,000.

GED Readiness

Problems 1 through 3 refer to the bar graph on page 82.

Problems 4 and 5 refer to the bar graph below.

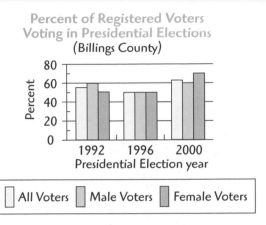

Percent of Registered Voters
Voting in Presidential Elections
(Billings County)

☐ All Voters ▨ Male Voters ▨ Female Voters

Concept

1 What total amount of interest would you pay on a 30-year $100,000 mortgage at an interest rate of 9%?

  ① about $50,000
  ② about $80,000
  ③ about $118,000
  ④ about $190,000
  ⑤ about $270,000

2 Suppose you borrow $100,000 to buy a house. For which mortgage would you pay about $200,000 more in interest than you would pay on a 15-year 6% mortgage?

  ① 15-year at 9%
  ② 15-year at 12%
  ③ 30-year at 6%
  ④ 30-year at 9%
  ⑤ 30-year at 12%

Procedure

3 Over the life of a 30-year mortgage at 6%, what is the average interest paid per year for a mortgage of $100,000? Round the average interest to the nearest $1,000.

Mark your answer in the circles in the grid.

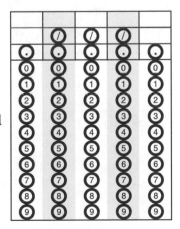

Application

4 In 2000, there were 40,400 registered male voters and 36,200 registered female voters in Billings County. About how many more women voted in the 2000 presidential election than men?

  ① about 4,000
  ② about 3,000
  ③ about 2,000
  ④ about 1,000
  ⑤ Not enough information is given.

5 Suppose 36,250 votes were cast in Billings County in the 1996 presidential election. How many more votes were cast in the 1992 election than the 1996 election?

  ① 1,653
  ② 1,024
  ③ 927
  ④ 5
  ⑤ Not enough information is given.

Understand a Circle Graph

Election results for a mayoral race are summarized in the circle graph. What percent of the votes did Gregg receive?

Mayoral Election Results
50,200 votes cast

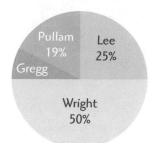

The answer 6% is recorded on the grid.

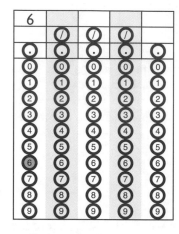

Circle Graphs

A circle graph, also called a pie graph, shows data as sections of a divided circle. Each section is in the shape of a cut piece of pie.

- An entire circle represents a whole amount. This graph represents 100% (all) of the votes cast in a mayoral election.

- Each section represents part of the whole. The largest section shows that Wright received 50% ($\frac{1}{2}$) of all votes. Gregg, represented by the smallest section, received the least number of votes. The percent of votes that Gregg received is not shown.

Solution

Set the sum of all percents equal to 100%:

To find the percent for Gregg, you can

- subtract the sum of the other percents from 100%

or

- subtract each other percent from 100%

% for Gregg + 50% + 25% + 19% = 100%

% for Gregg = 100% − (50% + 25% + 19%)

= 100% − 94%

= **6%**

or, % for Gregg = 100% − 50% − 25% − 19% = **6%**

You can use the calculator to do either subtraction.

this way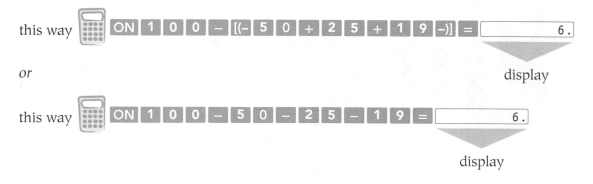

or

display

this way

display

GED Readiness

Problems 1 through 4 refer to the graph on page 84.

Concept

1 Which candidate received about $\frac{1}{5}$ of the votes cast?

① Gregg
② Pullam
③ Lee
④ Wright
⑤ Not enough information is given.

2 What percent of registered voters voted in this election?

① less than 30%
② between 30% and 60%
③ between 60% and 80%
④ more than 80%
⑤ Not enough information is given.

3 Which phrase best describes a comparison of votes for Lee to votes for Gregg?

① about the same
② about twice as many
③ about three times as many
④ about four times as many
⑤ about six times as many

Procedure

4 What is the ratio of votes for Wright to votes for Lee?

① 1 to 4
② 1 to 2
③ 2 to 1
④ 4 to 1
⑤ 4 to 3

Problems 5 through 7 refer to the graph below.

The Welty family budget is shown as *cents per budget dollar.*

Welty Family Budget
(cents per $1.00)

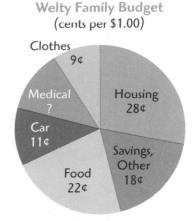

Concept

5 For which item does the Welty family spend half as much as they spend on food?

① car
② clothes
③ housing
④ savings, other
⑤ Not enough information is given.

6 For which two items does the Welty family spend about 50% of each budgeted dollar?

① food and housing
② clothes and housing
③ car and medical
④ medical and savings, other
⑤ food and car

Procedure

7 How many cents of each budget dollar does the Welty family spend on medical?

① 8¢   ④ 11¢
② 9¢   ⑤ 12¢
③ 10¢

Interpret a Circle Graph

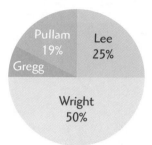

According to information provided by the graph, what number of votes did Lee receive?

① 2,500
② 6,245
③ 8,050
④ 9,500
⑤ 12,550

Mayoral Election Results
50,200 votes cast

Pullam 19%
Gregg
Lee 25%
Wright 50%

Solution

Write a sentence that describes the number of votes Lee received.

Votes for Lee = total votes × Lee's percent of total

Approach 1

Step 1

Write the percent of votes received by Lee as a fraction.

Reduce to lowest terms.

$$25\% = \frac{25 \div 25}{100 \div 25} = \frac{1}{4}$$

Step 2

Multiply 50,200 by $\frac{1}{4}$.

Votes for Lee = $50{,}200 \times \frac{1}{4}$

$= \frac{5{,}200}{4}$

$= \mathbf{12{,}550}$

Approach 2

Step 1

Write the percent of votes received by Lee as a decimal.

25% = **0.25**

Step 2

Multiply 50,200 by 0.25.

```
  5 0,2 0 0
    ×.2 5  ←— 2 decimal points
  ─────────
  2 5 1 0 0 0
1 0 0 4 0 0
─────────────
1 2,5 5 0.0 0  ←— 2 decimal points
```

Votes for Lee = 12,550

Using the calculator, you do not need to change the percent to either a fraction or a decimal. You can use the percent function of the calculator as follows:

percent function   display

GED Readiness

Problems 1 through 3 refer to the circle graph on page 86.

Problems 4 through 6 refer to the graph below.

The Welty family budget is shown as *cents per budget dollar.*

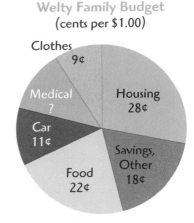

Welty Family Budget
(cents per $1.00)

Clothes 9¢
Medical ?
Car 11¢
Housing 28¢
Food 22¢
Savings, Other 18¢

Procedure

1. 🖩 According to information provided by the graph, what number of votes did Pullam receive?

    Mark your answer in the circles in the grid.

Application

2. Approximately how many more votes did Lee receive than Pullam?

    (1) 2,000
    (2) 3,000
    (3) 4,000
    (4) 5,000
    (5) 8,000

3. 🖩 In the city in which this election was held, there are 65,000 registered voters. About what percent of registered voters voted for Wright?

    (1) 60%
    (2) 50%
    (3) 40%
    (4) 30%
    (5) 12%

Concept

4. What is the approximate ratio of the amount the Weltys' budget for housing to the amount they budget for clothes?

    (1) $\frac{1}{3}$ (4) $\frac{2}{1}$

    (2) $\frac{1}{2}$ (5) $\frac{3}{1}$

    (3) $\frac{2}{3}$

Application

5. 🖩 If the Weltys earn $3,875 each month, how much of this income will most likely be spent for food?

    (1) about $650   (4) about $800
    (2) about $700   (5) about $850
    (3) about $750

6. 🖩 The Welty family income for last year was $46,500. About how much more did the Welty family spend on housing costs during the year than they spent on food?

    (1) $2,400   (4) $3,000
    (2) $2,600   (5) $3,200
    (3) $2,800

38 Use Two Sources of Data

Use the following graphs for problem 38.

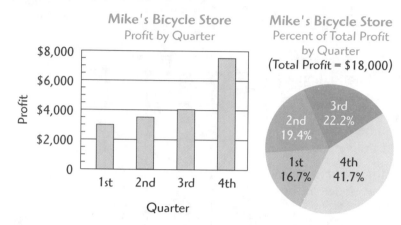

Mike's Bicycle Store
Profit by Quarter

Mike's Bicycle Store
Percent of Total Profit
by Quarter
(Total Profit = $18,000)

The profit for Mike's Bicycle Store for the four quarters of the year is shown. What is the store's mean (average) profit per quarter?

① $4,500
④ $6,800
② $5,600
⑤ $7,500
③ $6,250

Note

On the GED Test, there will likely be questions similar to this one: questions that you can answer most easily by first taking the time to look carefully at the data you are given.

In this problem, reading data values on the bar graph is not necessary.

Did you realize this when you first read the problem?

Solution

Graphs often show more information than you need. Before doing any math, take the time to see what information is available that may help you solve the question most easily. This can save you time and effort!

Approach 1

The circle graph gives the total profit for the four quarters in its title: $18,000. To find the average profit per quarter, divide the total profit by 4.

$18,000 ÷ 4 = **$4,500**

Approach 2

A longer solution is to use only the data in the bar graph.

Step 1 Add to find the total profit for the 4 quarters.

total profit = $3,000 + $3,500 + $4,000 + $7,500 = **$18,000**

Step 2 Divide the total profit by 4:

$18,000 ÷ 4 = **$4,500**

GED Readiness

Problems 1 through 4 refer to the two graphs on page 88.

Concept

1 Which expression tells the dollar amount of profit made during the 1st quarter?

① 1.67 × $13,000
② 1.67 × $18,000
③ 0.167 × $15,000
④ 0.167 × $18,000
⑤ Not enough information is given.

2 In which quarter is the profit most nearly equal to one quarter of the yearly profit?

① 1st quarter
② 2nd quarter
③ 3rd quarter
④ 4th quarter
⑤ Not enough information is given.

3 What is the approximate ratio of 4th quarter profit to 2nd quarter profit?

① 3 to 1
② 2 to 1
③ 1 to 1
④ 1 to 2
⑤ 1 to 3

Procedure

4 How much more total profit would Mike's Bicycle Store need to earn during the year to increase the average profit per quarter to $5,000?

① $2,000
② $1,500
③ $700
④ $500
⑤ $300

Application

Problems 5 and 6 refer to the graph and table below.

The table and graph show the pay rates and hours worked last week for four employees. The normal work week for each employee is 40 hours. Any additional hours are paid as overtime hours.

Employee	Regular	Overtime
Brown	$12.00	$18.00
Gonzales	$14.00	$21.00
Middleton	$11.00	$16.50
Yang	$12.00	$18.00

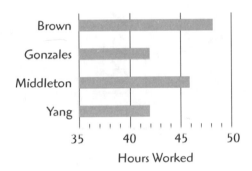

5 Which phrase best describes the overtime pay rate of these employees?

① time and a quarter
② time and a third
③ time and a half
④ double time
⑤ Not enough information is given.

6 How much more did Brown earn last week than Middleton earned?

① $15
② $25
③ $45
④ $65
⑤ $85

39 Probability

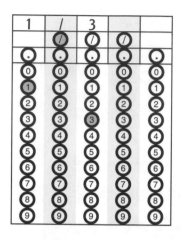

Regina is playing a game in which she draws marbles from a bag. If the bag contains 1 white marble, 2 gray marbles, and 3 green marbles, what is the probability that Regina will draw a gray marble on her first try?

The answer $\frac{1}{3}$ is recorded on the grid.

Probability

Probability is the likelihood of an event happening.

In the study of probability, each possible result is called an **outcome**. A particular outcome, such as Regina drawing a gray marble, is called a **favorable outcome**. The probability that a favorable outcome will occur is written as a fraction:

Probability of a favorable outcome $= \dfrac{\text{number of favorable outcomes}}{\text{number of all outcomes}}$

Solution

In this problem, Regina has an equal probability of drawing any of the six marbles.

So, the *number of all outcomes* = **6**

Of these six outcomes (marbles), two are gray in color.

So, the *number of favorable outcomes* = **2**

The probability that Regina will draw a gray marble is written as the fraction:

$\dfrac{\text{number of gray marbles}}{\text{total number of marbles}} = \dfrac{2}{6}$ which reduces to $\dfrac{1}{3}$

The probability that Regina will draw a gray marble is $\frac{1}{3}$.

Laws of Probability

According to the laws of probability, Regina has an equal opportunity of drawing any one of the 6 marbles in the bag: 1 out of 6 or $\frac{1}{6}$.

The laws of probability also apply when flipping coins. For example, when a penny is flipped, there is an equal likelihood of the penny landing heads up or landing tails up: 1 out of 2 or $\frac{1}{2}$.

GED Readiness

Concept

Problems 1 and 2 refer to the problem on page 90.

① What is the probability that, on her first try, Regina will **not** pick a gray marble?

① $\frac{4}{2}$ ② $\frac{4}{3}$ ③ $\frac{2}{3}$ ④ $\frac{1}{2}$ ⑤ $\frac{1}{3}$

② Suppose Regina takes two green marbles out of the bag. What is the probability that Regina will pick a gray marble now?

① $\frac{4}{2}$ ② $\frac{4}{3}$ ③ $\frac{2}{3}$ ④ $\frac{1}{2}$ ⑤ $\frac{1}{3}$

③ Elena thinks of a number from 1 to 50, and Sal tries to guess the number. Suppose Sal guesses the number 28. Which statement below is true?

  ① Sal is more likely to have guessed too low than too high.

  ② Sal is more likely to have guessed too high than too low.

  ③ Sal is equally likely to have guessed too high or too low.

  ④ Sal has zero probability of guessing the number on his first guess.

  ⑤ Nothing can be said about Sal's probability of guessing the number on his first try.

Procedure

④ Janine and her two children are attending Family Fun Night at the children's school. A drawing for a door prize will be held at 8:00 P.M. for all attending. If 390 people attend, what is the probability that someone in Janine's family will win the door prize?

① $\frac{1}{3}$ ④ $\frac{1}{130}$

② $\frac{1}{13}$ ⑤ $\frac{1}{180}$

③ $\frac{1}{39}$

⑤ Clara and her husband each bought 4 raffle tickets for a trip for two to Hawaii. What is the probability that a ticket either Clara or her husband bought will be the winning ticket?

① $\frac{1}{8}$

② $\frac{1}{4}$

③ $\frac{3}{8}$

④ $\frac{1}{2}$

⑤ Not enough information is given.

Application

Problems 6 and 7 refer to the table below.

Halia has a bag containing 5 marbles. She knows that some are red, some are blue, and some are green. Without looking in the bag, Halia takes a marble out, records its color, and returns it to the bag. She takes and returns a marble 10 times. Halia's results are shown in the table.

Halia's Results

Color	Number
red	2
blue	6
green	2

⑥ How many of the 5 marbles in the bag are most likely blue?

  ① 1
  ② 2
  ③ 3
  ④ 4
  ⑤ 5

⑦ How many of the 5 marbles in the bag are most likely green?

  ① 1
  ② 2
  ③ 3
  ④ 4
  ⑤ 5

Base Probability on Data

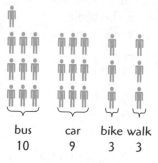

To understand parking needs, Michael asks each employee, "How do you get to work?" He records the results of the poll in the table.

Based on this data, how many of the next 15 employees Michael polls will say they ride a bus to work?

Transportation Poll	
Method	Number
Bus	10
Car	9
Bike	3
Walk	3

The answer 6 is recorded on the grid.

Basing Probability on Data

When you choose a marble from a bag, roll a number cube, or flip a coin, you base probability on *laws of probability*. You can also base probability on data or on past performance.

$$\text{Probability of an event} = \frac{\text{total number of favorable outcomes}}{\text{total number of all outcomes}}$$

When basing probability on data, you use the data to determine both favorable outcomes and total outcomes.

- A favorable outcome is the result you are asking about.

- Total outcomes are all the possible ways a result can happen.

Picture the Problem

25 Total Employees

bus	car	bike	walk
10	9	3	3

10 of 25 employees ride the bus.

The probability that any single employee rides the bus, P_{bus}, is based on this data:

$$P_{\text{bus}} = \frac{10}{25} = \frac{2}{5}$$

This same probability is assumed to be a good predictor for the next group of employees to be polled.

Solution

As a first step, find the probability that any single employee rides the bus. Based on the 25 employees polled so far, this probability is given as the following fraction:

$$\text{Probability an employee rides the bus} = \frac{\text{number of bus riders}}{\text{number of employees}} = \frac{10}{25}$$

Now, reduce the fraction: $\frac{10}{25} = \frac{10 \div 5}{25 \div 5} = \frac{2}{5}$

Next, to find the most likely number of the next 15 employees who ride the bus, multiply 15 by $\frac{2}{5}$, the probability that any single employee rides the bus.

$$15 \times \frac{2}{5} = \frac{\overset{3}{15}}{1} \times \frac{2}{\underset{1}{5}} = 6$$

6 of the next 15 employees polled are likely to ride the bus.

GED Readiness

Concept

① Look again at the table on page 92. Written as a fraction, what is the probability that an employee walks to work?

Mark your answer in the circles in the grid.

Problems 2 and 3 are based on the following passage.

Tamara, a basketball player, has made 20 free throw shots out of her past 50 attempts.

② What is the probability that Tamara will make her first free-throw attempt in tonight's game?

- ① $\frac{4}{5}$
- ② $\frac{2}{3}$
- ③ $\frac{1}{2}$
- ④ $\frac{2}{5}$
- ⑤ $\frac{1}{3}$

Procedure

③ How many of her next 25 free-throw attempts is Tamara most likely to make?

- ① 5
- ② 10
- ③ 15
- ④ 20
- ⑤ 25

④ Of the last 15 phone calls to the Ahrens family, 10 have been for Spencer. Of the next 6 calls, how many of the calls most likely will be for Spencer?

- ① 2
- ② 3
- ③ 4
- ④ 5
- ⑤ 6

Application

Problems 5 and 6 are based on the following passage and table.

Lam's Restaurant sells four types of omelets for breakfast. The table shows the omelets ordered by customers between 7:00 A.M. and 8:00 A.M. today.

Omelet	Number
Cheese	4
Ham	8
Vegetarian	5
Sausage	3

⑤ Expressed as a percent, what is the probability that the next omelet ordered will be ham?

- ① 40%
- ② 35%
- ③ 30%
- ④ 20%
- ⑤ 10%

⑥ How many of the next 15 omelets ordered are likely to be cheese?

- ① 1
- ② 2
- ③ 3
- ④ 4
- ⑤ 5

Evaluate a Formula

Use the temperature formula $^\circ C = \frac{5}{9}(^\circ F - 32^\circ)$ to find the Celsius temperature ($^\circ C$) when the Fahrenheit temperature is 50°F.

The answer 10°C is recorded on the grid.

The Temperature Formula

Two different temperature-measuring units are used in the United States: Fahrenheit units (°F) and Celsius units (°C). A temperature can be given in either unit. For example, water boils at 212°F, which is the same temperature as 100°C. The **temperature formula** is a rule that tells how to switch from one unit to another.

Solution

To evaluate the temperature formula, substitute 50° for °F and do the indicated operations.

Step 1
Substitute 50° for °F and evaluate the expression within parentheses.

$$^\circ C = \frac{5}{9}(^\circ F - 32^\circ)$$

$$^\circ C = \frac{5}{9}(50^\circ - 32^\circ)$$

$$^\circ C = \frac{5}{9}(18^\circ)$$

Step 2
Multiply.

$$^\circ C = \frac{5}{9}(18^\circ) = \frac{5}{\underset{1}{9}}(\overset{2}{18^\circ}) = 10^\circ$$

Answer: 10°C

Graphing the Temperature Formula

A graph of the temperature equation is shown below. Three values are indicated.

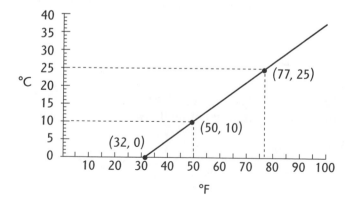

> A *formula* is an equation that shows a mathematical relationship.

> ### Order of Operations for Evaluating a Formula
>
> 1st Evaluate any expression within parentheses.
>
> 2nd Compute any power or root.
>
> 3rd Multiply or divide any coefficient.
>
> 4th Add or subtract any attached term.

GED Readiness

Use the temperature formula on page 94 to find the Celsius temperature (°C) when the Fahrenheit temperature is 98.6°F, the average human body temperature of a healthy person.

① 37°C
② 34.5°C
③ 32°C
④ 16.5°C
⑤ 0°C

2 What is the value of t in the formula

$t = 2(4h - 3w)^2$

when $h = 3$ and $w = 2$?

Mark your answer in the circles in the grid.

Application

3 The flow of electric current is given by the formula

$$i = \sqrt{\frac{v}{r}}$$

where i = electric current in amps
     v = voltage in volts
     r = resistance in ohms

About how many amps of electric current flow through a lightbulb when the voltage is 120 volts and the resistance is 150 ohms?

① 0.08
② 0.9
③ 1.4
④ 5.8
⑤ 9.0

The formula for the outside surface area of a cylinder is
$A_s = 2\pi \times r^2 + \pi \times d \times h$,
where r is the radius of the cylinder, d is the diameter of the cylinder (twice the radius), and h is the height of the cylinder.

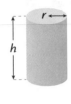

What is the surface area of a cylinder that has a radius of 1.5 inches and a height of 6 inches? Use $\pi = 3.14$.

① about 14 square inches
② about 42 square inches
③ about 57 square inches
④ about 71 square inches
⑤ about 159 square inches

5 The formula for the volume of metal used to make a hollow pipe is
$V = \pi \times l \times (r_1^2 - r_2^2)$,
where l = the length of the pipe, r_1 is the outside radius, and r_2 is the inside radius.

$\pi \approx 3.14$

What is the volume of metal in a pipe if $r_1 = 0.5$ m, $r_2 = 0.45$ m, and $l = 8$ m?

① about 0.2 cubic meters
② about 0.4 cubic meters
③ about 0.5 cubic meters
④ about 0.6 cubic meters
⑤ about 1.2 cubic meters

Write an Algebraic Expression

Jenni baked a batch of cookies. She kept 6 for herself and divided the rest equally among 4 friends. If Jenni baked a total of n cookies, which expression tells the number of cookies Jenni gave to each friend?

① $\dfrac{(n-4)}{6}$ ④ $4(n+6)$

② $\dfrac{(n+6)}{4}$ ⑤ $4(n-6)$

③ $\dfrac{(n-6)}{4}$

Solution

This is an example of a set-up question involving algebraic expressions. In this problem, the number of cookies each friend gets depends on the value of n, a number you are not given.

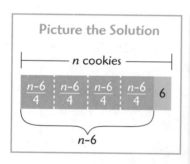

Picture the Solution

Approach 1: Write an Expression to Represent Known Facts

Jenni baked n cookies and kept 6 for herself. You do not need to know the value of n to solve this problem.

Jenni gave away "$n - 6$" cookies. [Think of "$n - 6$" as a single number.]

To divide the group of "$n - 6$" cookies into 4 equal parts, divide by 4. Write parentheses to indicate that the number "$n - 6$" is being divided by 4.

Each friend got $\dfrac{(n-6)}{4}$ cookies.

Answer choice 3 is correct.

Approach 2: Check Answer Choices

A second way to solve this problem is to choose a possible number for n. For example, choose $n = 18$.

• Jennifer baked 18 cookies and kept 6 for herself.

• You can conclude that she gave 12 to her friends. [$18 - 6 = 12$]

• Each friend received an equal share: $12 \div 4 = $ **3 cookies**

Now, substitute the value $n = 18$ into each answer choice:

① $\dfrac{(n-4)}{6} = \dfrac{(18-4)}{6} = \dfrac{14}{6} = 2.33$

② $\dfrac{(n+6)}{4} = \dfrac{(18+6)}{4} = \dfrac{24}{4} = 6$

③ $\dfrac{(n-6)}{4} = \dfrac{(18-6)}{4} = \dfrac{12}{4} = 3$

④ $4(n+6) = 4(18+6) = 4(24) = 96$

⑤ $4(n-6) = 4(18-6) = 4(12) = 48$

Only choice 3 gives the correct answer.

GED Readiness

Concept

1 Cole cuts a pizza into 12 equal slices. Cole takes n slices of the pizza and shares the remaining slices equally among 5 friends. Which expression tells the number of slices each friend gets?

① $\dfrac{(n-12)}{5}$

② $\dfrac{(n-5)}{12}$

③ $\dfrac{(12-5)}{n}$

④ $\dfrac{(12-n)}{5}$

⑤ $\dfrac{(5-n)}{12}$

2 Kitra runs for t minutes each Monday, Wednesday, and Friday. She also runs m minutes on Saturday. Which expression tells how many minutes Kitra runs each week?

① $3t + m$　　④ $3(t + m)$

② $3t - m$　　⑤ $3t + 3m$

③ $3(t - m)$

3 Terry is 2 years younger than 4 times his nephew's age. If c stands for his nephew's age, which expression stands for Terry's age?

① $4c + 2$

② $4c - 2$

③ $4(c + 2)$

④ $4(c - 2)$

⑤ Not enough information is given.

4 In Mitch's GED class there are m men in a class of n students. Which expression gives the ratio of **men to women** in this class?

① $\dfrac{m}{n}$

② $\dfrac{n}{m}$

③ $\dfrac{m}{m-n}$

④ $\dfrac{n}{n-m}$

⑤ $\dfrac{m}{n-m}$

5 The cost of n pounds of apples is \$3.88. At this rate, which expression gives the cost of k pounds of apples?

① $(\$3.88 + n) \times k$

② $(\$3.88 - n) \times k$

③ $\left(\dfrac{\$3.88}{k}\right) \times n$

④ $\left(\dfrac{\$3.88}{n}\right) \times k$

⑤ $\left(\dfrac{n}{\$3.88}\right) \times k$

Procedure

6 Which expression represents the area of the circle at right?

① $2(7)\pi$

② 14π

③ $7^2\pi$

④ $14^2\pi$

⑤ $(7\pi)^2$

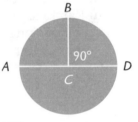

$\overline{AD}$ measures 14 inches.

$\overline{AC} = \overline{BC}$

7 On a test, Jeremy is asked to choose two ways to find n percent of 40. He is given these four choices.

A.　$\dfrac{n}{100} \times 40$

B.　$(n \times 0.01) \times 40$

C.　$(n \times 100) \div 40$

D.　$(n \div 0.01) \times 40$

Which two choices are correct?

① A and B

② A and D

③ B and C

④ B and D

⑤ C and D

Write an Equation to Solve a Word Problem

Kami, Maria, and Shannelle share living expenses. Kami pays $65 less each month than Maria. Shannelle pays twice as much each month as Kami. If total monthly living expenses are $985, which equation can be used to find Kami's share (k)?

① $4k + \$65 = \$985$ ④ $3k - \$65 = \$985$
② $4k - \$65 = \$985$ ⑤ $2k - \$65 = \$985$
③ $3k + \$65 = \$985$

Approach 1: Write Algebraic Expressions

Step 1

Write an expression to represent the amount of each person's share.

• Write the simplest expression first: Kami's share = k.

• Write each of the other expressions using this same variable k.

Kami's share = k
Maria's share = $k + \$65$ ($65 more than Kami's share)
Shannelle's share = $2k$ (twice Kami's share)

Step 2

Set the sum of the three shares equal to the total amount.

Sum = $k + k + \$65 + 2k = \$985$

Step 3

Simplify the sum by combining the k terms: $k + k + 2k = 4k$.

The equation simplifies to: $4k + \$65 = \$985$

Approach 2: Use a Drawing

You can also solve this problem by using a drawing. In the drawing, Kami's share is represented by the length k. Each of the other shares is based on the length k.

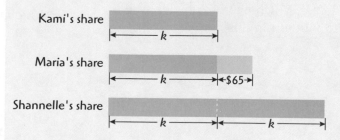

The sum of all three shares ($k + k + \$65 + 2k$) is $985

or, $4k + \$65 = \$985$.

Tip

Notice that each person's share is described in terms of Kami's share. So write each person's share in terms of Kami's share.

GED Readiness

Concept

1. Alan, Cory, and Marco together sold 92 tickets to a basketball fundraiser. Alan sold 12 more tickets than Cory. Marco sold three times as many as Alan. Which equation can be used to find a, the number of tickets Alan sold?

   ① $4a + 12 = 92$
   ② $4a - 12 = 92$
   ③ $5a + 12 = 92$
   ④ $5a - 12 = 92$
   ⑤ $3a - 12 = 92$

2. Shandell is paying an electrician a $30 home-service fee plus $40 per hour for time actually worked. Which equation below tells how to find t, the total amount Shandell will be charged, if the electrician works n hours?

   ① $t = \$30n + \$40$
   ② $t = \$30 + \$40n$
   ③ $t = (\$30 + \$40)n$
   ④ $t = \$40 + \$30n$
   ⑤ $t = (\$30 - \$40)n$

3. Marianna bought 8 packs of paper plates and 12 packs of paper cups for a picnic. She spent a total of $32.50. Each pack of paper plates cost $1.75.

   Which equation tells how to find c, the cost of each pack of cups?

   ① $8c = \$32.50 + \$1.75 \times 12$
   ② $8c = \$32.50 - \$1.75 \times 12$
   ③ $12c = \$32.50 \times \$1.75 - 8$
   ④ $12c = \$32.50 + \$1.75 \times 8$
   ⑤ $12c = \$32.50 - \$1.75 \times 8$

4. At Kelli's Restaurant, cooks make $350 more each month than servers. Kelli has 3 cooks and 5 servers working full time. Let s represent the monthly wages of each server.

   Which of the following shows the relationship between Kelli's monthly payroll P and the wages paid to her 8 employees?

   ① $P = 8(\$350 - s)$
   ② $P = 8(\$350 + s)$
   ③ $P = 3(\$350 + s) + 5s$
   ④ $P = 5(\$350 + s) + 3s$
   ⑤ Not enough information is given.

5. Keisha has $10.00 with her when she goes to the store. She buys a gallon of milk for $2.20 and as many muffins for 60¢ each as her money will allow. Which equation can be used to find n, the number of muffins she can buy?

   ① $n = 1,000 - (220 \div 60)$
   ② $n = (1,000 + 220) \div 60$
   ③ $n = (1,000 - 220) \div 60$
   ④ $n = 1,000 + (220 \div 60)$
   ⑤ $n - (1,000 - 60) \div 220$

6. Twyla pays a total amount t for p pounds of apples. If she pays d dollars per pound, which equation shows the relationship among the variables t, p, and d?

   ① $t = p \times d$
   ② $t = p \div d$
   ③ $t = d \div p$
   ④ $p = t \times d$
   ⑤ $d = p \times t$

Work with an Algebraic Expression

A **variable** is a letter that stands for an unknown number. The value of a variable can change. This is why it is called a variable.

This problem may represent a walkway.

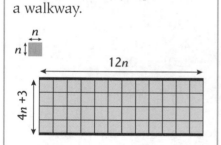

Alternate Solution

Substitute a value for the variable.
Example: $n = 1$

length $= 12 \times 1 = $ **12**
width $= 4 \times 1 + 3$
$\qquad = 4 + 3 = $ **7**

area $= 12 \times 7 = $ **84**

Substitute 1 for n in each answer choice. Only choice 2 equals 84.

② **$48n^2 + 36n$**
$= 48 \times 1^2 + 36 \times 1$
$= 48 + 36 = $ **84**

The dimensions of the rectangle are $12n$ and $4n + 3$.

Which expression gives the area of the rectangle?

① $96n^2 + 72n$
② $48n^2 + 36n$
③ $48n + 36$
④ $32n + 6$
⑤ $16n + 3$

Understanding the Drawing

The variable n stands for an unknown number and is part of each dimension.

• The length of the rectangle is 12 times n, written $12n$.

• The width of the rectangle is 4 times n plus 3, written $4n + 3$.

Suppose the rectangle represents a paved walk; n stands for the length, in inches, of the side of a square paving block. The walk is 12 blocks long and 4 blocks plus 3 inches wide. The extra 3 inches is the width of added edging material.

Because variables represent numbers, they follow the same rules as numbers. Variables can be added, subtracted, multiplied, and divided.

Solution

Write the formula for the area of the rectangle. Substitute the dimensions given. To simplify the product, use the rule:
$(a + b) \times c = (a \times c) + (b \times c)$.

area $=$ length $\times$ width
$\qquad = (4n + 3) \times 12n$
$\qquad = (4n \times 12n) + (3 \times 12n)$
$\qquad = (4 \times 12 \times n \times n) + (3 \times 12 \times n)$
$\qquad = $ **$48n^2 + 36n$**

The perimeter of the rectangle is also easily found. The terms containing the variable n are added together. The lone numbers are added together.

perimeter $=$ length $+$ width $+$ length $+$ width
$\qquad = 12n + (4n + 3) + 12n + (4n + 3)$
$\qquad = (12n + 4n + 12n + 4n) + (3 + 3)$
$\qquad = $ **$32n + 6$**

GED Readiness

Procedure

1 Which expression gives the area of this triangle?

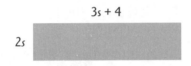
3x
4x

1. 7x
2. 12x
3. $6x^2$
4. $12x^2$
5. $12x^3$

Use the following diagram for problems 2 and 3.

3s + 4
2s

2 Which expression gives the perimeter of the rectangle?

1. $6s^2$
2. $6s^2 + 8s$
3. $10s^2 + 8s$
4. $5s + 4$
5. $10s + 8$

3 Which expression gives the area of the rectangle?

1. $5s^2 + 4$
2. $6s^2 + 8s$
3. $6s^2 + 4$
4. $6s + 4$
5. $10s + 8$

4 A circle is surrounded by a square. Which expression tells the area of the shaded section (the difference in area of the two figures)?

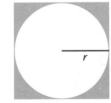
r

1. $4\pi \times r^2$
2. $4 - \pi r^2$
3. $4r - \pi r$
4. $4r^2 - \pi r^2$
5. $\pi r^2 - 4r^2$

Application

5 Square bricks, each 8 inches long and 8 inches wide, will be placed side-by-side to make an outdoor patio. The length and width of the patio are shown below.

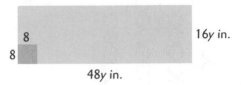
8
8
16y in.
48y in.

If *y* is a whole number, which expression tells how many bricks will be needed?

1. 12
2. 128
3. 8y
4. 12y
5. $12y^2$

6 Carrie is packing toy blocks in a box for shipment. The dimensions of the box she is using are given below.

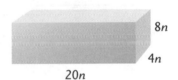
8n
4n
20n

The edge length of each block is 2n. Which expression tells how many blocks will fit inside the box?

2n
2n
2n

1. 80
2. 80n
3. $80n^2$
4. 160n
5. $160n^2$

Extend a Numerical Pattern

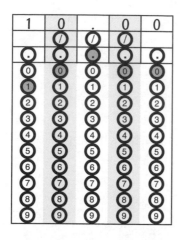

Movie rental prices at Video Circle are shown. Part of the price list is missing. If the price pattern continues, what is the cost of renting 5 movies for 1 week?

The answer $10.00 is recorded on the grid.

Video Circle	
Weekly Rental Rates	
1 movie	$3.00
2 movies	$5.50
3 movies	$7.50
4 movies	$9.00

Number Patterns

A number pattern is a sequence of numbers that are related.

Example: In the sequence 1, 2, 4, 7, 11, . . . the pattern is found by seeing that the numbers are related by addition:

$$1 \quad 2 \quad 4 \quad 7 \quad 11$$
$$+1 \quad +2 \quad +3 \quad +4$$

The next number in this sequence is 16, found by adding 5 to 11.

Solution

Approach 1

Look for the pattern in the increase in price for each added movie.

Weekly Rental Rates

1 movie	$3.00	
		+ $2.50
2 movies	$5.50	
		+ $2.00
3 movies	$7.50	
		+ $1.50
4 movies	$9.00	
		+ ?

Notice that each increase is $0.50 less than the previous increase. The next increase will be $1.00 ($0.50 less than $1.50). **So the price for 5 movies is $9.00 + $1.00 = $10.00.**

Approach 2

Look for the pattern in the *weekly cost per movie*. Divide the weekly rate by the number of movies.

a. Weekly Rental Cost	$3.00	$5.50	$7.50	$9.00	?
b. Number of Movies	1	2	3	4	5
c. Cost per Movie (a ÷ b)	$3.00	$2.75	$2.50	$2.25	$2.00

−$0.25 −$0.25 −$0.25 −$0.25

For 5 movies, the cost per movie is $2.00 ($2.25 − $0.25).

So, the cost of 5 movies = $2.00 × 5 = $10.00.

GED Readiness

Procedure

1 Which sequence of numbers is described by the rule "multiply by 3 and then subtract 2"?

① 2, 4, 8, 16, . . .
② 2, 4, 10, 28, . . .
③ 2, 4, 10, 20, . . .
④ 2, 6, 14, 28, . . .
⑤ 2, 6, 14, 30, . . .

2 Choose the rule that tells how the numbers change in the sequence below.

1, 4, ⁻2, 10, ⁻14, . . .

① multiply by ⁻2 and then add 6
② multiply by 2 and then add 2
③ add 10 and then subtract 7
④ multiply by ⁻1 and then add 5
⑤ add 5 and then subtract 2

Application

3 Allison is attending a musical fundraiser with her family. The cost of admission follows the pattern that is started on the table below.

Fundraiser Prices by Number in Family

1	2	3	4	5
$4.50	$6.25	$8.00		

What will be the total cost if Allison and four other family members attend the fundraiser?

① $7.00   ④ $10.50
② $9.25   ⑤ $11.50
③ $9.75

4 While working over a weekend, Harry laid $9\frac{1}{2}$ feet of concrete blocks for his new driveway. He hopes to finish the driveway in the evenings after work. He records his progress in the table below.

Driveway Construction Progress

Day	Weekend	Mon.	Tues.	Wed.
Length (feet)	$9\frac{1}{2}$	$14\frac{1}{4}$	19	$23\frac{3}{4}$

If this pattern continues, what will be the driveway's length on Friday?

① $33\frac{1}{4}$ feet

② 33 feet

③ $31\frac{3}{4}$ feet

④ 29 feet

⑤ $28\frac{1}{2}$ feet

5 Jenni has her choice of two jobs. The job at Cohen Electronics pays $18,000 per year with yearly raises of $800. The job at Swanson Company pays $16,400 per year with yearly raises of $1,200. In how many years will the two annual salaries be equal?

① 6   ② 5   ③ 4   ④ 3   ⑤ 2

6 Maurice is thinking of buying one of two used cars. The Toyota costs $9,500 and will depreciate (lose value) at the rate of about $600 each year. The Ford costs $11,000 and will depreciate at the rate of about $1,100 each year. Using these estimates, in how many years will the values of the two cars be equal?

① 6   ② 5   ③ 4   ④ 3   ⑤ 2

Identify Values Represented by an Equation

Cab fares in Springfield are given by the equation:

$$F = \$2.50 + \$1.50n$$

where F = total fare

and n = number of miles driven

Which table shows a set of values represented by this equation?

①

n	F
1	$2.50
2	$4.00
3	$5.50
4	$7.00
5	$8.50

②

n	F
1	$1.00
2	$2.50
3	$4.00
4	$5.50
5	$7.00

③

n	F
1	0
2	$1.50
3	$3.00
4	$4.50
5	$6.00

④

n	F
1	$5.50
2	$7.00
3	$8.50
4	$10.00
5	$11.50

⑤

n	F
1	$4.00
2	$5.50
3	$7.00
4	$8.50
5	$10.00

Another Approach
See the Pattern in the Table

Miles	Fare	
		$2.50
1	$4.00	+$1.50
2	$5.50	+$1.50
3	$7.00	+$1.50
4	$8.50	+$1.50
5	$10.00	+$1.50

Total Fare = $2.50 + $1.50n

Approach 1: Use Substitution

To find the values represented by the equation $F = \$2.50 + \$1.50n$, substitute values for n and solve the equation for F.

n	F = $2.50 + $1.50n	F
$n = 1$	$F = \$2.50 + \$1.50(1) = \$2.50 + \$1.50 = \$4.00$	
$n = 2$	$F = \$2.50 + \$1.50(2) = \$2.50 + \$3.00 = \$5.50$	
$n = 3$	$F = \$2.50 + \$1.50(3) = \$2.50 + \$4.50 = \$7.00$	
$n = 4$	$F = \$2.50 + \$1.50(4) = \$2.50 + \$6.00 = \$8.50$	
$n = 5$	$F = \$2.50 + \$1.50(5) = \$2.50 + \$7.50 = \$10.00$	

These values for F are found only in **answer choice 5**.

See the Pattern in the Graph

Notice that the graph starts at $2.50 and increases a constant amount, $1.50, for each mile.

Approach 2: Graph the Equation

Graph the equation using two points.

Example:

$n = 0$, $F = \$2.50$

and $n = 1$, $F = \$4.00$

Draw a straight line that passes through these two points. Now identify the F values for each n.

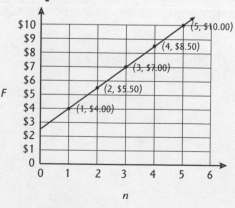

The F values, indicated by dots on the graph, match values found only in **answer choice 5**.

GED Readiness

Concept

1 The volume of a cube is given by the formula $V = edge^3 = s^3$, where s is the length of each edge. Which graph best represents how the value of V depends on the value of s?

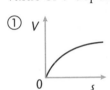

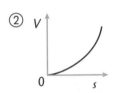

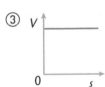

2 For what value of x is the value of y equal to 0 in the following equation?

$$y = (x - 3)^2$$

① $^-3$
② $^-1$
③ 0
④ 1
⑤ 3

3 In the following equation n is a positive whole number {1, 2, 3, 4, 5, . . .}.

$$z = 6n - 23$$

What is the least value of n for which z is positive?

① 1
② 2
③ 3
④ 4
⑤ 5

Procedure

4 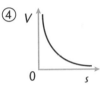 The formula that tells how to find the temperature in degrees Fahrenheit (°F) when you know the temperature in degrees Celsius (°C) is:

$$°F = \frac{9}{5}°C + 32°$$

According to the formula, which of the following statements is **not** true?

① $212°F = 100°C$
② $86°F = 30°C$
③ $50°F = 10°C$
④ $32°F = 0°C$
⑤ $0°F = 32°C$

Application

5 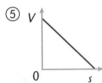 Mira is visiting Dinosaur Mountain Theme Park. She must pay an admission fee and buy ticket booklets for rides. The cost of Mira's visit to Dinosaur Mountain is represented by the equation

$$C = \$15.00 + \$2.25n$$

where n is the number of ticket packages Mira buys. Each ticket package is good for 3 rides.

Not counting the cost of admission, how much does each ride cost?

① \$0.75
② \$1.50
③ \$2.25
④ \$6.75
⑤ \$17.25

Identify an Equation from a Table of Values

Jake, a plumber, charges customers a fixed amount for traveling time and an hourly rate for each hour spent on the job. The table below shows the total cost (C) that Jake charges. The variable n stands for the number of hours Jake works at the job site.

n	0	1	2	3	4	5
C	$25	$60	$95	$130	$165	$200

Which equation tells how the value of C depends on the value of n?

① $C = \$40n$

② $C = \$60n + 25$

③ $C = \$25n + \$25$

④ $C = \$35n + \$25$

⑤ $C = \$35n - \$25$

You can see the pattern in the table.

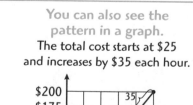

n	c	
0	$25	◀ $25
1	$60	◀ +$35
2	$95	◀ +$35
3	$130	◀ +$35
4	$165	◀ +$35
5	$200	◀ +$35

Total Cost = $35n + 25

Approach 1: Represent What the Data Says

Step 1 When n is 0, the total cost C is $25 (Jake's traveling time charge).

State the equation as:

$C = \$25 + $ (amount charged for hours worked)

Step 2 Now, determine the amount Jake charges each hour. To do this, subtract one hourly cost from the one before it.

1st hour: $60 − $25 = $35

2nd hour: $95 − $60 = $35

> As n changes by 1, C changes by $35.

and so on.

So, Jake charges $35 for each hour worked.

The equation becomes:

$C = \$25 + \$35n$, which you can also write as $C = \$35n + \$25$

You can also see the pattern in a graph.
The total cost starts at $25 and increases by $35 each hour.

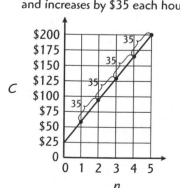

Approach 2: Check Each Answer Choice

A second way to find the correct equation is to check each answer. For example, find the value of each choice for n = 1.

① $C = \$40 = \$40(1) = \$40$

② $C = \$60n + 25 = \$60(1) + \$25 = \$85$

③ $C = \$25n + \$25 = \$25(1) + \$25 = \$50$

④ $C = \$35n + \$25 = \$35(1) + \$25 = \mathbf{\$60}$

⑤ $C = \$35n - \$25 = \$35(1) - \$25 = \$10$

Only choice 4 gives the correct value of $60 for C.

GED Readiness

Application

1 Cora's monthly rent (R) is shown in the table below. For each day she pays the rent before the due date, Cora is given a small discount.

n	0	1	2	3	4
R	$485	$482	$479	$476	$473

Which equation tells how the value of R depends on the value of n, the number of days early that Cora pays the rent?

① $R = \$485n - \$3$
② $R = (\$485 + \$3)n$
③ $R = (\$485 - \$3)n$
④ $R = \$485 + \$3n$
⑤ $R = \$485 - \$3n$

2 The following table shows how the cost (C) of the daily rental price of videos at Video Central depends on the number of videos rented.

Video Central
video rental prices

n	1	2	3	4
C	$3.00	$4.50	$6.00	$7.50

Which equation tells how the value of C depends on the value of n?

① $C = \$4.50 - \$1.50n$
② $C = \$2.00 - \$1.50n$
③ $C = \$1.509 + \$1.50n$
④ $C = \$3.00n$
⑤ $C = \$3.00n - \$1.50$

3 The table below shows the distance d (in feet) an object falls through the air in a time t (in seconds) due to Earth's gravity.

t	0	1	2	3	4
d	0	16	64	144	256

Which equation tells how the value of d depends on the value of t?

① $d = 32 - 16t$
② $d = 16t + 16$
③ $d = 32t - 16$
④ $d = (16t)^2$
⑤ $d = 16t^2$

4 City Library charges a late fee (F) of 25¢ on an audio book if the book is not more than 7 days late. An additional 10¢ is charged for each day beyond 7 days.

The table shows the late fee charged on an audio book that is up to 10 days late.

The letter n stands for the number of days beyond the due date.

City Library
audio book late fees

n	due	1-7	8	9	10
F	0	25¢	35¢	45¢	55¢

For values of n greater than 7, which equation tells how the value of F depends on the value of n?

① $F = 25¢ + (n + 7) \times 10¢$
② $F = 25¢ + (n - 7) \times 10¢$
③ $F = 25¢ - (n - 7) \times 10¢$
④ $F = 25¢ + (7 \times 10¢)n$
⑤ $F = 25¢ - (7 \times 10¢)n$

48

Identify Points on a Linear Equation

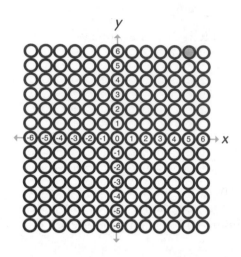

The point (3,2) is a point on the line defined by the equation $y = 2x - 4$. This line is shown on the graph.

What point on this graphed line has a *y*-value of 6?

The answer (5,6) is recorded on the coordinate plane grid.

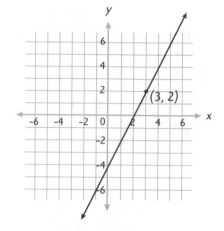

Approach 1: Use the Equation

Each point on the line has an *x*-value and a *y*-value such that $y = 2x - 4$. If you know the value of one variable, you can easily find the other.

For $y = 6$, the equation becomes: $6 = 2x - 4$

To find the value of *x*, isolate *x* on one side of the equals sign.

First, add 4 to each side: $6 + 4 = 2x - 4 + 4$

$$\text{or, } 10 = 2x \text{ (because } 6 + 4 = 10$$
$$\text{and } -4 + 4 = 0)$$

Then divide both sides by 2: $\frac{\overset{5}{\cancel{10}}}{\underset{1}{\cancel{2}}} = \frac{\overset{1}{\cancel{2}x}}{\underset{1}{\cancel{2}}}$ or $5 = x$

The point is **(5,6)**.

Reminder

A point on a coordinate plane is written as an **ordered pair:** (*x*,*y*).

- The first number, the *x*-coordinate, tells how far the point is to the right (positive *x*) or left (negative *x*) of the *y*-axis.

- The second number, the *y*-coordinate, tells how far the point is above (positive *y*) or below (negative *y*) the *x*-axis.

Approach 2: Use the Graph

Locate the point $y = 6$ on the *y*-axis. Move directly right of the *y*-axis until you reach the graphed line.

- On the graphed line, mark the point where the $y = 6$ line intersects the graphed line.

- From the marked point, scan directly down to the *x*-axis. Read the *x*-value.

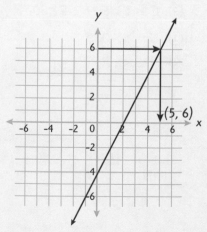

The *x*-value is 5.

The point is **(5,6)**.

GED Readiness

Concept

1 The point (2,2) is a point on a line that also passes through the origin (0,0). What is the point on this line that has a *y*-coordinate of ⁻5?

Mark your answer on the coordinate plane grid below.

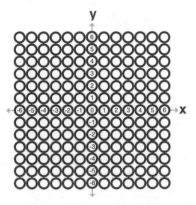

2 Use the identified points on the graphed line to find the equation represented by the line.

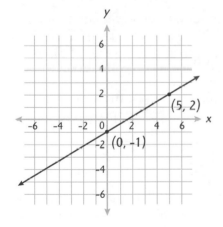

① $y = 2x - 1$

② $y = x - 1$

③ $y = \frac{3}{5}x + 2$

④ $y = \frac{3}{5}x - 1$

⑤ Not enough information is given.

3 The point (0,2) is a point on the line defined by the equation $y = 3x + 2$. Which point on this line has a *y*-value of 8?

① (4,8)

② (2,8)

③ (8,2)

④ (8,0)

⑤ (1,3)

Procedure

4 On the graph on page 108, at what point does the graphed line intersect the *y*-axis? [This point is called the *y*-intercept.]

Mark your answer on the coordinate plane grid below.

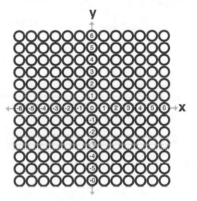

5 Which of the following lines contains the point (3,1)?

① $y = 2x + 1$

② $y = 2x + 2$

③ $y = \frac{2}{3}x - 2$

④ $y = \frac{2}{3}x - 1$

⑤ Not enough information is given.

Write an Equivalent Equation

Which equation is equivalent to the following equation?

$$y = 3x + 6$$

① $x = y - \frac{6}{3}$ ④ $x = \frac{1}{3}y + 2$

② $x = y + \frac{6}{3}$ ⑤ $x = 3y - 6$

③ $x = \frac{1}{3}y - 2$

Inverse Operations

Operations are **inverse operations** if one undoes the other. The following pairs are inverse operations:

• Addition and Subtraction

$$y = x + 2$$
$$y - 2 = x + 2 - 2$$
$$y - 2 = x$$

$$y = x - 5$$
$$y + 5 = x - 5 + 5$$
$$y + 5 = x$$

• Multiplication and Division

$$y = 4x$$
$$\frac{y}{4} = \frac{4x}{4}$$
$$\frac{1}{4}y = x$$

$$y = \frac{x}{9}$$
$$9 \times y = \frac{x}{9} \times 9$$
$$9y = x$$

• Square and Square Root

$$y = x^2$$
$$\sqrt{y} = \sqrt{x^2}$$
$$\sqrt{y} = x$$

$$y = \sqrt{x}$$
$$y^2 = (\sqrt{x})^2$$
$$y^2 = x$$

Solution

The equation $y = 3x + 6$ shows a relationship between x and y. The equation tells you how to find y when you know x.

Rearranging terms in an equation does not change the relationship. Rearranging terms results in an **equivalent equation**.

You can rearrange terms in the equation $y = 3x + 6$ to write an equivalent equation that tells how to find x when you know y.

Step 1 Remove the 6 that is added to $3x$.

• To remove an added number from one side of an equation, subtract that number from **both sides** of the equation. Subtraction is the inverse of addition and results in moving the 6 from one side of the equation to the other.

Subtract 6: $y - 6 = 3x + 6 - 6$ $(6 - 6 = 0$, so these   6's can be dropped)

     Or, $\mathbf{y - 6 = 3x}$

Step 2 Remove the 3 that multiplies x.

• To remove a coefficient (a number multiplying a variable), divide **both sides** of the equation by that number. Division is the inverse of multiplication and results in both sides of the equation being divided by the same number.

Divide by 3: $\frac{y - 6}{3} = \frac{3x}{3}$ (On the right, the 3's cancel, leaving x alone.)

         $\frac{y}{3} - \frac{6}{3} = x$ (On the left, 3 divides each term.)

    So, $\frac{1}{3}y - 2 = x$

        Or, $x = \frac{1}{3}y - 2$

GED Readiness

Procedure

1 Which equation for x is equivalent to the following equation for y?

$$y = 2x - 8$$

① $x = \frac{1}{2}y + 4$

② $x = \frac{1}{2}y + 8$

③ $x = \frac{1}{2}y - 4$

④ $x = \frac{1}{8}y + 8$

⑤ $x = \frac{1}{8}y - 4$

2 The formula for the area A of a circle is $A = \pi \times \text{radius}^2$, or $A = \pi r^2$. Which equation tells you how to find r when you know the value of A?

① $r = \left(\frac{1}{\pi}\right)\sqrt{A}$ ④ $r = (\pi A)^2$

② $r = \left(\frac{1}{\pi}\right)A$ ⑤ $r = \pi A$

③ $r = \sqrt{\frac{A}{\pi}}$

3 The formula that tells how to find the temperature in degrees Celsius (°C) when you know the temperature in degrees Fahrenheit (°F) is written:

$$°C = \frac{5}{9}(°F - 32°)$$

Which formula tells how to find the temperature in °F when you know it in °C?

① $°F = \frac{9}{5}(°C \times 32°)$

② $°F = \frac{9}{5}(°C - 32°)$

③ $°F = \frac{9}{5}(°C + 32°)$

④ $°F = \frac{9}{5}°C - 32°$

⑤ $°F = \frac{9}{5}°C + 32°$

Application

4 The area of a square is given by the formula $A = \text{side}^2$, or $A = s^2$. If the floor area of a square dining hall is about 175 square feet, which is the best estimate of the length of each side?

① between 12 and 13 feet
② between 13 and 14 feet
③ between 14 and 15 feet
④ between 15 and 16 feet
⑤ between 16 and 17 feet

5 The simple interest formula is written interest earned = principal × rate × time, or $i = prt$. Suppose \$3,500 is left in the bank for 1 year and 6 months. If a total interest of \$210 is earned, what is the interest rate?

① 2%
② 3%
③ 4%
④ 5%
⑤ Not enough information is given.

6 The volume of a cylinder is given by the formula $V = \pi \times \text{radius}^2 \times \text{height}$, or $V = \pi r^2 h$. James estimated the volume of a cylindrical can to be 124 cubic inches. He used the values $r = 2$ inches and $h = 10$ inches. He estimated the value of π. What value did James use for π?

① 3
② 3.1
③ 3.14
④ 3.18
⑤ Not enough information is given.

cube

Jennifer is preparing to move to a new home. She is packing her clothes in a box shaped like a cube. If Jennifer uses another box the same shape but whose edges are double in length, how does the box volume change?

1. The volume becomes 2 times its original amount.
2. The volume becomes 4 times its original amount.
3. The volume becomes 6 times its original amount.
4. The volume becomes 8 times its original amount.
5. The volume becomes 16 times its original amount.

The volume of a cube is given by the formula:

Volume of a cube $= \text{edge}^3 = \text{edge} \times \text{edge} \times \text{edge}$

The question is asking, "How does V change when the length of each edge is doubled?"

Approach 1: Use Simple Numbers

One way to solve this problem is to use simple numbers to compare different volumes. To do this, imagine two boxes **(cubes)** of different sizes as shown at left. Next, find the volume of each.

- Choose the length of the edge of box A to be 1.

- Choose the length of the edge of box B to be 2, twice the length of the side of box A.

  Volume of box A $= 1 \times 1 \times 1 = 1^3 = \mathbf{1}$

  Volume of box B $= 2 \times 2 \times 2 = 2^3 = \mathbf{8}$

The volume of box B is **8 times** the volume of box A.

Numerical Approach

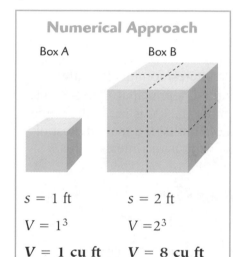

Box A   Box B

$s = 1$ ft $s = 2$ ft

$V = 1^3$ $V = 2^3$

$V = 1$ cu ft $V = 8$ cu ft

Box B can be pictured as 8 smaller boxes, each the size of box A.

Algebraic Approach

Cube A   Cube B

y $2y$

$V = y^3$ $V = (2y)^3 = 8y^3$

Approach 2: Use Algebra

A second way to solve this problem is to use algebra. To use algebra, represent the boxes as cubes. Represent the edge of each cube with a variable.

Let $y = $ length of the edge of cube A

Then $2y = $ length of the edge of cube B

Volume of cube A $= y \times y \times y = \mathbf{y^3}$

Volume of cube B $= 2y \times 2y \times 2y = 2^3y^3 = \mathbf{8y^3}$

The volume of cube B is **8 times** the volume of cube A.

The algebraic result shows that the relationship between the two cube volumes is true for any value of y.

GED Readiness

Concept

1. Suppose both the length and width of a rectangle are doubled. How does the perimeter of the new rectangle compare with the perimeter of the original rectangle?

   ① 2 times the original perimeter
   ② 4 times the original perimeter
   ③ 6 times the original perimeter
   ④ 8 times the original perimeter
   ⑤ 16 times the original perimeter

Application

2. Casey makes jewelry boxes that are 10 inches long, 6 inches wide, and 5 inches high. He will start making boxes that are 12 inches long, 6 inches wide, and 5 inches high. What is the ratio of the volume of the larger box to the volume of the smaller box?

   ① $\frac{6}{5}$ ④ $\frac{2}{3}$

   ② $\frac{5}{4}$ ⑤ $\frac{5}{3}$

   ③ $\frac{4}{5}$

3. Juan owns a small bakery and has 3 employees. His weekly payroll is shown in the table. How much will Juan's weekly payroll increase if he raises each employee's salary by 25¢ per hour?

Employee	Hours per Week	Hourly Wage
Garcia	32	$9.00
Jansen	20	$7.50
Lopez	40	$11.50

   ① $31.25
   ② $28.00
   ③ $25.50
   ④ $23.00
   ⑤ $19.75

4. At Sadik's Pizzeria, pizzas come in two sizes. The large size has twice the diameter of the small size. About how much more cheese topping is on the large size than on the small size? [The formula for the area of a circle is: area = π × radius²]

   ① 2 times as much
   ② 2π times as much
   ③ 4 times as much
   ④ 4π times as much
   ⑤ 8 times as much

5. The formula $t = \frac{d}{r}$ tells the time of travel in hours, where d is the distance in miles, and r is the rate (speed) in miles per hour (mph). If Jon is planning to drive a distance of 120 miles, how would his time of travel change if he drives at 60 mph rather than at 40 mph?

   ① decrease by 60 minutes
   ② decrease by 45 minutes
   ③ decrease by 30 minutes
   ④ increase by 45 minutes
   ⑤ increase by 60 minutes

6. Lisa has 2 storage boxes in the shape of cubes. Each edge of the larger box is 1.25 yards long. Each edge of the smaller box is 1 yard long. By about what percent is the volume of the larger box greater than the volume of the smaller box?

   ① 150%
   ② 95%
   ③ 66%
   ④ 50%
   ⑤ 33%

Taking the GED Test

Congratulations on completing the instruction part of this book. You are now very familiar with the kinds of questions and answer formats you will see on the actual GED Test. As you ready yourself to take the Posttest, you may want to think about good test-taking strategies:

• work carefully
• use estimates to eliminate answer choices and to check your answers
• answer every question
• check to make sure that each answer makes sense

Simulating the test conditions may help you set a good pace for answering the 50 questions on the actual GED Test. Pacing is important.

• Difficult questions may precede easy ones. Because all questions have the same point value, you will want to make sure you have an opportunity to answer all of the easier questions. Don't spend a lot of time on a difficult question. Put a question mark beside the question number. Then mark the answer that you think is most likely correct. So answer every question. If you have time at the end of the test, go back and think about each question that you found difficult.

• Allow 45 minutes to complete the 25 questions in Part 1. You may use a calculator to help you answer any of these 25 questions for which you find a calculator helpful.

• Allow 45 minutes to complete the 25 questions in Part 2. Do NOT use a calculator to help you answer any of these 25 questions.

• If you finish Part 2 before using all 45 minutes, you may go back and work more on Part 1, but you may not use the calculator.

• A formula page that appears in the GED Test booklet is reproduced on the following page. You have already used most of these formulas as you worked the problems in this book. Take the time to remind yourself of these formulas so that you may find them quickly and use them accurately.

Formulas

AREA of a:	
square	Area = side^2
rectangle	Area = length × width
parallelogram	Area = base × height
triangle	Area = $\frac{1}{2}$ × base × height
trapezoid	Area = $\frac{1}{2}$ × (base$_1$ + base$_2$) × height
circle	Area = π × radius^2; π is approximately equal to 3.14

PERIMETER of a:	
square	Perimeter = 4 × side
rectangle	Perimeter = 2 × length + 2 × width
triangle	Perimeter = side$_1$ + side$_2$ + side$_3$
CIRCUMFERENCE of a circle:	Circumference = π × diameter; π is approximately equal to 3.14

VOLUME of a:	
cube	Volume = edge^3
rectangular solid	Volume = length × width × height
square pyramid	Volume = $\frac{1}{3}$ × (base edge)^2 × height
cylinder	Volume = π × radius^2 × height; π is approximately equal to 3.14
cone	Volume = $\frac{1}{3}$ × π × radius^2 × height; π is approximately equal to 3.14

COORDINATE GEOMETRY	distance between points = $(x_2 - x_1)^2 + (y_2 - y_1)^2$; (x_1, y_1) and (x_2, y_2) are two points in a plane. slope of a line = $\frac{y_2 - y_1}{x_2 - x_1}$; (x_1, y_1) and (x_2, y_2) are two points on the line.

PYTHAGOREAN RELATIONSHIP	$a^2 + b^2 = c^2$; a and b are legs and c the hypotenuse of a right triangle

MEASURES OF CENTRAL TENDENCY	**mean** = $\frac{x_1 + x_2 + \ldots + x_n}{n}$, where the x's are the values for which a mean is desired, and n is the total number of values for x **median** = the middle value of an odd number of *ordered* scores, and halfway between the two middle values of an even number of *ordered* scores

SIMPLE INTEREST	interest = principal × rate × time
DISTANCE	distance = rate × time
TOTAL COST	total cost = (number of units) × (price per unit)

GED Posttest Part 1

You may use a calculator for questions on this part of the test.

1. The ingredients in each pound of Swan's Mixed Nuts are listed in the table below.

Swan's Mixed Nuts
(ingredients by weight in a 1-pound mixture)

Peanuts	0.4 lb
Filberts	0.125 lb
Pecans	0.125 lb
Cashews	0.25 lb
Other	

What part of a pound is represented by the word *Other* on the table?

① 0.1
② 0.2
③ 0.25
④ 0.35
⑤ Not enough information is given.

2. An engineer is designing a support beam for a church steeple. She determines that the weight of the beam (in hundreds of pounds) is given by the expression:

Weight = $3 \times (5 - 2)^2 + \sqrt{5^2 - 3^2}$

What is the weight of the beam?

① 400 pounds
② 900 pounds
③ 1,400 pounds
④ 2,300 pounds
⑤ 3,100 pounds

3. Yann earns *time and three quarters* for each hour of overtime he works on Saturday. His overtime pay rate is found by multiplying his regular pay rate of $10.40 by 1.75.

How much will Yann earn on a Saturday if he works a regular 8-hour shift and 2.5 hours of overtime?

① $92.90
② $101.80
③ $128.70
④ $145.60
⑤ $191.10

4. The two thermometers show the daily high and low temperatures for a winter day in Chicago. What is the difference between the high and low temperatures?

① 15°F
② 20°F
③ 32°F
④ 50°F
⑤ 65°F

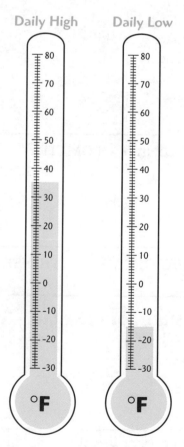

5. Mary Lou's favorite recipe for corn chowder calls for $\frac{1}{3}$ cup of cream. To have enough for each guest at her party, Mary Lou wants to make 8 times as much as a single recipe. How much cream does she need?

① $2\frac{2}{3}$ cups

② 2 cups

③ $1\frac{3}{4}$ cups

④ $1\frac{2}{3}$ cups

⑤ $1\frac{1}{2}$ cups

6. At Alonzo's Radio, the best-selling radio is available in two colors: dark gray and silver. Shown below are the radios left in stock.

What percent of these radios are dark gray 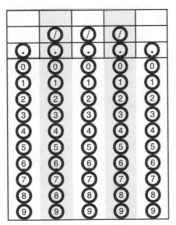?

Mark your answer in the circles in the grid.

7. The walking paths in Central Park meet in a triangle around the play area.

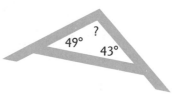

Which expression gives the measure of the third angle in this triangle?

① $180° + (49° + 43°)$
② $180° - (49° + 43°)$
③ $90° - (49° + 43°)$
④ $90° + (49° - 43°)$
⑤ $360° - (49° + 43°)$

8. Maximum recommended heart rate during strenuous exercise for adults between the ages of 25 and 65 is given by the equation:

$M = 195 - (n - 25)$
  where M = maximum heart rate
  and n = age in years

How does the recommended maximum heart rate (M) change over a 10-year period for a woman who begins an exercise program in her 30s?

① decreases 5 beats per minute
② decreases 10 beats per minute
③ increases 5 beats per minute
④ increases 10 beats per minute
⑤ stays the same

9. The point (4,1) is a point on a line defined by the equation $y = 2x - 7$. What point on this line has an *x*-value of 3?

Mark your answer on the coordinate plane grid below.

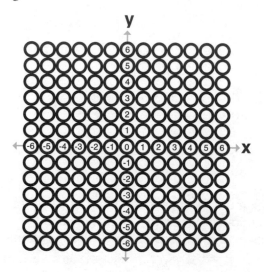

Problem 10 is based on the following table.

Mia's Pizza Shop

Sale Item	Original Price	Sale Price
Large Pizza	$18.00	$16.00
Medium Pizza	$14.00	$11.50
Small Pizza	$10.00	$7.50
Single Pizza	$6.50	$5.00

10. Which expression shows how to determine the percent discount being offered on medium pizzas?

① $\dfrac{\$11.50 - \$2.50}{\$14.00} \times 100\%$

② $\dfrac{\$14.00 - \$11.50}{\$11.50} \times 100\%$

③ $\dfrac{\$14.00 - \$11.50}{\$25.50} \times 100\%$

④ $\dfrac{\$14.00 - \$11.50}{\$2.50} \times 100\%$

⑤ $\dfrac{\$14.00 - \$11.50}{\$14.00} \times 100\%$

Problem 11 refers to the graph below.

Yearly Interest Rates

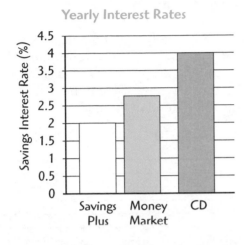

11. A customer of Evergreen Bank plans to place $4,000 in a savings account for a period of 6 months. The bank offers 3 savings plans:

- In the Savings Plus plan, money can be withdrawn at any time without penalty.
- In the Money Market plan, interest is earned only for full months at a time.
- In the CD (certificate of deposit) plan, money must be left for a full 6 months or an early withdrawal fee is charged.

If the customer's money remains deposited for the full 6 months, how much more interest would be earned in a CD account than in a Savings Plus account?

① $20   ④ $60
② $24   ⑤ $80
③ $40

12. The storage compartment of a freezer has a volume of 22.5 cubic feet. If the height of the storage compartment is 5 feet, which could be its length and width?

① length = 2.75 ft; width = 2 ft
② length = 2.4 ft; width = 2.1 ft
③ length = 2.5 ft; width = 2 ft
④ length = 2.25 ft; width = 2 ft
⑤ length = 2.25 ft; width = 2.5 ft

13. Manuel measures the length of the shadow of a flagpole. At the same time of day, he also measures the length of the shadow of a yardstick. Manuel's measurements are shown below.

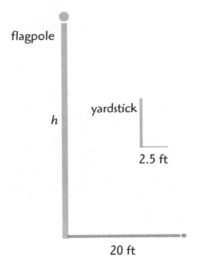

Which proportion can be used to find h, the height in feet of the flagpole?

① $\frac{h}{3} = \frac{20}{2.5}$

② $\frac{h}{3} = \frac{2.5}{20}$

③ $\frac{h}{1} = \frac{20}{2.5}$

④ $\frac{h}{1} = \frac{2.5}{20}$

⑤ $\frac{h}{20} = \frac{2.5}{3}$

14. A set of towels that regularly sells for $24.00 is on sale at a 30% discount. What is the total cost of the set of towels if the sales tax is 5%?

Mark your answer in the circles in the grid.

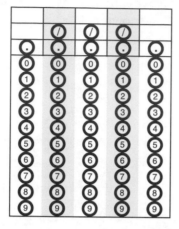

15. Body mass index (BMI) is a measure of body fat, based on height and weight. BMI applies to both men and women and is defined by the following formula:

$$BMI = \frac{703w}{h^2}$$

where h is the height in inches, and w is the weight in pounds.

Weight categories based on BMI for both men and women are defined as follows:

BMI	Weight Description
below 18.5	Underweight
18.5 to 24.9	Normal weight
25 to 29.9	Overweight
30 or greater	Very overweight

To the nearest whole number, what is the BMI of a 70-inch-tall man who weighs 185 pounds?

① 24
② 27
③ 29
④ 30
⑤ 33

Problems 16–18 are based on the following graph and information.

Over a 7-day period, the manager of CD Circle had a sale on music CDs. Each day he reduced the price by $1.00. The sales results are graphed below. A line of best fit is drawn to show the trend of the data.

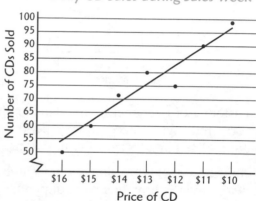

16. Based on the line of best fit, about how many more CDs sell for each reduction of $1.00 in price? Round your answer to the nearest whole number.

① 2
② 3
③ 5
④ 7
⑤ 9

17. Which is the best estimate of the ratio of the actual number of CDs sold at $10 to the number sold at $16?

① 2 to 3
② 3 to 2
③ 2 to 1
④ 3 to 1
⑤ 4 to 1

18. What is the median number of sales per day during the 7-day period shown?

Mark your answer in the circles in the grid.

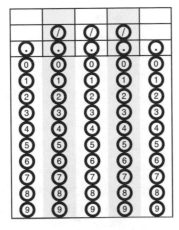

19. Georgia walks from her home (*H*) to the theater (*T*) by taking the shortcut through the park as shown by the arrows. What distance in blocks will Georgia walk?

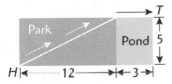

All distances are in blocks.

① 13
② 15
③ 16
④ 17
⑤ 20

20. Debra is planning to buy either a square rug or a circular rug as shown in the drawing. About how many square feet larger is the square rug than the circular rug? Use $\pi = 3.14$.

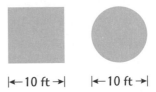

|←10 ft →| |←10 ft →|

① 18
② 22
③ 25
④ 29
⑤ 32

21. Lucinda is bowling 3 games in tonight's league competition. The scores for her first 2 games are 148 and 161. If Lucinda wants the average (mean) of her 3 games to be 160, what score does she need in her third game?

Mark your answer in the circles in the grid.

Problems 22 and 23 refer to the information and circle graph below.

In a recent Internet poll, the following question was asked: "On the average, how many hours of sleep do you get each weeknight?" The poll results are shown in the circle graph below.

Average Hours of Sleep on Weeknights
3,250 People Responding

34% 7 hours
18% 8 hours
7% more than 8 hours
less than 5 hours
10% 5 hours
27% 6 hours

22. What percent of the people who responded said *less than 5 hours*?

Mark your answer in the circles in the grid.

23. How many of the people who responded said 7 hours?

① 996
② 1,017
③ 1,026
④ 1,105
⑤ Not enough information is given.

24. Kira is having her living room carpeted. A pad that is $\frac{5}{8}$ inch thick will be placed on the floor. Then the carpet will be placed over the pad. If the carpet is $\frac{3}{4}$ inch thick, what is the total thickness of the pad and the carpet together?

① $\frac{2}{3}$ inch
② $\frac{7}{8}$ inch
③ $1\frac{1}{8}$ inches
④ $1\frac{1}{4}$ inches
⑤ $1\frac{3}{8}$ inches

25. An assembly-line worker found 6 defects in the 265 computers he tested. At this rate, how many defects, to the nearest whole number, will be found in 1,200 computers?

Mark your answer in the circles in the grid.

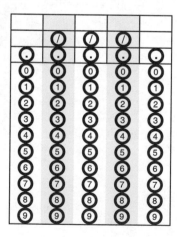

GED Posttest Part 2

You may **not** use a calculator for questions on this part of the test.

26. Orange juice concentrate is on sale for $0.99 per can if you buy a case of 24 cans. Which is the best estimate of the amount you save by buying at this sale price compared with the cost of buying 24 cans at the regular price of $1.21 each?

    ① $1
    ② $2
    ③ $3
    ④ $4
    ⑤ $5

27. Armano has five guitar strings that have the following thicknesses given in inches: 0.098, 0.204, 0.3, 0.03, and 0.026.

    How many of the strings have a thickness greater than 0.2 inch?

    ① 5
    ② 4
    ③ 3
    ④ 2
    ⑤ 1

28. Julianna wants to drill a hole that is wider than $\frac{1}{2}$ inch but narrower than $\frac{5}{8}$ inch. She has a box containing five drill bits. The diameters, in inches, of the drill bits are:
    $\frac{3}{4}, \frac{13}{32}, \frac{7}{16}, \frac{9}{16}, \frac{1}{4}$

    Which drill bit should Julianna use?

    ① $\frac{3}{4}$

    ② $\frac{13}{32}$

    ③ $\frac{9}{16}$

    ④ $\frac{7}{16}$

    ⑤ $\frac{1}{4}$

29. Roberto is making silver bracelets to sell at his booth at the Fall Festival. For each bracelet he uses 7 inches of chain. How many bracelets can Roberto make if he has 3 pieces of silver chain, each $2\frac{1}{2}$ feet long?

    Mark your answer in the circles in the grid.

30. Mount McKinley in Alaska is the highest mountain in North America. What is the approximate height of Mount McKinley?

    ① 13,700 millimeters
    ② 6,200 meters
    ③ 650 kilometers
    ④ 450 centimeters
    ⑤ 140 meters

Problem 31 refers to the table below.

Length (U.S. Customary)		
1 foot	=	12 inches
1 yard	=	3 feet
1 mile	=	5,280 feet

31. Elyssa bought 9 inches of lace trim to make dollhouse curtains. The price of the trim is $1.89 per yard. Which expression tells how to find the fraction of a yard that Elyssa purchased?

① $\dfrac{12}{9 \times 3}$

② $\dfrac{9 \times 3}{12}$

③ $\dfrac{3 \times 12}{9}$

④ $\dfrac{9}{12 \times 3}$

⑤ $\dfrac{9 \times 12}{3}$

32. Leticia works as a server at The Gas Light Restaurant. On the average she serves 12 tables each hour. She earns $7 each hour and keeps her tips, which average $3.00 for each table she serves. How many tables can Leticia expect to serve during a shift of 3 hour and 45 minutes on Saturday?

Mark your answer in the circles in the grid.

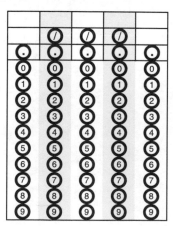

Problem 33 refers to the drawing below.

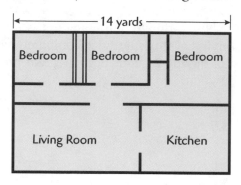

33. Heather drew the sketch of several rooms shown above. She measured the width of the sketch to be 7 inches. Which scale should Heather write below her sketch?

① 1 inch = 6 feet
② 1 inch = 12 yards
③ 1 inch = 3 feet
④ 1 inch = 4 feet
⑤ Not enough information is given.

Problem 34 refers to the diagram below.

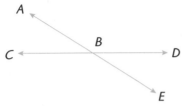

∠ ABC and ∠ ABD combine
to form a straight angle.

34. The measure of ∠ABC is 40°. Which of the
following gives the correct name and measure
of an angle that is supplementary to ∠ABC?

① ∠DBE, which has a measure of 40°
② ∠DBE, which has a measure of 50°
③ ∠CBE, which has a measure of 140°
④ ∠ABD, which has a measure of 50°
⑤ ∠ABD, which has a measure of 320°

Problem 35 refers to the diagram below.

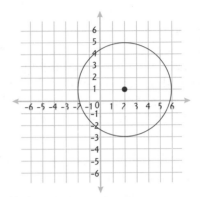

35. Suppose the circle is moved 3 units to the
right and 4 units down. What will be the new
coordinates of the circle's center?

Mark your answer on the coordinate plane
grid below.

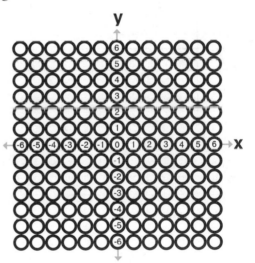

Problems 36–38 refer to the information and graph below.

Corey needs her car's engine rebuilt. She checks prices at three auto repair shops. Each shop has its own way of charging for labor, and each shop has estimated that the total time for the repairs should take "no longer than 6 hours." The cost for parts will be about the same in each shop.

- Sam's Auto charges $325 for labor, no matter how long it takes.
- Auto House charges $100 *plus* an hourly charge for each hour worked.
- Central Auto charges only for the hours actually worked on the car.

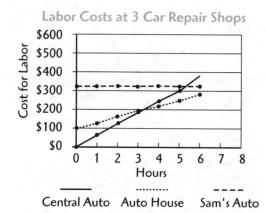

36. How much does Central Auto charge for each hour of labor?

  ① $80
  ② $60
  ③ $40
  ④ $20
  ⑤ Not enough information is given.

37. If Corey's car engine takes 5 hours to rebuild, about how much would Corey save by having the work done at Auto House rather than at Central Auto?

  ① about $125
  ② about $100
  ③ about $75
  ④ about $50
  ⑤ about $25

38. If Corey's car engine takes more than 6 hours to rebuild, about how much would Corey save by having the work done at Auto House rather than at Central Auto?

  ① about $75
  ② about $100
  ③ about $125
  ④ about $150
  ⑤ Not enough information is given.

Problem 39 refers to the graph below.

The graph shows the population of Harney County between the years 1950 and 2000.

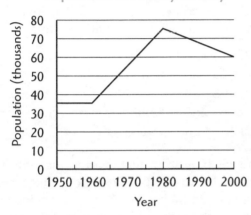

Population of Harney County

39. Between 1960 and 1980, what was the average yearly increase in Harney County population?

① 2,000
② 5,000
③ 10,000
④ 20,000
⑤ Not enough information is given.

40. Six friends have pooled $50 to buy raffle tickets for a Hawaiian vacation. The prices are $5.00 each or 5 for $20.00. A total of 6,000 tickets will be sold. If the friends buy the maximum tickets possible, what is the probability that one of the friends will win the vacation?

① $\frac{1}{1000}$
② $\frac{1}{800}$
③ $\frac{1}{600}$
④ $\frac{1}{500}$
⑤ $\frac{1}{50}$

Problems 41 and 42 refer to the graphs below.

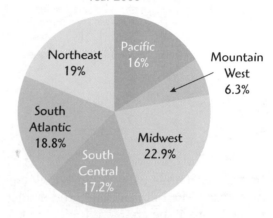

Where People Live in the U.S. by Region
Year 2000

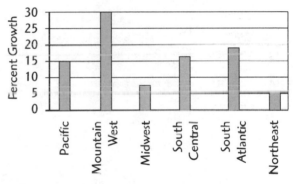

U.S. Population Growth By Region
1990 to 2000

41. Which region of the United States had the greatest population in the year 2000?

① South Atlantic
② Midwest
③ South Central
④ Northeast
⑤ Mountain West

42. In which region did the population increase by about one-third during the 1990s?

① South Atlantic
② Midwest
③ South Central
④ Northeast
⑤ Mountain West

43. Shailan has made 18 out of 24 field goal attempts this season. What is the probability that Shailan will **not** make her first field goal attempt in today's game?

① $\frac{3}{4}$

② $\frac{3}{5}$

③ $\frac{1}{4}$

④ $\frac{2}{3}$

⑤ $\frac{1}{2}$

44. The Sanders family eats dinner Friday night at Lou's Pizza. The bill is $21.50, and a sales tax of n percent will be charged. Including tax, which expression tells the total cost of dinner?

① $(\frac{n}{100} \times \$21.50)$

② $(\frac{n}{100} \div \$21.50)$

③ $\$21.50 - (\frac{n}{100} \times \$21.50)$

④ $\$21.50 + (\frac{n}{100} \times \$21.50)$

⑤ $\$21.50 \times (\frac{n}{100} + \$21.50)$

45. Joyce and Daffney run a housecleaning service. Because Joyce provides all of the supplies, she earns $250 more each month than Daffney. In May, Joyce and Daffney together earned a total of $3,280.

Which equation can be used to find Joyce's share (*J*) of the income earned in May?

① $2J = \$3,280 + \$250$

② $J = \$3,280 - \$250$

③ $2J = \$3,280 - \$125$

④ $J = \$3,280 + \$350$

⑤ $2J = \$3,280 - \$250$

46. Andrew is building a rectangular brick patio in his backyard. He is using bricks that have a length of $2n$ inches and a width of n inches. He places the long side of each brick parallel to the length of the patio as shown below.

Andrew will place 25 bricks along the length of the patio and 30 bricks along the width. Not counting the space between the bricks, which expression gives the area of the completed patio?

① $1,500n^2$ square inches

② $750n^2$ square inches

③ $1,500n$ square inches

④ $750n$ square inches

⑤ 750 square inches

Problems 47 and 48 refer to the following information and table.

Benton County Fair charges an admission price and a fee for each thrill ride. The total cost for admission and a number (*n*) of rides is shown in the table below.

County Fair
Admission and Ride Cost

n	0	1	2	3	4
C	$4.50	$5.10	$5.70	$6.30	$6.90

47. If this cost pattern continues, what total amount will Joel spend going to the fair and paying for 10 rides?

  ① $12.50
  ② $10.50
  ③ $9.70
  ④ $8.40
  ⑤ $6.00

48. Which equation tells how the value of *C* depends on the value of *n*?

  ① $C = \$4.50 + n$
  ② $C = \$0.60n$
  ③ $C = \$0.60n + \$4.50$
  ④ $C = \$4.50n + \$0.60$
  ⑤ $C = (\$4.50 + \$0.60)n$

49. Which graph best represents the relationship between the circumference, *C*, of a circle and its diameter, *d*?

①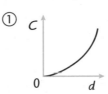
④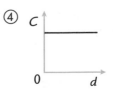
②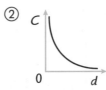
⑤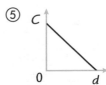
③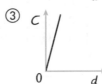

50. The volume for a square pyramid is given by the formula:

Volume $= \frac{1}{3} \times$ (base edge)$^2 \times$ height
In symbols, this formula is $V - \frac{1}{3} \times s^2 \times h$.

Which formula tells you how to find the height *h* of a square pyramid when you know *V* (the volume) and *s* (the length of the base edge)?

  ① $h = \frac{V}{3s^2}$

  ② $h = \frac{3}{Vs^2}$

  ③ $h = \frac{s^2}{3V}$

  ④ $h = \frac{3s^2}{V}$

  ⑤ $h = \frac{3V}{s^2}$

Posttest Evaluation Chart

Circle the number of any problem you missed. The column after the problem number tells you the skill. The next column tells you the pages to review in this book. The last column indicates the pages in Contemporary's *GED Mathematics* where the skill is taught in greater detail.

Part 1

Problem Number	Skill Name	Review Pages	GED Math
1	Decimals	18–19	75–98
2	Order of Operations	20–21	43–45
3	Decimals	22–23	75–98
4	Scales	42–43	190–194
5	Fractions	28–29	103–136
6	Fractions, Decimals, Percents	30–31	150–155
7	Triangles	58–59	259–262
8	Values	112–113	292–322
9	Linear Equations	108–109	329–330
10	Percent	38–39	149–182
11	Simple Interest	48–49	176–178
12	Volume	64–65	252–258
13	Similar Figures	50–51	263–270
14	Discount and Sales Tax	32–33	174–175
15	Formulas	94–95	234–239
16	Line of Best Fit	76–77	---
17	Ratios	34–35	137–139
18	Central Tendency	70–71	197
19	Pythagorean Relationship	60–61	271–275
20	Area	62–63	240–248
21	Missing Terms	72–73	140–144
22	Circle Graphs	84–85	197–211
23	Circle Graphs	86–87	197–211
24	Fractions	26–27	103–136
25	Proportions	36–37	140–145

Part 2

Problem Number	Skill Name	Review Pages	GED Math
26	Estimation	14–15	25, 61, 116
27	Decimals	16–17	75–98
28	Fractions	24–25	103–136
29	Measurement	54–55	183–194
30	Units	40–41	183–194
31	Units of Measure	44–45	183–194
32	Rate	46–47	137–148
33	Scale Drawing	52–53	190–194
34	Angles	56–57	223–280
35	Coordinate Plane	66–67	323–346
36	Slope	68–69	331–335
37	Multiple Line Graph	80–81	197–222
38	Interpolate and Extrapolate	74–75	---
39	Single Line Graph	78–79	197–222
40	Probability	90–91	197–222
41	Data	88–89	197–222
42	Bar Graphs	82–83	197–222
43	Probability	92–93	197–222
44	Algebraic Expressions	96–97	292–322
45	Equation Word Problems	98–99	292–322
46	Algebraic Expressions	100–101	292–322
47	Numerical Patterns	102–103	17–50
48	Values	106–107	292–322
49	Equations	104–105	294–322
50	Equations	110–111	294–322

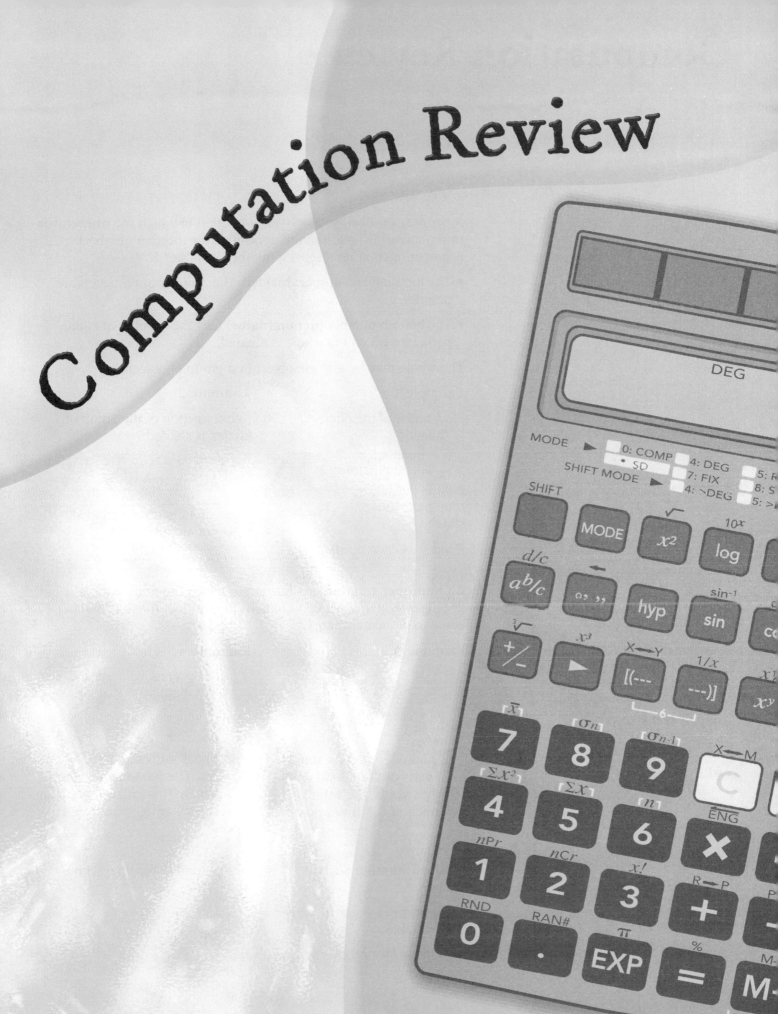

Computation Review

Computation Review

Fractions and Mixed Numbers

A **proper fraction**, such as $\frac{1}{2}$, is a fraction in which the **numerator** (top number) is less than the **denominator** (bottom number). A proper fraction represents a number less than 1.

- The top number (**numerator**) tells the number of parts you are describing.

- The bottom number (**denominator**) tells the number of equal parts into which the whole is divided.

The whole may be a single object or a group of objects.

Example 1

How much of the circle is shaded?

$\frac{2}{3}$ ← numerator
← denominator

2 parts out of 3 total parts are shaded.

Read $\frac{2}{3}$ as "two thirds."

Example 2

What fraction of the group of circles is shaded?

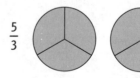

3 out of 4 circles are shaded.

$\frac{3}{4}$ ← numerator
← denominator

An **improper fraction** is a fraction in which the numerator is equal to or greater than the denominator. An improper fraction is either equal to or greater than 1.

Example 3

$\frac{3}{3}$

This improper fraction stands for 3 parts out of 3 total parts. In other words, the value of this fraction is 1 (the whole).

Example 4

$\frac{5}{3}$

One whole is divided into 3 pieces. The numerator 5 refers to 5 pieces. This improper fraction represents 1 whole *plus* 2 more pieces.

A **mixed number** such as $1\frac{2}{3}$ is a whole number together with a fraction.

- The number 1 stands for one whole object.

- $\frac{2}{3}$ stands for part of a second object.

$1\frac{2}{3}$

An **improper fraction** can always be written as a **mixed number**. A mixed number can always be written as an improper fraction:

Examples

a) $\frac{5}{3} = \frac{3}{3} + \frac{2}{3}$
$= 1\frac{2}{3}$

b) $2\frac{2}{3} = \frac{6}{3} + \frac{2}{3}$
$= \frac{8}{3}$

132

Try These

Change a Mixed Number to an Improper Fraction

1. $2\frac{3}{4} = \frac{}{4}$

2. $5\frac{1}{2} = \frac{}{2}$

Write an Equal Fraction

3. $\frac{3}{4} = \frac{}{16}$

4. $\frac{6}{4} = \frac{}{8}$

Simplify Each Fraction or Mixed Number

5. $\frac{6}{12} = \frac{}{2}$

6. $\frac{12}{16} = \frac{}{4}$

7. $1\frac{8}{16} =$

8. $3\frac{6}{8} =$

Writing Equivalent Fractions

There is more than one way to write a fraction to represent a given amount. For example, the two cups contain equal amounts of milk.

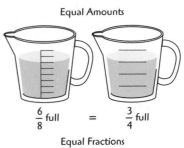

Equal Amounts

$\frac{6}{8}$ full $=$ $\frac{3}{4}$ full

Equal Fractions

- The cup at the left is divided into 8 equal measuring units.
- The cup at the right is divided into 4 equal measuring units.

The fractions $\frac{3}{4}$ and $\frac{6}{8}$ represent the same amount. The two fractions are called **equivalent fractions**, or **equal fractions**.

To find equivalent fractions, multiply the numerator and denominator of a fraction by the same number.

Examples

$$\frac{3}{4} = \frac{6}{8} \qquad \frac{1}{2} = \frac{4}{8} \qquad \frac{5}{3} = \frac{15}{9}$$

Simplifying Fractions and Mixed Numbers

To **simplify a fraction** (also called **reducing a fraction to lowest terms**) is to write the fraction as an equivalent fraction using the lowest numbers possible.

Examples $\frac{4}{8}$ reduces to $\frac{1}{2}$ $\quad$ $\frac{6}{9}$ reduces to $\frac{2}{3}$ $\quad$ $\frac{4}{16}$ reduces to $\frac{1}{4}$

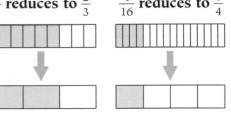

To reduce a fraction to lowest terms, divide both numerator and denominator by the greatest number that divides evenly into both.

Examples

$$\frac{4}{8} = \frac{1}{2} \qquad \frac{6}{9} = \frac{2}{3} \qquad \frac{4}{16} = \frac{1}{4}$$

Improper fractions and **mixed numbers** can also be simplified.

Examples

$$\frac{12}{8} = \frac{3}{2} \ \left(\text{or, } 1\frac{1}{2}\right) \qquad 2\frac{6}{9} = 2\frac{2}{3}$$

Like Fractions

1. $\frac{1}{2} + \frac{1}{2} =$

2. $\frac{2}{4} - \frac{1}{4} =$

3. $\frac{5}{8} + \frac{1}{8} = \frac{}{8} = \frac{}{4}$

4. $\frac{7}{16} - \frac{3}{16} = \frac{}{16} = \frac{}{4}$

Unlike Fractions

5. $\frac{1}{4} + \frac{1}{2} =$

6. $\frac{1}{9} + \frac{2}{3} =$

7. $2\frac{1}{3} + \frac{1}{2} =$

8. $\frac{3}{4} - \frac{1}{2} =$

9. $\frac{1}{2} - \frac{3}{16} =$

10. $1\frac{1}{2} - \frac{1}{3} =$

Adding and Subtracting Fractions with Like Denominators

Like fractions are fractions that have the same denominator.

Like Fractions: $\frac{5}{8}$ and $\frac{1}{8}$ $\frac{7}{16}$ and $\frac{3}{16}$

To add like fractions, add the numerators and write the sum over the denominator. Reduce the answer to lowest terms.

To subtract like fractions, subtract one numerator from the other. Write the difference over the denominator. Reduce the answer to lowest terms.

Example 1 $\frac{5}{8} + \frac{1}{8} = \frac{6}{8} = \frac{3}{4}$ **Example 2** $\frac{3}{4} + \frac{2}{4} = \frac{5}{4} = 1\frac{1}{4}$

Example 3 $\frac{11}{12} - \frac{5}{12} = \frac{6}{12} = \frac{1}{2}$ **Example 4** $\frac{5}{2} - \frac{1}{2} = \frac{4}{2} = 2$

Adding and Subtracting Fractions with Unlike Denominators

Unlike fractions are fractions that do **not** have the same denominator.

Unlike Fractions: $\frac{1}{2}$ and $\frac{1}{4}$ $\frac{5}{6}$ and $\frac{1}{3}$

To add or subtract unlike fractions, rewrite them as like fractions. You follow the same procedure here as you use when you compare unlike fractions.

• First, choose a common denominator.

• Second, write each fraction using the common denominator.

Example 1 Add: $\frac{1}{2} + \frac{1}{4}$

Step 1 Change $\frac{1}{2}$ to $\frac{2}{4}$.

Step 2 Add: $\frac{2}{4} + \frac{1}{4} = \frac{3}{4}$

Answer $\frac{3}{4}$

Example 2 Subtract: $\frac{5}{6} - \frac{1}{3}$

Step 1 Change $\frac{1}{3}$ to $\frac{2}{6}$

Step 2 Subtract: $\frac{5}{6} - \frac{2}{6} = \frac{3}{6}$

Step 3 Reduce $\frac{3}{6}$ to lowest terms.

Answer $\frac{3}{6} = \frac{1}{2}$

Multiplying Fractions and Mixed Numbers

To multiply a fraction by a fraction is to find part of a part.

The drawings below show three fraction products:

$\frac{1}{2}$ of $\frac{1}{2}$ $\frac{1}{2}$ of $\frac{1}{4}$ $\frac{1}{3}$ of $\frac{1}{4}$

$\frac{1}{2} \times \frac{1}{2} = \frac{1}{4}$ $\frac{1}{2} \times \frac{1}{4} = \frac{1}{8}$ $\frac{1}{3} \times \frac{1}{4} = \frac{1}{12}$

Both like fractions and unlike fractions are multiplied in the same way:

- Multiply the numerators to find the numerator of the answer.

- Multiply the denominators to find the denominator of the answer.

- Reduce products to lowest terms possible.

Try These

Multiply Fractions

1. $\frac{2}{3} \times 3 =$

2. $\frac{3}{8} \times 2 =$

3. $\frac{3}{4} \times 2 =$

4. $\frac{2}{3} \times \frac{1}{2} =$

5. $\frac{1}{8} \times \frac{1}{2} =$

Multiply Mixed Numbers

6. $1\frac{1}{3} \times 3 =$

7. $2\frac{1}{2} \times 6 =$

8. $4\frac{3}{1} \times 4 =$

9. $1\frac{1}{3} \times \frac{1}{2} =$

10. $2\frac{1}{2} \times \frac{1}{2} =$

Example 1

Multiply: $\frac{1}{3} \times \frac{2}{3} = \frac{2}{9}$

Example 2

Multiply: $\frac{2}{3} \times \frac{3}{4} = \frac{6}{12} = \frac{1}{2}$

To multiply any combination of fractions, whole numbers, or mixed numbers, the first step is to change each whole number or mixed number to an improper fraction. Then multiply as usual.

Example 3

Multiply: $\frac{3}{4} \times 8 =$

Step 1 Rewrite 8 as $\frac{8}{1}$.

Step 2 Multiply the fractions.

$\frac{3}{4} \times \frac{8}{1} = \frac{24}{4} = 6$

Answer 6

Example 4

Multiply: $3\frac{1}{2} \times \frac{1}{4} =$

Step 1 Rewrite $3\frac{1}{2}$ as an improper fraction.

$3\frac{1}{2} = \frac{6}{2} + \frac{1}{2} = \frac{7}{2}$

Step 2 Multiply the fractions.

$\frac{7}{2} \times \frac{1}{4} = \frac{7}{8}$

Answer $\frac{7}{8}$

Divide Fractions

1. $\frac{5}{8} \div \frac{1}{8} =$

2. $\frac{3}{4} \div \frac{1}{4} =$

3. $\frac{2}{3} \div \frac{1}{3} =$

4. $\frac{1}{2} \div \frac{1}{4} =$

5. $\frac{3}{4} \div \frac{1}{16} =$

6. $\frac{2}{3} \div \frac{2}{3} =$

Dividing a Fraction by a Fraction

To divide is to find out how many times one number is contained in a second number. This is also true with fractions.

Example To find how many $\frac{1}{8}$-inch-wide washers must be placed next to each other to span a distance of $\frac{3}{4}$ inch, divide $\frac{3}{4}$ by $\frac{1}{8}$.

$$\frac{3}{4} \div \frac{1}{8} = ?$$

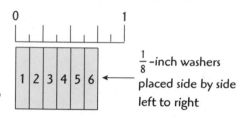

$\frac{1}{8}$-inch washers placed side by side left to right

As shown in the drawing, the answer is **6**.

Dividing fractions involves two more steps than multiplying fractions:

- First, invert the divisor (the number you are dividing by).

- Second, change the division sign to a multiplication sign.

Then multiply the two fractions.

Invert the Divisor

To **invert** means to turn a fraction upside down—interchange the numerator and denominator. In other words, switch the top and bottom numbers.

Example Divide: $\frac{3}{4} \div \frac{1}{8}$

Step 1 Invert the divisor: $\frac{1}{8}$ is inverted to become $\frac{8}{1}$

Step 2 Change the division sign to a multiplication sign.

invert the divisor

$$\frac{3}{4} \div \frac{1}{8} = \frac{3}{4} \times \frac{8}{1} = \frac{24}{4} = 6$$

change the sign

Answer: 6

Dividing Fractions, Whole Numbers, and Mixed Numbers

To divide fractions and whole numbers or mixed numbers:

- Change a whole-number divisor to an improper fraction by placing the whole number over 1.
- Change a mixed number divisor to an improper fraction.
- Invert the divisor.
- Change the division sign to a multiplication sign.
- Multiply the fractions.

Try These

Divide Fractions and Mixed Numbers

1. $\frac{1}{2} \div \frac{7}{8} =$

2. $\frac{3}{2} \div \frac{3}{4} =$

3. $2 \div \frac{1}{2} =$

4. $3 \div \frac{1}{3} =$

5. $\frac{7}{8} \div 2 =$

6. $\frac{1}{2} \div 4 =$

7. $1\frac{1}{3} \div \frac{1}{3} =$

8. $2\frac{1}{2} \div \frac{3}{4} =$

Type of Divisor	Example	Write the Divisor as a Fraction	Invert the Divisor and Change the Sign
proper fraction	$\frac{3}{4} \div \frac{7}{8}$	$\frac{3}{4} \div \frac{7}{8}$	$\frac{3}{4} \times \frac{8}{7} = \frac{24}{28} = \frac{6}{7}$
improper fraction	$\frac{2}{3} \div \frac{4}{3}$	$\frac{2}{3} \div \frac{4}{3}$	$\frac{2}{3} \times \frac{3}{4} = \frac{6}{12} = \frac{1}{2}$
whole number	$\frac{1}{2} \div 3$	$\frac{1}{2} \div \frac{3}{1}$	$\frac{1}{2} \times \frac{1}{3} = \frac{1}{6}$
mixed number	$\frac{3}{4} \div 1\frac{3}{8}$	$\frac{3}{4} \div \frac{11}{8}$	$\frac{3}{4} \times \frac{8}{11} = \frac{24}{44} = \frac{6}{11}$

Example Divide: $\frac{1}{4} \div 1\frac{1}{2}$

Step 1 Rewrite $1\frac{1}{2}$ as $\frac{3}{2}$.

So the problem becomes: $\frac{1}{4} \div \frac{3}{2}$

Step 2 Invert the divisor: $\frac{3}{2}$ inverted is $\frac{2}{3}$.

Change the $\div$ sign to a $\times$ sign.

Step 3 The division problem becomes a multiplication problem:

$\frac{1}{4} \div \frac{3}{2} = \frac{1}{4} \times \frac{2}{3} = \frac{2}{12} = \frac{1}{6}$

Answer $\frac{1}{6}$

Ratios

A ratio is a comparison of two numbers. If there are 8 women and 5 men in your class, the ratio of women to men is 8 to 5. In this class, the ratio of men to women is 5 to 8.

There are three ways to write the ratio 8 to 5, but each is read as "8 to 5":

using the word *to*	writing a fraction	using a colon
8 to 5	$\frac{8}{5}$	8:5

In a ratio, the order in which numbers are written is very important. The ratio 8 to 5 is not the same as the ratio 5 to 8.

Reduce Each Ratio

4. $\frac{4}{8}$ =

5. $\frac{16}{4}$ =

6. 6 to 9 =

7. 15 to 10 =

8. 5:25 =

9. 32:8 =

Rules for Writing a Ratio

- Reduce a ratio to lowest terms. Reduce a ratio in the same way you reduce a fraction. $6 \text{ to } 12 = \frac{6}{12} = \frac{1}{2}$

- Leave an improper-fraction ratio as an improper fraction. $9 \text{ to } 6 = \frac{9}{6} = \frac{3}{2}$

- Write a whole-number ratio as an improper fraction. $8 \text{ to } 2 = \frac{8}{2} = \frac{4}{1}$

Rates

A **rate** is a ratio that compares two different measured units, such as miles and hours or dollars and pounds. A **unit rate** is the rate for one unit of a quantity, such as miles per hour *or* dollars per pound.

To find a unit rate, divide the two numbers in the ratio. The word *per* is often used with rates. *Per* means *for each*.

Example

Donnelle walks 9 miles in 2.5 hours. What is Donnelle's walking rate in miles per hour?

To find Donnelle's walking rate in miles per hour, divide the number of miles by the number of hours.

$$\text{Walking rate} = \frac{\text{number of miles}}{\text{number of hours}} = \frac{9 \text{ miles}}{2.5 \text{ hours}} = \textbf{3.6 miles per hour}$$

Answer: 3.6 miles per hour

Proportions

A **proportion** is made up of two equal ratios. When you write ratios as fractions, you write a proportion as a pair of **equivalent fractions**.

Example

Suppose you add 1 cup of punch concentrate to 3 cups of water. The ratio of *concentrate to water* is 1 to 3. You get the same flavor of punch if you add 2 cups of punch concentrate to 6 cups of water. These two mixtures form a proportion.

Written as equivalent fractions: $\frac{1}{3} = \frac{2}{6}$

You read a proportion as two equal ratios connected by the word *as*.

$\frac{1}{3} = \frac{2}{6}$ is read "1 is to 3 as 2 is to 6"

Cross Products

In a proportion, the cross products are equal. To find cross products, multiply each numerator by the opposite denominator.

Cross Multiplication	**Equal Cross Products**
$\frac{1}{3} \diagtimes \frac{2}{6}$	$1 \times 6 = 3 \times 2$
	$6 = 6$

Finding a Missing Number in a Proportion

Sometimes you are asked to find a missing number in a proportion. To find the missing number, follow these steps:

- Write n (or some other letter) to stand for the missing number.
- Write equal cross products. Notice that one cross product contains n.
- To find n, divide each cross product by the number that multiplies n.

Example 1

Find the value of n: $\frac{n}{4} = \frac{9}{12}$

Step 1 Cross multiply: $12n = 36$

Step 2 To find n, divide each side by 12.

Answer: $n = \frac{36}{12} = 3$

Proportion $\frac{3}{4} = \frac{9}{12}$

Example 2

Find the value of x: $\frac{2}{x} = \frac{10}{15}$

Step 1 Cross multiply: $10x = 30$

Step 2 To find x, divide each side by 10.

Answer: $x = \frac{30}{10} = 3$

Proportion $\frac{2}{3} = \frac{10}{15}$

Try These

Solve Each Proportion

1. $\frac{4}{8} = \frac{n}{12}$ $n = $ _____

2. $\frac{3}{4} = \frac{x}{20}$ $x = $ _____

3. $\frac{16}{4} = \frac{4}{n}$ $n = $ _____

4. $\frac{20}{m} = \frac{4}{5}$ $m = $ _____

5. $\frac{y}{12} = \frac{15}{6}$ $y = $ _____

6. $9:12 = 15:p$ $p = $ _____

7. $r:4 = 6:8$ $r = $ _____

Fractions, Decimals, and Percents

Percent is another way to write part of a whole.

- Percent is the *number of parts out of 100 equal parts.*
- The symbol % is used to indicate percent.
- 5 percent means 5 parts out of 100 equal parts.
- 5 percent is written 5%.

Examples

One dollar is equal to 100 cents. Coins can be thought of as a percent of a dollar.

 = 1% of    = 10% of

 = 5% of    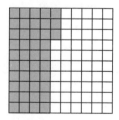 = 25% of

When calculating with percents, the first step is to change the percent to a decimal or a fraction.

- Percent has the same value as a two-place decimal. 43% is equal to 0.43.
- Percent has the same value as a fraction that has a denominator of 100: $43\% = \frac{43}{100}$.

43% is shaded.
0.43 is shaded.
$\frac{43}{100}$ is shaded.

Try These

Write as a Percent

1. 35¢ = _____% of $1

2. 8¢ = _____% of $1

3. 2¢ = _____% of $1

Write as a Decimal

4. 15% =

5. 6% =

6. 4.5% = 0.045

Write as a Percent

7. 0.61 = 61%

8. 0.25 = 25%

9. 0.08 = 8%

10. 0.055 = 5.5%

Write as a Percent

11. $\frac{1}{2}$ =

12. $\frac{3}{4}$ =

13. $\frac{2}{3}$ =

Memory Aid

To write a percent as a decimal, let the two 0s in % remind you of two decimal places.

To write percent as a fraction, let the two 0s in % remind you of two 0s in the denominator.

Special Fractions

The fractions $\frac{1}{3}$ and $\frac{2}{3}$ are special fractions because their decimal and percent forms include a fraction.

$\frac{1}{3} = 0.33\frac{1}{3} = 33\frac{1}{3}\%$ and $\frac{2}{3} = 0.66\frac{2}{3} = 0.66\frac{2}{3}\%$

Adding Decimals

To add decimals:

- Write the numbers in a column and line up the decimal points.
- Use placeholding 0s as needed to give all numbers the same number of decimal places.
- Add the columns.
- Place a decimal point in the answer directly below the decimal points of the numbers being added.

Try These

No Regrouping

1. 3.4
    + 1.5

2. 23.5
    + 12.1

3. 3.7
    − 2.1

4. $4.75
    − 1.25

Example 1

Add: 12.4 + 4.68 + 0.375

$$\underset{\text{Line up the decimal points.}}{}$$

12.400 ← Write two placeholding 0s.
4.680 ← Write one placeholding 0.
+ 0.375
17.455 ← Add the columns.

Place a decimal point in the answer.

Answer: 17.455

Example 2

Add: 6 + 2.45

6.00 Place a decimal point to the
+ 2.45 right of 6.
8.45 Add two placeholding 0s.

Answer: 8.45

Subtracting Decimals

To subtract decimals:

- Write the numbers in a column and line up the decimal points.
- Use placeholding 0s as needed to give all numbers the same number of decimal places.
- Subtract the columns just as you would whole numbers.
- Place a decimal point in the answer directly below the decimal points of the numbers being subtracted.

Regrouping

5. 4.5
    + 1.9

6. 19.375
    + 8.240

7. 15.60
    − 8.75

8. $5.00
    − 2.89

Example

Subtract: 7 − 2.483

Place a decimal point to the right of 7. Line up the decimal points.

7.000 ← Write three placeholding 0s.
− 2.483
4.517 ← Subtract the columns.

Place a decimal point in the answer.

Answer: 4.517

Multiplying Decimals

To multiply decimals:

- Multiply the numbers as you would whole numbers.

- Count the number of decimal places in both of the numbers you are multiplying. This total tells you the number of decimal places in the product (answer).

- Place a decimal point in the product.

Example 1

Multiply: 3.24×4

$$
\begin{array}{r}
3.24 \leftarrow \text{ 2 decimal places} \\
\times \quad 4 \leftarrow + \text{ 0 decimal places} \\
\hline
12\,96 \quad \text{ 2 decimal places}
\end{array}
$$

Place the decimal point so that the answer has 2 decimal places.

Answer: 12.96

Example 2

Multiply: 1.37×2.6

$$
\begin{array}{r}
1.37 \leftarrow \text{ 2 decimal places} \\
\times \quad 2.6 \leftarrow + \text{ 1 decimal place} \\
\hline
8\,2\,2 \quad \text{ 3 decimal places} \\
2\,7\,4 \\
\hline
3\,5\,6\,2
\end{array}
$$

Place the decimal point so that the answer has 3 decimal places.

Answer: 3.562

Try These

No Regrouping

1. $\begin{array}{r} 3.1 \\ \times\ 1.2 \\ \hline \end{array}$

2. $\begin{array}{r} \$4.23 \\ \times\quad 2 \\ \hline \end{array}$

3. $2\overline{)6.4}$

4. $3\overline{)9.66}$

Regrouping

5. $\begin{array}{r} 16.25 \\ \times\quad 7 \\ \hline \end{array}$

6. $\begin{array}{r} 4.75 \\ \times\ 1.3 \\ \hline \end{array}$

7. $\begin{array}{r} \$8.50 \\ \times\quad 3.5 \\ \hline \end{array}$

8. $2.5\overline{)9}$

9. $1.6\overline{)5.2}$

Dividing Decimals

To divide decimals:

- Move the decimal point in the divisor all the way to the right.

- Move the decimal point in the dividend an equal number of places to the right. Add placeholding 0s if needed.

- Divide the numbers.

- Place a decimal point in the quotient directly above the point in the dividend.

Example

Divide: $1.4\overline{)4.48}$

Step 1 Change the divisor (1.4) to a whole number. Do this by moving the decimal point one place to the right. Then move the decimal point in the dividend (4.48) one place to the right.

$1.4\overline{)4.48}$

Step 2 Divide 14 into 44.8.

$$
\begin{array}{r}
3.2 \\
14.\overline{)44.8} \\
-42 \\
\hline
2\,8 \\
-2\,8 \\
\hline
\end{array}
$$

Answer: 3.2

Working with Percents

A **percent statement** contains three important numbers: the **percent**, the **whole**, and the **part**.

Example 1

25% of 200 is 50.

percent   whole   part

Example 2

75% of $24 is $18.

percent   whole   part

A percent question asks you to find one of these three numbers when you know the other two.

- Find the **part** when you know the percent and the whole.
  Example: What is 30% of $40?
  percent = 30%, whole = $40, part = ?

- Find the **percent** when you know the whole and the part.
  Example: What percent of 60 is 12?
  whole = 60, part = 12, percent = ?

- Find the **whole** when you know the percent and the part.
  Example: If 50% of a number is 80, what is the number?
  percent = 50%, part = 80, whole = ?

Try These

$P = \% \times W$
Find the Part

1. 30% of $40: _____

2. 25% of 16: _____

3. 10% of 125: _____

4. 2% of $14: _____

5. 4.5% of $20: _____

Finding the part:

To find the part, multiply the percent times the whole.

How to do it: Change the percent to a decimal or a fraction; then multiply.

Example A $65 jacket is on sale for 30% off. How much can you save by buying this jacket on sale?

Think: You save 30% of $65.

Method 1

Step 1 Change 30% to a decimal.

$$30\% = 0.30 = 0.3$$

Step 2 Multiply $65 by 0.3.

$$\begin{array}{r} \$65 \\ \times\ 0.3 \\ \hline 19.5 = \$19.50 \end{array}$$

Answer: $19.50

Method 2

Step 1 Change 30% to a fraction.

$$30\% = \frac{30}{100} = \frac{3}{10}$$

Step 2 Multiply $65 by $\frac{3}{10}$.

$$\frac{65}{1} \times \frac{3}{10} = \frac{195}{10}$$

$$\frac{195}{10} = 19.5$$

Answer: $19.50

143

Finding the percent:

To find the percent, divide the part by the whole.

How to do it: Write the fraction $\frac{\text{part}}{\text{whole}}$. Reduce this fraction if possible.

Then change the fraction to a %. One way to change a fraction to a percent is to multiply the fraction by 100%.

Example Out of his salary of $2,000 per month, Miguel has $400 withheld for taxes and health insurance. What percent of Miguel's income is withheld?

Step 1 Write the fraction: $\frac{\text{part}}{\text{whole}} = \frac{400}{2,000}$

Step 2 Reduce the fraction: $\frac{400}{2,000} = \frac{4}{20} = \frac{1}{5}$

Step 3 Change the fraction to a percent.

Multiply the fraction by 100%:

$\frac{1}{5} \times 100\% = \frac{100\%}{5} = \mathbf{20\%}$

Answer: 20%

Finding the whole:

To find the whole, divide the part by the percent.

How to do it: Change the percent to a decimal or a fraction; then divide.

Example 40% of the students in Gail's writing group are men. If 12 men are in the group, how many people (men and women) are in the group?

In other words, 12 is 40% of what number?

Method 1

Step 1 Change 40% to a decimal.

$40\% = 0.40 = 0.4$

Step 2 Divide 12 by 0.4.

$$0.4\overline{)12.0}\quad\substack{3\,0}$$

Answer: 30

Method 2

Step 1 Change 40% to a fraction.

$40\% = \frac{40}{100} = \frac{4}{10} = \frac{2}{5}$

Step 2 Divide 12 by $\frac{2}{5}$.

$12 \div \frac{2}{5} = \frac{12}{1} \times \frac{5}{2}$

$= \frac{60}{2} = 30$

Answer: 30

Try These

Find the Percent

$\% = \dfrac{P}{W}$

1. What percent of 30 is 6?

_____

2. What percent of $150 is $50?

_____

Find the Whole

$W = \dfrac{P}{\%}$

3. 25 is 50% of what number?

_____

4. 48 is 75% of what number?

_____

5. $24 is $33\frac{1}{3}$% of what amount?

_____

Try These

Write as a Power

1. $5 \times 5 \times 5 =$ 5^3

2. $2 \times 2 \times 2 \times 2 =$

3. $10 \times 10 \times 10 =$

4. $6.5 \times 6.5 =$ $\lfloor 5.5^2$

5. $\frac{1}{4} \times \frac{1}{4} =$

6. $\frac{2}{3} \times \frac{2}{3} \times \frac{2}{3} =$ $\left(\frac{2}{3}\right)^3$

Write as a Product

7. $3^4 =$

8. $7^3 =$

9. $2.5^2 =$

10. $10^5 =$

Find Each Square Root

11. $\sqrt{25} =$

12. $\sqrt{49} =$

13. $\sqrt{121} =$

14. $\sqrt{196} =$

Powers

A **power** is the product of a number multiplied by itself one or more times. For example, "5 to the third power" means "$5 \times 5 \times 5$." A power usually is written as a base and an exponent.

$5 \times 5 \times 5$ is written 5^3 ← exponent
↑ base

The exponent (3) tells how many times to write the base (5) in the product. To find the value of a power, multiply and find the total. The value of 5^3 is $5 \times 5 \times 5 = 125$.

Product	As a Base and Exponent	Word Expression	Value
4 x 4	4^2	4 squared	16
3 x 3 x 3	3^3	3 cubed	27
10 x 10 x 10 x 10	10^4	10 to the fourth power	10,000
$\frac{1}{4} \times \frac{1}{4} \times \frac{1}{4}$	$\left(\frac{1}{4}\right)^3$	$\frac{1}{4}$ cubed	$\frac{1}{64}$

Note: A number to the second power is *squared*. A number to the third power is *cubed*. These are the only two powers that have special names.

Square Roots

The opposite of squaring a number is finding a square root. To find the square root of 36 you ask, "What number times itself equals 36?" The answer is 6 because $6 \times 6 = 36$.

The symbol for square root is $\sqrt{\ }$. Using symbols, $\sqrt{36} = 6$.

Perfect Squares

Below is a table of squares of numbers from 1 to 15. The numbers 1, 4, 9, and so on are called perfect squares because their *square roots are whole numbers*.

Table of Perfect Squares				
$1^2 = 1$	$4^2 = 16$	$7^2 = 49$	$10^2 = 100$	$13^2 = 169$
$2^2 = 4$	$5^2 = 25$	$8^2 = 64$	$11^2 = 121$	$14^2 = 196$
$3^2 = 9$	$6^2 = 36$	$9^2 = 81$	$12^2 = 144$	$15^2 = 225$

You can also use the table to find the square roots of the first 15 perfect squares.

For example, the square root of 81 is 9 because $9^2 = 81$. Thus, $\sqrt{81} = 9$.

Adding Signed Numbers

Try These

Add

1. $9 + 3 =$

2. $8 + (^-3) =$

3. $(^-4) + 9 =$

4. $7 + 12 =$

5. $(^-12) + (^-3) =$

6. $(^-34) + (^-7) =$

Subtract

7. $15 - (^-6) =$

8. $^-8 - (^-4) =$

9. $15 - (^-5) =$

10. $20 - (^-10) =$

11. $^-16 - (^-12) =$

12. $25 - (^-8) =$

> **Rule for adding numbers that have the same sign:**
>
> Add the absolute values of the numbers and give the sum the same sign.

Examples $7 + 6 = 13$

$(^-6) + (^-5) = ^-11$

> **Rule for adding numbers that have opposite signs:**
>
> First, find the difference between the absolute values of the numbers. Then give that difference the sign of the number that had the greatest absolute value.

Examples $9 + (^-5) = |9| - |5| = 4$ Now give 4 a positive sign: $^+\mathbf{4}$ or **4**

$3 + (^-9) = |9| - |3| = 6$ Now give 6 a negative sign: $^-\mathbf{6}$

$^-11 + (4) = |11| - |4| = 7$ Now give 7 a negative sign: $^-\mathbf{7}$

Subtracting Signed Numbers

> **Rule for subtracting signed numbers:**
>
> Change the sign of the number being subtracted, and then add the numbers. When adding, follow the rules for adding signed numbers.

Examples $12 - (^-5) = 12 + (^+5) = \mathbf{17}$

$^-7 - (^-12) = ^-7 + (^+12) = |12| - |7| = \mathbf{5}$

$11 - (^-8) = 11 + (^+8) = \mathbf{19}$

Multiplying Signed Numbers

Try These
Multiply

1. $6 \times 5 =$

2. $9 \times (^-3) =$

3. $(^-2) \times 2 =$

4. $(^-8) \times 3 =$

5. $(^-10) \times (^-5) =$

6. $34 \times (^-2) =$

Rules for multiplying signed numbers:

- If the signs of the numbers are alike, multiply the numbers and give the product a positive sign:

  positive $\times$ positive = positive   negative $\times$ negative = positive

- If the signs of the numbers are different, multiply the numbers and give the product a negative sign.

  positive $\times$ negative = negative   negative $\times$ positive = negative

Examples $6 \times 5 = \mathbf{30}$

$(^-6) \times (^-5) = \mathbf{30}$

$6 \times (^-5) = ^-\mathbf{30}$

$(^-6) \times 5 = ^-\mathbf{30}$

$(^-3)^4 = (^-3) \times (^-3) \times (^-3) \times (^-3) = 9 \times (^-3) \times (^-3) = ^-27 \times (^-3) = \mathbf{81}$

$(^-5)^3 = (^-5) \times (^-5) \times (^-5) = 25 \times (^-5) = ^-\mathbf{125}$

Divide

7. $25 \div (^-5) =$

8. $(^-16) \div (^-4) =$

9. $(^-35) \div 5 =$

10. $20 \div (^-10) =$

11. $(^-36) \div (^-12) =$

12. $45 \div 5 =$

Dividing Signed Numbers

Rules for dividing signed numbers:

- If the signs of the numbers are alike, divide the numbers and give the quotient a positive sign:

  positive $\div$ positive = positive   negative $\div$ negative = positive

- If the signs of the numbers are different, divide the numbers and give the quotient a negative sign.

  positive $\div$ negative = negative   negative $\div$ positive = negative

Examples $28 \div 7 = 4$

$(^-28) \div (^-7) = 4$

$28 \div (^-7) = ^-4$

$(^-28) \div 7 = ^-4$

Try These

Write in Scientific Notation

1. 50 =

2. 125 =

3. 2,450 =

4. 35,875 =

5. 164,000 =

6. 2,750,000 = 2.750×10^6

7. 0.5 =

8. 0.025 =

9. 0.00075 =

Write in Standard Form

10. 4×10^2 =

11. 3.5×10^3 =

12. 5.75×10^3 =

13. 1.25×10^4 =

14. 8×10^5 =

15. 7.5×10^{-1} =

16. 9×10^{-2} =

17. 7×10^{-5} =

Scientific Notation

Scientific notation is a shorthand way to write very large numbers or very small numbers. Written in scientific notation, many numbers are easier to read, to write, and to compare than when written in standard form.

In scientific notation, a number is written as the product of two factors:

• a number between 1 and 10

• a power of 10 [10^1, 10^2, 10^3, 10^4, and so on]

The power of 10 tells how many places to move the decimal point when changing from scientific notation to standard form. Each factor of 10 moves the decimal point one place.

The sign of the exponent tells the direction to move the decimal point.

• A positive exponent means *move the decimal point to the right*.

• A negative exponent means *move the decimal point to the left*. A negative exponent does **not** represent a negative number.

Positive Exponents

Standard Form	Scientific Notation
63	6.3×10^1
845	8.45×10^2
12,670	1.267×10^4
294,300,000	2.943×10^8

Negative Exponents

Standard Form	Scientific Notation	
0.6	6×10^{-1}	A positive number
0.078	7.8×10^{-2}	A negative number
0.004	4×10^{-3}	

Example During a typical lifetime, a human heart beats about 2,800,000,000 times. To write this number in scientific notation:

• Write the first factor as a number between 1 and 10: 2.8.

• Count the number of places the decimal point must move:

2,800,000,000   The exponent is 9.

9 places

Answer: 2,800,000,000 = **2.8×10^9**

Table of Measurements

U.S. Customary Units	Metric Units

Length

1 foot (ft) = 12 inches (in.)	1 centimeter (cm) = 10 millimeters (mm)
1 yard (yd) = 3 feet = 36 inches	1 meter (m) = 100 centimeters
1 mile (mi) = 1,760 yards = 5,280 feet	1 kilometer (km) = 1,000 meters

Capacity (Liquid Measurement)

1 cup (c) = 8 fluid ounces (fl oz)	1 liter (L) = 1,000 milliliters (mL)
1 pint (pt) = 2 cups	1 kiloliter (kL) = 1,000 liters
1 quart (qt) = 2 pints	
1 gallon (gal) = 4 quarts	

Weight

1 pound (lb) = 16 ounces (oz)	1 gram (g) = 1,000 milligrams (mg)
1 ton (T) = 2,000 pounds	1 kilogram (kg) = 1,000 grams
	1 metric ton (t) = 1,000 kilograms

Time
Both Systems

1 minute (min) = 60 seconds (sec)

1 hour (hr) = 60 minutes

1 day = 24 hours

1 week (wk) = 7 days

1 year (yr) = 365 days

Converting Between the U.S. Customary and the Metric Systems

Length	Capacity	Weight
1 mile ≈ 1.6 kilometers	1 gallon ≈ 3.8 liters	1 pound ≈ 0.45 kilogram
1 yard ≈ 0.9 meter	1 fluid ounce ≈ 30 milliliters	1 ounce ≈ 28 grams
1 foot ≈ 30 centimeters		
1 inch ≈ 2.5 centimeters		

Annotated Answer Key

Pretest

Annotated answers are on each skill page.

Skill 1 Page 15

1. ❸ 4,300

2. ❷ $320
   $324.99 is greater than $320 but less than $325
   (halfway between $320 and $330).

3. ❺ $4,000
   $200 × 20 = $4,000

4. ❷ $50
   $2,500 ÷ 50 = $50

5. ❹ 600
   (600 + 500 + 600 + 500 + 700 + 700) ÷ 6 = 600

6. ❶ very close to the actual amount
   ($20 × 24) + $50 = $530

7. ❸ between 750 and 850 miles
   40 × 20 = 800

Skill 2 Page 17

1. ❸ $2.30

2. ❶ 123C
   the part number opposite 6.09

3. ❷ 6
   From top of table: 6.78, 7.09, 6.7, 7.3, 7.28, 7.076

4. ❷ 1
   6.09

5. ❹ 0.07, 0.6, 0.76. 0.8

6. ❺ 11.79 sec
   The fastest time is the least number of seconds.

7. ❸ 7.26 m
   the shortest rope longer than 6.4 m

Skill 3 Page 19

1. ❹ $0.10

2. ❹ $10.00 − ($2.25 + $0.75)
   75¢ = $0.75; $10 minus the cost of what Alice
   buys

3. ❶ 70 − (13.9 + 20.65 +0.3)
   the total weight minus the weight taken so far

4. 1.844 sec
   (25.000 sec − 23.156 sec)

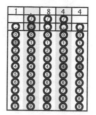

5. ❶ $0.0215
   $0.1165 − $0.095

6. ❷ $561.42
   $589.86 − $18.12 − $50.43 + $40.11

Skill 4 Page 21

1. ❸ $5(153 + 207)
   Add to find the number of tickets sold. Then
   multiply the sum by $5 to find the value of the
   tickets sold.

2. ❺ (15 × $12) + (20 × $10)
   Find the amounts Cole earns at each job. Then add
   them to find the total Cole earns.

3. ❹ (3 × $16) + (2 × $22) + $11
   Add the cost for the shirts, the cost for the
   sweatshirts, and the shipping cost.

4. ❹ exactly 5 cm
   $\sqrt{3^2 + 4^2} = \sqrt{9 + 16} = \sqrt{25} = 5$
   Remember to square the numbers within the square
   root sign before adding and taking the square root.

5. ❸ $8 - (7.3 - 2.3)^2 \div \sqrt{25} = 8 - (5)^2 \div \sqrt{25}$
   $= 8 - 25 \div 5 = 8 - 5 = 3$

6. ❶ 6 km
   $5 + \frac{\sqrt{5^2 - 4 \times 2 \times 2}}{3} = 5 + \frac{\sqrt{25 - 16}}{3} = 5 + \frac{\sqrt{9}}{3} =$
   $5 + \frac{3}{3} = 6$
   When using a calculator, the easiest approach
   would be to solve for the value inside the square
   root sign and then take the square root.

Skill 5 Page 23

1. ❸ $2.50
   10 × $0.25 = $2.50

2. ❺ (11.3 − 0.5) ÷ (2 × 12)
   Subtract to find the weight of the cans and then
   divide by 2 dozen to find the weight of one can.

3. ② $5.50

$22 ÷ 4 = $5.50 The bill is divided among 4 people.

4. ④ 71.6

The total miles for Mon., Wed., Fri.: 4.3 × 3 = 12.9
The total miles for Tues., Thurs.: 2.5 × 2 = 5
Add to find the total for each week: 12.9 + 5 = 17.9
Multiply to find the miles for 4 weeks: 17.9 × 4 = 71.6

5. ④ $45.82

Cost of towels & pillow: ($15.97 × 2) + 5.97 = $37.87
Cost for standard shipping on a $37.91 order: $7.95
Add to find total costs: $37.91 + $7.95 = $45.82

6. ① $19.00

Cost for 3 pairs of shorts: $43.50
1-day shipping cost: $26.95
Standard shipping costs: $7.95
Difference: $26.95 − $7.95 = $19.00

Skill 6 Page 25

1. ④ $\frac{1}{6}$

$\frac{47}{307} \approx \frac{50}{300} = \frac{1}{6}$

2. ① a little less than $\frac{1}{4}$ cup

$\frac{4}{16} = \frac{1}{4}$ so $\frac{3}{16}$ is a little less than $\frac{1}{4}$.

3. ④ $\frac{1}{2}$ lb, $\frac{2}{3}$ lb

For a fraction to be $\frac{1}{2}$ or greater, the numerator must be at least half the denominator.
1 is half of 2, so $\frac{1}{2} = \frac{1}{2}$.
2 is more than half of 3, so $\frac{2}{3}$ is more than $\frac{1}{2}$.

4. ⑤ $\frac{2}{9}$

A yard is 36 inches. So 8 inches is $\frac{8}{36}$ yd.
$\frac{8}{36} = \frac{8 ÷ 4}{36 ÷ 4} = \frac{2}{9}$

5. ② $1\frac{3}{8}$ inches

$1\frac{6}{16} = 1\frac{3}{8}$

6. ④ Nicole

The fastest runner ran the greatest distance.
Rewrite the fractional distances greater than 1 mile using the greatest common denominator: 8.
$1\frac{1}{2} = 1\frac{4}{8}; 1\frac{1}{4} = 1\frac{2}{8}; 1\frac{5}{8} = 1\frac{5}{8}; 1\frac{3}{4} = 1\frac{6}{8}$
Compare numerators. The greatest numerator is 6.
So $1\frac{3}{4}$ is the greatest distance.

Skill 7 Page 27

1. ④ 5

Round each distance to the nearest whole number:

$\frac{1}{8}$ rounds to 0

$2\frac{3}{4}$ rounds to 3

$2\frac{1}{3}$ rounds to 2

Then add the numbers: 0 + 2 + 3 = 5

2. $\frac{3}{4}$

$147\frac{1}{2} − 146\frac{3}{4} = \frac{3}{4}$ pound

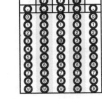

3. ② $3\frac{3}{8}$ in.

$68\frac{3}{8} − 65 = 3\frac{3}{8}$ inches

4. ⑤ $1\frac{1}{8}$ yards

Add: $\frac{5}{8} + \frac{1}{2} + \frac{3}{4} = 1\frac{7}{8}$
Then subtract what Janice has from the 3 yards she needs: $3 − 1\frac{7}{8} = 1\frac{1}{8}$ yards

5. ④ Only B and C are true.

A. Not true—Jake was the slowest.
B. True—Calvin improved $\frac{3}{8}$ mi and so did Luis.
C. True—The difference between Calvin and Jake in June was 1 mi and in December $\frac{1}{8}$ mi.

Skill 8 Page 29

1. ③ 13 + 20 × 2

The approximate weight of the railroad car (13 tons) plus 20 pickup trucks at about 2 tons each

2. 12

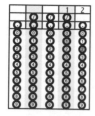

Three pounds divided into $\frac{1}{4}$-pound patties:
$3 \div \frac{1}{4} = 3 \times 4 = 12$
Note: Here is another way to think about this problem. Lucy can get 4 quarter-pound patties from 1 lb of hamburger. With 3 lb she can get three times as much. $4 \times 3 = 12$

3. ② 15 hr
$\frac{3}{4} \times 20 = \frac{3}{4} \times \frac{20}{1} = \frac{60}{4} = 15$

4. ① $\frac{1}{20}$
$\frac{1}{2}$ of $\frac{1}{10}$ is $\frac{1}{10} \times \frac{1}{2} = \frac{1}{20}$

5. ④ $32.94
Keith can cut only one $3\frac{1}{4}$-ft length from a 6-foot board. If he needs six $3\frac{1}{4}$-ft boards, Keith will have to purchase six 6-ft boards. $5.49 \times 6 = $32.94

6. ③ $18.50
First eliminate using the 6-foot boards because they are too expensive. Keith can cut 2 shelves from the 8-foot boards, so he will need 3 to make the 6 shelves. Keith can cut 3 shelves from the 10-foot boards so he will need 2 to make the 6 shelves.
$6.93 \times 3 = $20.79; $9.25 \times 2 = $18.50

Skill 9 Page 31

1. ④ $\frac{2}{3}$
Estimate: $\frac{2}{3}$ is the only fraction listed that is greater than $\frac{1}{2}$ (50%). So it must be the correct choice.
Or, $\frac{2}{3} \times 100\% \approx 67\%$.

2. ③ 25%
$\frac{1}{4} \times 100\% = 25\%$

3. ⑤ 75%
$\frac{15}{20} \times 100\% = 75\%$

4. ④ $\frac{4}{5}$
$0.8 = \frac{8}{10} = \frac{4}{5}$

5. ① 5.07%
$\frac{3}{4}\% = 0.75\%$; $4.32\% + 0.75\% = 5.07\%$

6. 42.5%
$\frac{3}{8} = 37.5\%$ $\left[\frac{3}{8} \times 100\% = 37.5\%\right]$
$80\% - 37.5\% = 42.5\%$

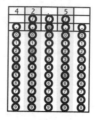

Skill 10 Page 33

1. ⑤ $39.99 × 1.085
Total cost = the price of the dishes + the sales tax.
= $39.99 + $39.99 × 0.085
= $39.99(1 + 0.085)
= $39.99 × 1.085

2. ④ $360
$400 − $40   [$40 = 10% of $400]
or, $400 × 0.90 [sales price is 90% of regular price]

3. ④ B and D
B: 25% discounted price = 75% of
    original price = 0.75 × $250
D: 25% discounted price =
    100% − 25% × original price
= (100% − 25%) × $250 = (1 − 0.25) × $250

4. ① $15.23
$14.50 + $14.50 × 0.05 = $15.225
or, $14.50 × 1.05 = $15.225

5. $13.23
Sale price: $18 − $18 × 0.30 = $12.60
Total cost = $12.60 + $12.60 × 0.05
= $13.23

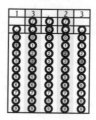

6. ⑤ $732.72
Sale price = $860 − $860 × 0.20 = $688
Total cost = $688 + $688 × 0.065 = $732.72

Skill 11 Page 35

1. $\frac{4}{11}$

   Number of women = 15 − 11 = 4
   Number of men = 11

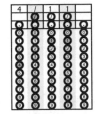

2. ❶ $\frac{1}{3}$

   January clothing = $60; February clothing = $180

   $\frac{60}{180} = \frac{60 \div 60}{180 \div 60} = \frac{1}{3}$

3. ❷ $\frac{7}{6}$

   January utilities: $210; January childcare: $180

   $\frac{210}{180} = \frac{210 \div 30}{180 \div 30} = \frac{7}{6}$

4. ❷ 26%

   Amount going to taxes = $300 + $100 +
   $124 = $524

   Gross earnings = $2,000

   Percent going to taxes = $\frac{524}{2,000} \times 100\% = 26.2\%$

5. ❶ $\frac{1}{3}$

   $\frac{\text{Materials}}{\text{Labor}} = \frac{25}{75} = \frac{25 \div 25}{75 \div 25} = \frac{1}{3}$

Skill 12 Page 37

1. ❷ $\frac{c}{45} = \frac{150}{30}$

   The ratio of calories used in 45 minutes $\left(\frac{c}{45}\right)$ equals

   the ratio of calories used in 30 minutes $\left(\frac{150}{30}\right)$.

2. ❹ $\frac{4}{5} \times 240$

   $\frac{4}{5} = \frac{n}{240}$ so, $\frac{4}{5} \times 240 = n$

   Or think: The number of people who preferred

   Amy's Catering is $\frac{4}{5}$ of all employees: $\frac{4}{5} \times 240$.

3. ❹ 80,000

   $\frac{n}{200,000} = \frac{2}{5}$

   or $n = \frac{2}{5} \times 200,000$

   $\frac{2}{5}$ of the 200,000 people walk to work.

   $\frac{2}{5} \times 200,000 = 80,000$

4. ❶ 1,228

   The total number of manufacturing jobs, 1,395, is
   found in the graph's title.

   $\frac{n}{1,395} = \frac{88}{100}$

   or $n = \frac{88}{100} \times 1,395 \approx 1,228$

   or $n = 88\%$ of $1,395 \approx 1,228$

   $1,395 \times 88\% = 1,395 \times 0.88 = 1,227.6 \approx 1,228$

Skill 13 Page 39

1. ❺ $\frac{\$20 - \$15}{20} \times 100\%$

   The percent discount = $\frac{\text{difference in price}}{\text{original price}} \times 100\%$

2. ❹ 12.5%

   % discount = $\frac{\$36.00 - \$31.50}{\$36} = \frac{\$4.50}{\$36} = 0.125 =$ 12.5%

3. ❺ gloves

   Estimation is very useful here. Gloves is the only
   item for which the sale price is half the original
   price. The sale price for all the other items is more
   than half price. So gloves have the greatest percent
   discount.

   Shirt: 25% discount [(20 − 15) ÷ 20]
   Sweater: 12.5% discount [(36 − 31.5) ÷ 36]
   Jacket: about 18% discount [(60 − 49) ÷ 60]
   Shoes: 30% discount [(50 − 35) ÷ 50]
   Gloves 50% discount [(24 − 12) ÷ 24]

4. ❶ 11%

   (15.5 − 14) ÷ 14 = 0.107 = 10.7% ≈ 11%

5. ❶ Only A is true.

Store	$	% Discount	$ Discount	Sale Price
Great Photo	$599.99	15%	$90.00	$509.99
Photo Snap	$479.99	20%	$96.00	$383.99
Shutter Time	$419.00	25%	$104.75	$314.25
Dave's Camera	$347.00	10%	$34.70	$312.30

Skill 14 Page 41

1. ❺ ounce

   In the US, postage for a letter is given according to
   weight in ounces.

2. ❷ 2.1 meters

   1 meter is a little more than 3 feet. The basketball
   player's height would be between 6 and 7 feet tall.
   A millimeter is about the width of a tiny ant.
   A centimeter is about the length of a ladybug.
   A kilometer is a little more than half a mile.

3. ④ 677 kilometers
Only kilometers is a metric distance used to measure distances between cities. One kilometer is a distance of about 0.6 miles. A distance of 677 kilometers is equal to a distance of about 406 miles.

4. ④ 500 milliliters
500 milliliters is half a liter (1,000 milliliters) or about 2 cups.

5. ② 1 centimeter
A centimeter is about the length of a ladybug.
A millimeter is about the width of a tiny ant.
A meter is a little longer than a yard.
A liter is a measure of capacity, not length.

6. ① 1 gram
A gram is about the weight of a pin.
A pound is the weight of 4 sticks of butter.
A kilogram is about the weight of 8 sticks of butter.
An ounce is the weight of a letter to a friend.
A liter is a measure of capacity, not length.

7. ④ 0.75 cup
0.75 gram is a weight lighter than a pin.
0.75 gallon is $\frac{3}{4}$ gallon, or 12 cups. [1 gallon = 16 cups]
7.5 liters is about 2 gallons.
0.75 cup is $\frac{3}{4}$ cup.
7.5 pints is 15 cups. [1 pint = 2 cups]

8. ② 1.25 m
A meter is about 3 feet, so…
0.125 meter is about a tenth of a meter, about 4 inches.
1.25 meters is about 4 feet.
12.5 meters is about 40 feet.
125 meters is about 400 feet.
1,250 meters is about a half-mile.

Skill 15 page 43

1. ③ 5 fl oz
The liquid level in the measuring cup is halfway between the $\frac{1}{2}$ (4 fluid ounces) and $\frac{3}{4}$ (6 fluid ounces) marks.

2. ② 47°F below freezing
32°F − (⁻15°F) = 32 + 15 = 47°F

3. ④ 1 hr 45 min
In 45 minutes the time will be 11:30 A.M.
After 1 more hour the time will be 12:30 P.M.
Total time at rink = 45 min + 1 hour
= 1 hour 45 minutes

4. ① $260
9:30 A.M. to 4:30 P.M. is a 7-hour period. During this time, Luis could give 13 lessons, each lasting 30 minutes, and could take one 30-minute lunch.
$20 × $13 = $260

5. ② $3.50
Ask what would Marleena pay for 7 pounds of apples. At $0.50 per pound (2 pounds for $1), she would pay $3.50.

6. ⑤ $\frac{15}{16}$ in.
To find this distance, count the number of $\frac{1}{16}$-inch divisions along the width of the walnut strip, or, subtract $1\frac{1}{2} - \frac{9}{16}$, the measurements of the strip.

Skill 16 Page 45

1. ⑤ (100 × 2) ÷ (4 × 4)
number of gallons needed = number of cups divided by the number of cups in one gallon
number of cups needed = 100 × 2
number of cups in 1 gallon = 4 × 4

2. ② 0.3 m
1 cm = 0.01 m
So, 31.5 cm = 31.5 (0.01 m) = 0.315 m ≈ 0.3 m

3. ② 5 × 10³
5 kilometers = 5,000 meters
5,000 can be written 5 × 1,000 = 5 × 10³

4. ② $\frac{2}{3}$
2 feet = 24 inches = $\frac{24}{36}$ yd = $\frac{2}{3}$ yd
or, 3 feet = 1 yard so 2 feet = $\frac{2}{3}$ yard

5. ③ 0.06 mi
1 mile = 1,760 yards (5,280 ÷ 3)
100 yards = $\frac{100}{1,760}$ mile = 0.056818181 ≈ 0.06

6. ⑤ $228,228.00
total cost = cost per foot × number of feet
number of feet = 5,280 × 1.3 = 6,864
total cost = 6,864 × $33.25 = $228,228.00

Skill 17 Page 47

1. ③ $\frac{165}{3}$
rate = $\frac{distance}{time} = \frac{165\ hours}{3\ hours}$

2. ① $\frac{t}{3} = \frac{\$48}{5}$
Each ratio is: $\frac{amount\ earned}{number\ of\ hours\ worked}$

3. 22.5

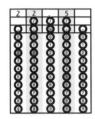

$d = r \times t$
$d = 4.5 \text{ mph} \times 5 \text{ hr}$
$\quad = 22.5 \text{ mi}$

4. ⑤ either B or C
The price per tablet for A is $5.40 ÷ 60 = $0.09.
The price per tablet for B is $7.80 ÷ 100 = $0.078.
The price per tablet for C is $11.70 ÷ 150 = $0.078.

5. ④ 770
Let n = number of calories in 4 ounces.
$\dfrac{\text{calories}}{\text{ounces}} : \dfrac{n}{4} = \dfrac{230}{1.2}$
$n = \dfrac{230 \times 4}{1.2} = \dfrac{920}{1.2} = 766.666\ldots \approx 770$

6. ④ 95
Write 2 hours 30 minutes as 2.5 hours
(or $2\frac{1}{2}$ hours).
Multiply 2.5 hours times Wendy's hourly reading rate:
$38 \times 2.5 = 95$ (or $38 \times 2\frac{1}{2} = 95$)

Skill 18 Page 49

1. ④ A and D
By definition, 6% means 6 parts out of 100 equal parts. 6 out of 100 can be written as the fraction $\frac{6}{100}$ or the decimal 0.06.

2. ② $400 \times \frac{1}{25} \times \frac{5}{2}$
$4\% = \frac{4}{100} = \frac{1}{25}$; 2 yr 6 mo = $2\frac{1}{2}$ yr = $\frac{5}{2}$ yr

3. ⑤ Not enough information is given.
To know the amount of interest earned, you must know the amount deposited—the principal.

4. ④ $360.00
In this problem, it may be easier to work the problems using decimals, rather than fractions:
interest = $2,000 × 0.12 × 1.5 = $240 × 1.5 = $360

5. ③ $3,618.13
In this problem, it may be easier to work the problems using decimals, rather than fractions:
total = $3,500 + ($3,500 × 0.045 × 0.75) = $3,618.13

6. ② $7,437.50
In this problem, it may be easier to work the problems using fractions, rather than decimals:
total owed = $7,000 + ($7,000 × $\frac{1}{20}$ × $\frac{5}{4}$) = $7,437.50

Skill 19 Page 51

1. ③ $\dfrac{d}{15} = \dfrac{34}{9}$
The two triangles are similar. The corresponding side to side d is the side that is 15 yards long. These two sides are the heights of the two triangles. The corresponding widths are labeled 34 yd and 9 yd.

2. ④ 3.2 inches
$\dfrac{\text{width of copy}}{\text{width of original}} = \dfrac{\text{height of copy}}{\text{height of original}}$;
$\dfrac{w}{8} = \dfrac{4}{10}$ width of copy = $\dfrac{4 \times 8}{10} =$
$\dfrac{32}{10} = 3.2$

3. ① 19 feet
$\dfrac{\text{height of large tree}}{\text{height of small tree}} = \dfrac{\text{length of large shadow}}{\text{length of small shadow}}$
$\dfrac{h}{8} = \dfrac{48}{20}$
$h = \dfrac{48 \times 8}{20} = \dfrac{384}{20} = 19.2$

Skill 20 Page 53

1. ① $\dfrac{0.5}{15} = \dfrac{5.25}{d}$
$\dfrac{\text{map distance in inches}}{\text{actual distance in miles}}$

2. ④ 3 feet 6 inches
actual length = 24 inches × $1\frac{3}{4} = 6 \times \frac{7}{1} = 42$
42 inches − 3 feet 6 inches

3. ③ between 36 and 40 miles
actual distance = 15 miles × $2\frac{1}{2} = 15 \times \frac{5}{2} -$
37.5 miles

4. ② 1 inch = 5 feet
$\dfrac{\text{drawing in inches}}{\text{actual in feet}} = \dfrac{8}{40} = \dfrac{1}{5}$
1 in. in drawing = 5 ft

5. ③ 18 feet
actual width = 2.25 × 8 feet = 18 feet

6. ④ about 37 feet
width of deck = 2.25 × 8 feet = 18 feet
length of deck = 4 × 8 feet = 32 feet
length of diagonal = $\sqrt{(18)^2 + (32)^2}$ =
$\sqrt{324 + 1,024}$ = $\sqrt{1,348}$ = 36.7151195 ≈ 37 feet

Skill 21 Page 55

1. ⑤ $n = 75 \div 2\frac{1}{3}$

20 seconds = $\frac{20}{60}$ minutes = $\frac{1}{3}$ minute

Divide the available minutes on the disk (75) by
the length of one song ($2\frac{1}{3}$).

2. ① 13
8 m = 800 cm; 800 cm ÷ 60 = $13\frac{1}{3}$

3. 40

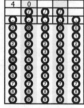

3,140 ÷ 80 = $39\frac{1}{4}$
To do the entire job, Aaron must buy 39 + 1
packages.

4. ② 4
7 feet = 84 inches; 84 ÷ 26 = 3 (3 gifts per roll)
For 10 gifts, 4 rolls are needed.

5. ② $10.80
$2\frac{1}{4}$ hr = 120 min + 15 min = 135 min
135 min × $0.08 = $10.80

6. ① $\frac{7}{100}$
8 fluid ounces of orange juice has 105 calories:
420 ÷ 4
$\frac{105}{1,500} = \frac{21}{300} = \frac{7}{100}$

Skill 22 Page 57

1. ④ 135°
The pictured angle is greater than a right angle
(90°) but less than a straight angle (180°).

2. ① supplementary
∠A and ∠C together form a straight angle.

3. ④ ∠D, ∠E, and ∠H
When two parallel lines (Oak Street and Pine
Street) are crossed by a transversal (1st Street),
each obtuse angle formed at an intersection
has equal measure with each other obtuse
angle formed.

4. 34.7

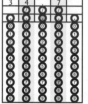

Any two angles whose measures add to 90° are
complementary angles.
90° − 55.3° = 34.7°

5. ③ $\frac{1}{4}$
The three oregano sections each have 90° angles
which, when added, total 270°. Subtract the total
of the oregano sections from the total degrees in a
circle: 360° − 270° = 90°. The rosemary sections
of the garden total 90° or, $\frac{90°}{360°} = \frac{1}{4}$ of the garden.

This problem can also be solved visually. Since the
oregano sections take up $\frac{1}{4}$ of the circle each for a
total of $\frac{3}{4}$, the rosemary section must fill the
remaining $\frac{1}{4}$ of the garden.

Skill 23 Page 59

1. ① 15°
∠A is a small angle, much less than 90°, and much
less than 45° (half of a right angle).

2. ⑤ 180° − (90° + 20°)
The sum of the measures of the three angles within
a triangle is 180°. This is true for any shape
triangle.
The measure of a missing angle is found by
subtracting the two known measures from 180°.

3. ③ $\frac{180}{3}$
Each of the 3 angles has equal measure because
each of the sides has equal measure. The sum of
the 3 measures is 180°.

4. ④ 40°
∠DBC = 180° − (90° + 50°) =
180° − (140°) = 40°

5. ⑤ Not enough information is given. Without knowing the measure of $\angle ABC$, there is no way to know the measure of $\angle BAC$. Using this drawing, there is no way to determine the measure of $\angle ABC$.

6. ③ 40°
Notice that the measure of $\angle ABC$ is 55°. And the measure of $\angle ACB$ is 85° (180° − 95°).
So the measure of $\angle BAC$ is found by subtracting the sum of the measures of $\angle ABC$ and $\angle ACB$ from 180°.
$\angle BAC = 180° - (55° + 85°) =$
$180° - (140°) = 40°$

Skill 24 Page 61

1. ③ between 3 and 6 meters
An estimate using the Pythagorean relationship gives a length of a little more than 5 meters.
$\sqrt{6^2 + 3^2} = \sqrt{36 - 9} = \sqrt{27} > \sqrt{25} = 5$

2. ③ $d = \sqrt{6^2 + 2^2}$
d is the length of the side of the hypotenuse of a right triangle whose sides are 6 mi and 2 mi.

3. ③ $35.00
The length of the picture's diagonal in inches can be found by using the Pythagorean relationship:
length of diagonal $= \sqrt{6^2 + 8^2} = \sqrt{36 + 64} =$
$\sqrt{100} = 10$
$3.50 × 10 = $35.00

4. ⑤ 12 feet
The distance along the bottom of the ramp in feet can be found by using the Pythagorean relationship:
distance $= \sqrt{13^2 - 5^2} = \sqrt{169 - 25} = \sqrt{144} = 12$

5. ① 7 feet
The first step is to notice that the unknown length is equal to an equal length of a right triangle whose hypotenuse is 25 feet and whose longest side is 24 feet.
Next, use the Pythagorean relationship to find the unknown length in feet:
length $= \sqrt{25^2 - 24^2} = \sqrt{625 - 576} = \sqrt{49} = 7$

Skill 25 Page 63

1. ⑤ $(6 × 4) \div \left(\frac{2}{3} × \frac{2}{3}\right)$
number of tiles = area of entryway (in square feet) divided by area of a single tile (in square feet)
area of entryway = 6 × 4 square feet
area of single tile $= \left(\frac{2}{3} × \frac{2}{3}\right)$ square foot

2. ④ $(20 × 10) − (5 × 4)$
The area of the deck can be thought of as the area of a rectangle 20 ft long by 10 ft wide minus the right hand corner part (area 5 ft by 4 ft) that is not part of the deck.

3. ① 120
area of triangle $= \frac{1}{2} ×$ base × height $=$
$\frac{1}{2} × 12 × 20 = 120$

4. ③ 192
number of tiles = area of floor (in square feet) divided by area of a single tile (in square feet)
area of floor = 12 × 9 = 108 square feet
area of single tile $= \frac{3}{4} × \frac{3}{4} = \frac{9}{16}$ square foot
number of tiles $= 108 \div \frac{9}{16} = 108 × \frac{16}{9} = 192$

5. ② $60.00
area of mirror $= \pi × r × r = 3.14 × 12 × 12 \approx$
450 sq in
cost of mirror $= 450 × $0.14 = $63.00 \approx $60.00

6. ④ 900 square feet
area of walkway − area of outer rectangle minus area of pool
Notice that the outer rectangle has a length of 60 ft (50 ft + 5 ft + 5 ft) and a width of 40 ft (30 ft + 5 ft + 5 ft).
area of walkway = (60 × 40) − (50 × 30) =
2,400 − 1,500 = 900 square feet
You can also find this area by adding the areas of the 4 rectangles that make up the walkway:
area of walkway = (60 × 5) + (60 × 5) +
(30 × 5) + (30 × 5) − 300 + 300 + 150 + 150 −
900 sq ft

Skill 26 Page 65

1. ④ $(\pi × r^2) × (6 × r)$
The volume of the cylinder is the area of the base $(\pi × r^2)$ times the height of the cylinder $(6 × r)$.
[The height of each ball is $2 × r$; the height of all three balls is $3 × 2 × r = 6 × r$.]

2. ① $25 × 16 × 0.5$
The volume of a rectangular solid is found by multiplying the length times the width times the height, where each dimension is in the same unit—in this case, feet. So, 6 inches is written as 0.5 feet.

3. ① 70 cubic feet
$V = \frac{1}{3} × \pi × r^2 × h$
$= \frac{1}{3} × 3.14 × 4^2 × 4 \approx 66.987 \approx 70$ cubic feet

4. ⑤ about 1,200 pounds
weight = volume in cubic feet × 62 pounds
$= 6 \times 5 \times \frac{2}{3} \times 62 = 20 \times 62 = 1{,}240$ pounds

5. ③ 24
Divide the volume of the box by the volume of a single block:
box volume = $8 \times 6 \times 4 = 192$ cubic inches
block volume = $2 \times 2 \times 2 = 8$ cubic inches
number of blocks = $192 \div 8 = 24$

6. ② about 90 gallons
capacity = volume in cubic feet × 7.5
$= \pi \times r^2 \times h \times 7.5$
$= 3.14 \times 1^2 \times 4 \times 7.5 = 94.2$ gallons

Skill 27 Page 67

1. ③ *x*-value negative; *y*-value negative

2. ⑤ (⁻3,4)
3 units left of the *y*-axis
4 units above the *x*-axis

3. ① (2,1)
Add +5 to the *x*-value of the filled-in point.
Subtract 3 from the *y*-value of the filled-in point.
$(^-3 + 5, 4 - 3) = (2,1)$

4. (2,⁻1)

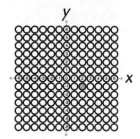

The move is made by adding +1 to the *x*-value of point *A* and adding +3 to the *y*-value of point *A*. Add these same numbers to point *C*: $(1,^-4) =$
$(1 + 1, ^-4 + 3) = (2,^-1)$

5. (1,⁻2)

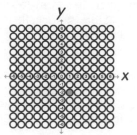

A parallelogram has two pairs of parallel sides. You can easily determine the 4th vertex by visually identifying where the lines must meet: Opposite sides are parallel and have equal length.

Skill 28 Page 69

1. ② negative
Moving from left to right, the line slopes downward.

2. ④ $\frac{1-0}{5-2}$
slope = $\frac{\text{change in } y\text{-value}}{\text{change in } x\text{-value}}$

3. ④ $\frac{2}{5}$
slope = $\frac{\text{change in } y\text{-value}}{\text{change in } x\text{-value}} = \frac{4-2}{6-1} = \frac{2}{5}$

4. ③ $15.00
$\frac{\$1{,}000 - \$400}{60 \text{ yr} - 20 \text{ yr}} = \frac{\$600}{40 \text{ yr}} = \$15$ per year

5. ② $7.50
$\frac{\$500 - \$200}{60 \text{ yr} - 20 \text{ yr}} = \frac{\$300}{40 \text{ yr}} = \$7.50$ per year

Skill 29 Page 71

1. ① None of the statements.
Check the truth of each statement:

A. The mean of any set of numbers is **not** always a whole number.
Example, the mean of the set
{1,2} is $(1 + 2) \div 2 = 1.5$
B. The mean of any set of numbers is **not** always a number in the set.
Example, the mean of {2,4} is $(2 + 4) \div 2 = 3$
C. The median of any set of numbers is **not** always a number in the set.
Example, the mean of {1,1,2,2} is the average of the 2 middle numbers: $(1 + 2) \div 2 = 1.5$

2. ⑤ None would change.
The mean of 80 and 100 is 90; the mean of 80, 90, and 100 is also 90.
The median of 80 and 100 is 90; the median of 80, 90, and 100 is 90.
The range of 80 and 100 is 20 (100 − 80); the range of 80, 90, and 100 is also 20.
Neither set has a mode.

3. ② $\frac{15 + 5 + 0 + 20}{4}$
The average is found by adding all 4 scores, even if one of the scores is 0. To find the average, the sum of all scores is divided by the number of scores.

4. ④ $102
The median is the middle value of the three values: $80, $102, and $145.

5. ③ $257
The mean is found by adding the three food amounts and then dividing the sum by 3.
average cost $= \frac{\$256 + \$214 + \$301}{3} = \frac{\$771}{3} = \$257$

6. ② 17.9 mph
average mileage $= \frac{\text{total miles driven}}{\text{total number of gallons used}}$
$= \frac{287 + 310 + 298}{17.5 + 16.8 + 15.7} = \frac{895}{50} = 17.9$

Skill 30 Page 73

1. ⑤ A, B, or C
Any of the three, A, B, or C, can be used to find the total sales for the first three quarters. Once you know this total sales number, you can find what the 4th quarter sales must be so that total sales for the year can be equal to $280,000 ($70,000 × 4).

2. ① $100,000
For the average quarterly sales to be $80,000, the total sales for the year must be $320,000 ($80,000 × 4).
So far, Chandra has sales of $220,000.
So $220,000 + n = $320,000; n = 4th quarter sales
n = $100,000

3. ⑤ $160,000
If the average of the 3rd and 4th quarters is $120,000, then the total of 3rd and 4th quarter sales must be $240,000.
So Chandra's 4th quarter sales are found by subtracting $80,000 from $240,000.
$240,000 − $80,000 = $160,000

4. ④ 85
average $= \frac{90 + 80 + 85}{3} = \frac{255}{3} = 85$

5. ⑤ 88.75
highest average $= \frac{90 + 80 + 85 + 100}{4} = \frac{355}{4} = 88.75$

6. ② 97
For the lowest score Josh needs to get an A, assume his final average is 88:
average $= \frac{90 + 80 + 85 + n}{4} = 88$
To find n, multiply 88 by 4, and then subtract Josh's first three scores:
Multiply: 88 × 4 = 352
Subtract: 352 − (90 + 80 + 85) = 352 − 255 = 97

Skill 31 Page 75

1. ⑤ about 650 servings
halfway between 750 (at 40°F) and 550 (at 50°F)

2. ④ 55°F
If you connect the dots, the two lines would cross (have equal value) at about 55°F. The number of sales of each drink at this point is about 375.

3. ② 63°F
The maximum value of lemonade sales shown is about 840. Half of this number is 420. The temperature at which 420 lemonades sell is a little greater than 60°F. Choice ② is the best answer.

4. ① 45°F
The maximum value of hot chocolate sales shown is about 990. Two-thirds of this number is 660. The temperature at which about 660 hot chocolates sell is about 45°F.

5. ④ 800 feet
halfway between 600 feet and 1,000 feet

6. ⑤ Not enough information is given.
There is no way to know from the graph what the trend in the altitude of Highway 20 is at the 100-mile point.

Skill 32 Page 77

1. ⑤ about 69 inches
Identify the point on the line of best fit that lies directly above 10.5 on the horizontal axis. This point is directly across from 69 on the vertical axis.

2. ① about 8 inches
Identify the point on the line of best fit that is directly across from 62 on the vertical axis. This point is directly above point 8 on the horizontal axis.

3. ③ 10 inches

Find the average of the two middle values of foot length. Both of these points correspond to a foot length of 10 inches. There are 7 points to the left of 10 inches and 7 points to the right of 10 inches. So the median is 10 inches.

4. ① about 1 inch

The average height of these two students is 69 inches ($\frac{67 + 71}{2}$). The line of best fit shows about 68 inches. The difference is about 1 inch.

5. ② 72

Identify the point on the line of best fit that lies directly above 5 on the horizontal axis. This point is directly across from about 72 on the vertical axis.

6. ③ 4

This rate is equal to the slope of the line of best fit. Finding this slope from the 1-hour and 10-hour points gives the following answer:

rate of learning = slope of line = $\frac{93 - 56}{10 - 1} = \frac{36}{9} = 4$

Skill 33 Page 79

1. ③ about 50 miles

Read this point on the graphed line above the 1-hour point on the horizontal axis.

2. ④ 7th hour

Jocelyn's speed is the greatest at points where the line is the steepest (has the greatest slope). Of the answer choices given, only the 7th hour corresponds to the steepest slope of the line.

3. ④ about 65 miles per hour

Jocelyn's average speed during the final 3 hours is the slope of the line during this time. Finding this slope from the 5-hour and 8-hour points gives the following answer:

speed = slope of line = $\frac{375 - 175}{3} = \frac{200}{3} \approx 65$ mph

4. ② 54 miles per hour

The average overall speed is the total distance Jocelyn traveled (375 miles) divided by the total driving time (7 hours).

Overall average speed = $\frac{375}{7} \approx 54$ miles per hour

5. ② 70 beats per minute

The resting heart rate is shown both before the exercise period begins and at the end of the recovery period.

6. ⑤ about 23 beats per minute

During the first 3 minutes of recovery, the patient's heart rate decreases from 140 beats per minute to 70 beats.

average rate of decrease = $\frac{70}{3} \approx 23$

Skill 34 Page 81

1. ④ $12.00

This is the point at which the 58WTR line intersects the horizontal axis: the point where months = 0.

2. ③ about $31

This point is on the 65WS line above the 12-month point on the horizontal axis.

3. ⑤ about 9 months

The purchase price of the 13WSR is about $7. With an operating cost of $14, the total cost is $21. The $21 point on the graphed line is directly above the 9-month point on the horizontal axis.

4. ① about $1.00

The monthly operating cost is the slope of the line. Choosing the 0-month and 12-month points, this slope is given as follows:

monthly operating cost = slope = $24 - \frac{12}{12} = \$1.00$

5. ④ 2000

This is the point where the Benton and Lynn lines cross.

6. ③ about $\frac{4}{3}$

ratio of rent in Lynn to Marion in 2000 = $\frac{600}{450} = \frac{4}{3}$

7. ⑤ about 80%

Between 1980 and 2000, rent in Marion increased from about $250 to about $450.

percent increase = $\frac{\$450 - \$250}{\$250} = \frac{\$200}{\$250} = \frac{4}{5} = 80\%$

Skill 35 Page 83

1. ④ about $190,000

The middle bar over the 30-year label represents a 9% mortgage. The top of this bar is directly across from the $190,000 reading on the vertical axis.

2. ⑤ 30-year at 12%

The 30-year at 12% loan has a total interest of about $270,000. This is greater than $200,000 more than the $53,000 (or so) interest on a 15-year loan at 6%.

3. $4,000

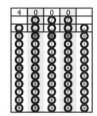

Total interest paid on a 30-year loan at 6% is about $118,000.

$$\text{average} = \frac{\$118,000}{30}$$
$$= \$3,933$$
$$\approx \$4,000$$

4. ④ about 1,000
votes cast in 2000 by female voters:
= 70% of 36,200 = 0.7 × 36,200 = 25,340
votes cast in 2000 by male voters:
= 60% of 40,400 = 0.6 × 40,400 = 24,240
female voters − male voters
= 25,340 − 24,240 = 1,100 ≈ 1,000

5. ⑤ Not enough information is given. To compute the number of votes cast in the 1992 election, you must first know the number of voters.

Skill 36 Page 85

1. ② Pullam
Pullam received 19% of the votes, about $\frac{1}{5}$ or 20% of the votes cast.

2. ⑤ Not enough information is given.
Although the number of votes cast is given, the number of registered voters is not. So there is no way to know what percent of registered voters actually voted.

3. ④ about 4 times as many
The sum of percents represented by the entire circle must be 100%. This means that the percent for Gregg is 6%. 25% is about 4 times 6%.

4. ③ 2 to 1
$$\frac{\text{percent of votes for Wright}}{\text{percent of votes for Lee}} = \frac{50\%}{25\%} = \frac{2}{1} \ (2 \text{ to } 1)$$

5. ① car
The Weltys spend 11% for car expenses, half of the 22% they spend on food.

6. ① food and housing
Food (22%) and housing (28%) together make up half (50%) of the Weltys' budget.

7. ⑤ 12¢
The sum of the amounts represented by all segments is $1.00 = 100¢.
medical (¢) = 100¢ − (9¢ + 28¢ + 18¢ + 22¢ + 11¢) = 100¢ − 88¢ = 12¢

Skill 37 Page 87

1.   9,538

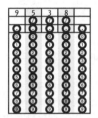

votes for Pullam = 19% of 50,200
= 0.19 × 50,200
= 9,538

2. ② 3,000
Lee received 6% more of the vote than Pullam: 25% − 19%.
6% of 50,200 = 0.06 × 50,200 ≈ 3,000
or, 12,550 − 9,538 = 3,012 ≈ 3,000

3. ③ 40%
Wright received 25,100 votes (50% of 50,200).
percent of registered voters voting for Wright =
$\frac{25,100}{65,000} = \frac{251}{650} = 0.386\ldots \approx 40\%$

4. ⑤ $\frac{3}{1}$
housing to clothes ratio = $\frac{28}{9} \approx \frac{3}{1}$

5. ⑤ about $850
22¢ is 22% (0.22) of each budgeted dollar:
food cost = $3,875 × 0.22 = $852.50 ≈ $850

6. ③ $2,800
Last year the Weltys spent 6¢ more per dollar on housing than on food: 28¢ − 22¢.
6¢ is 6% (0.06) of each budgeted dollar.
$46,500 × 0.06 = $2,790 ≈ $2,800

Skill 38 Page 89

1. ④ 0.167 × $18,000
16.7% is changed to a decimal by moving the decimal point two places to the left: 16.7% = 0.167.
3rd quarter profit = 16.7% of $18,000 = 0.167 × $18,000

2. ③ 3rd quarter

Of the 4 quarters, the profit in the 3rd quarter (22.2%) is most nearly equal to one quarter (25%) of the yearly profit.

3. ② 2 to 1

$$\text{ratio} = \frac{4^{\text{th}} \text{ quarter profits}}{2^{\text{nd}} \text{ quarter profits}} = \frac{41.7\%}{19.4\%} \approx \frac{2}{1}$$

4. ① $2,000

To raise the average profit per quarter to $5,000, Mike's Bicycle Store would need to earn a total yearly profit of $20,000. The total yearly profit shown above the circle graph is $18,000: $20,000 − $18,000 = $2,000.

5. ③ time and a half

For each employee, the overtime hourly pay rate is 1.5 times the regular hourly pay rate. Example: Brown's overtime rate of $18.00 is 1.5 × $12.00, his regular rate.

6. ⑤ $85

Brown earned: ($12.00 × 40) + ($18.00 × 8)
= $480.00 + $144.00 = $624.00
Middleton earned: ($11.00 × 40) + ($16.50 × 6)
= $440.00 + $99.00 = $539.00
difference = $624 − $539 = $85

Skill 39 Page 91

1. ③ $\frac{2}{3}$

There are 4 marbles in the bag that are not gray.

probability of not gray marble = $\frac{4}{6} = \frac{2}{3}$

2. ④ $\frac{1}{2}$

After 2 green marbles are taken out, the bag would then contain only 4 marbles: 2 gray, 1 white, and 1 green.
probability of gray marble now = $\frac{2}{4} = \frac{1}{2}$

3. ② Sal is more likely to have guessed too high than too low.

There are more numbers between 1 and 28 than there are between 28 and 50. So it is more likely that the correct number is less than 28 than greater than 28.

4. ④ $\frac{1}{130}$

Janine and her children together have 3 tickets.

probability = $\frac{3}{390} = \frac{1}{130}$

5. ⑤ Not enough information is given.

Unless you know the total number of tickets that were sold, you cannot determine this probability.

6. ③ 3

Picking a blue marble 6 times out of 10 times is a clue that $\frac{6}{10}$ or $\left(\frac{3}{5}\right)$ of the marbles are blue: $\frac{3}{5}$ of 5 is 3.

7. ① 1

Picking a green marble 2 times out of 10 times is a clue that $\frac{2}{10}$ or $\left(\frac{1}{5}\right)$ of the marbles are blue: $\frac{1}{5}$ of 5 is 1.

Skill 40 Page 93

1. $\frac{3}{25}$

3 out of 25 employees walk to work.

2. ④ $\frac{2}{5}$

probability of Tamara making her next free-throw shot: $\frac{20}{50}$ which reduces to $\frac{2}{5}$

3. ② 10

Tamara is likely to make $\frac{2}{5} \times 25 = 10$ of her next 25 free throws.

4. ③ 4

probability that the next call is for Spencer: $\frac{10}{15} \times 6 = 4$.
Of the next 6 calls, $\frac{2}{3} \times 6 = 4$ are likely to be for Spencer.

5. ① 40%

probability next omelet will be ham:
$\frac{8}{20} = \frac{2}{5} = 40\%$

6. ③ 3

The probability that the next omelet will be cheese is $\frac{4}{20} = \frac{1}{5}$. Of the next 15 omelets, $\frac{1}{5} \times 15 = 3$ are likely to be cheese.

Skill 41 Page 95

1. ① 37°C

$°C = \frac{5}{9}(°F − 32°) = \frac{5}{9}(98.6°F − 32°)$
$= \frac{5}{9}(66.6°) = \frac{333}{9°} = 37°$

2. 72

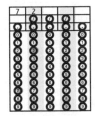

$t = 2(4 \times 3 - 3 \times 2)^2$
$= 2(12 - 6)^2$
$= 2(6)^2$
$= 2(36)$
$= 72$

3. ② 0.9

$i = \sqrt{\dfrac{120}{150}} = \sqrt{0.894\ldots} \approx 0.9$ amps

4. ④ about 71 square inches

surface area $= 2(3.14) \times (1.5)^2 + 3.14 \times 3 \times 6$
$= 6.28 \times 2.25 + 9.42 \times 6$
$= 14.13 + 56.52$
$= 70.65 \approx 71$ square inches

5. ⑤ about 1.2 cubic meters

volume $= 3.14 \times 8 \times (0.5^2 - 0.45^2)$
$= 3.14 \times 8 \times (0.25 - 0.2025)$
$= 3.14 \times 8 \times (0.0475)$
$= 25.12 \times 0.0475 = 1.1932 \approx 1.2$ cubic meters

Skill 42 Page 97

1. ④ $\dfrac{(12 - n)}{5}$

The number of pieces that is shared is represented by the expression $12 - n$.

2. ① $3t + m$

Three days each week, Kitra runs t minutes; this total is $3t$. To $3t$ is added m, the time Kitra runs Saturday.

3. ② $4c - 2$

$4c$ stands for four times the nephew's age. Subtracting 2 from this gives $4c - 2$.

4. ⑤ $\dfrac{m}{n - m}$

The number of men is represented by m; the number of women is represented by $n - m$. The ratio of *men to women* can be written as a fraction with a numerator of m and a denominator of $n - m$.

5. ④ $\left(\dfrac{\$3.88}{n}\right) \times k$

The cost per pound of apples is the rate $\dfrac{\$3.88}{n}$.
To find the total cost of k pounds, multiply this rate (cost per pound) times k.

6. ③ $7^2\pi$

area of the circle $= \pi \times r^2 = \pi \times 7^2 = 7^2 \times \pi = 7^2\pi$
Notice that the times sign ($\times$) does not need to be written in the expression; it is a guide to the eye but is not necessary.

7. ① A and B

Percent means "out of 100 equal parts." The term "n percent" can be written as $\dfrac{n}{100}$ or as $0.01n$ (which is equal to $n \times 0.01$).
Example: 5% can be written as $\dfrac{5}{100}$ or as 0.05.

Skill 43 Page 99

1. ④ $5a - 12 = 92$

a = number of tickets Alan sold
$a - 12$ = number of tickets Cory sold
$3a$ = number of tickets Marco sold
Add: $a + a + 3a - 12$ = total number of tickets = 92, or, $5a - 12 = 92$

2. ② $t = \$30 + \$40n$

home service fee = \$30
charge for working n hours = \$40n
Add: \$30 + \$40n = total (t)
or, $t = \$30 + \$40n$

3. ⑤ $12c = \$32.50 - \$1.75 \times 8$

cost of paper plates = \$1.75 $\times$ 8
cost of paper cups = $c \times 12 = 12c$
cost of cups = \$32.50 − cost of plates
or, $12c = \$32.50 - \$1.75 \times 8$

4. ③ $P = 3(\$350 + s) + 5s$

monthly amount earned by 5 servers = 5s
monthly amount earned by 1 cook = s + \$350
monthly amount earned by 3 cooks = $3(s + \$350)$
Add to find total payroll P:
$P = 3(\$350 + s) + 5s$

5. ③ $n = (1{,}000 - 220) \div 60$

Keisha has \$10.00 − \$2.20 to spend on muffins, each costing 60¢. To find n, the number of muffins Keisha can buy, divide the money she has left to spend by the cost of each muffin. One way to do this division is to write each amount as a number of pennies:
$n = (1{,}000 - 220) \div 60$

6. ① $t = p \times d$

total price = price per pound times number of pounds:
$t = p \times d$

Skill 44 Page 101

1. ③ $6x^2$

   area of triangle $= \frac{1}{2} \times$ base $\times$ height $= \frac{1}{2}(4x)(3x)$
   $= \frac{1}{2}(12x^2) = 6x^2$

2. ⑤ $10s + 8$

   perimeter = sum of the lengths of all four sides
   perimeter $= 2s + (3s + 4) + 2s + (3s + 4) =$
   $10s + 8$

3. ② $6s^2 + 8s$

   area = length $\times$ width $= 2s \times (3s + 4)$
   $= 2s \times 3s + 2s \times 4$
   $= 6s^2 + 8s$

4. ④ $4r^2 - \pi r^2$

   difference in area $= (2r)^2 - \pi \times r^2$
   $= 4r^2 - \pi \times r^2$
   $= 4r^2 - \pi r^2$

5. ⑤ $12y^2$

   area of patio $= 48y \times 16y = 768y^2$ square inches
   area of brick $= 8 \times 8 = 64$ square inches
   number of bricks needed $= 768y^2 \div 64$
   $= (768 \div 64)y^2 = 12y^2$
   Or, you can see that a row of $6y$ blocks ($48y \div 8$)
   can be placed along length of patio. And you can
   see that there are $2y$ rows of blocks ($16y \div 8$).
   number of blocks needed $= 6y \times 2y = 12y^2$

6. ① 80

   number of blocks = volume of box $\div$ volume of
   block
   $= (20n \times 4n \times 8n) \div (2n \times 2n \times 2n)$
   $= 640n^3 \div 8n^3 = 640 \div 8 = 8$
   Or, you can see that a row of 10 blocks ($20n \div 2n$)
   can be placed along the length of the box; a row of
   2 blocks ($4n \div 2n$) can be placed along the width
   of the box; and a row of 4 blocks ($8n \div 2n$) can be
   placed along the height of the box.
   number of blocks needed $= 10 \times 2 \times 4 = 80$

Skill 45 Page 103

1. ② 2, 4, 10, 28, . . .

   Try the rule on each sequence. The rule is true only
   for choice ②.

2. ① multiply by ⁻2 and then add 6

   Try this rule on the sequence, and you will see that
   it predicts each next number; no other rule does.

3. ⑤ $11.50

   Each guest beyond the first person pays $1.75
   for the fundraiser. For a total of 5 people, the total
   cost is $4.50 + ($1.75 $\times$ 4), which is $11.50.

4. ① $33\frac{1}{4}$

   Each day, Harry lays $4\frac{3}{4}$ feet of concrete blocks. To
   find the total length on Friday, add the following:
   $23\frac{3}{4} + 4\frac{3}{4} + 4\frac{3}{4} = 33\frac{1}{4}$.

5. ③ 4

   After 4 years, each job will pay $21,200:
   Cohen: $18,800; $19,600; $20,400; $21,200
   Swanson: $17,600; $18,800; $20,000; $21,200

6. ④ 3

   After 3 years, each car will have the same value:
   Toyota: $8,900; $8,300; $7,700
   Ford: $9,900, $8,800, $7,700

Skill 46 Page 105

1. ②

   Notice, when $s = 0$, $V = 0$. V increases at an
   ever-increasing rate as s increases.

2. ⑤ 3

   For $y = 0$, the term $x - 3$ must be 0, which means
   $x = 3$.
   $(3 - 3)^2 = 0^2 = 0 \times 0 = 0$

3. ④ 4

   When $n = 3$, $z = 6(3) - 23 = 18 - 23 = ^-5$
   When $n = 4$, $z = 6(4) - 23 = 24 - 23 = 1$

4. ⑤ $0°F = 32°C$

   If $°C = 32$, then
   $\frac{9}{5}(32°) + 32° = 89\frac{3}{5}°F$, not $0°F$. Two positive
   numbers never add to give 0.

5. ① $0.75

   A ticket package costs $2.25 and is good for 3 rides.
   So, a single ride costs $2.25 \div 3 = $0.75.

Skill 47 Page 107

1. ⑤ $R = \$485 - \$3n$
This equation agrees with the table:
when $n = 0$, $R = \$485$: $R = \$485 - \$3(0) = \$485$
when $n = 1$, $R = \$482$: $R = \$485 - \$3(1) = \$482$
and so on.

2. ③ $C = \$1.50 + \$1.50n$
This equation agrees with the table:
when $n = 1$, $C = \$3.00$: $C = \$1.50 + \$1.50(1) = \$3.00$
when $n = 2$, $C = \$4.50$: $C = \$1.50 + \$1.50(2) = \$4.50$

3. ⑤ $d = 16t^2$
This equation agrees with the table:
when $t = 0$, $d = 0$: $d = 16(0)^2 = 16 \times 0 = 0$
when $t = 1$, $d = 16$: $d = 16(1)^2 = 16 \times 1 = 16$
when $t = 2$, $d = 64$: $d = 16(2)^2 = 16 \times 4 = 64$
and so on.

4. ② $F = 25¢ + (n - 7) \times 10¢$
This equation agrees with the table:
when $n = 8$, $F = 35¢$: $F = 25¢ + (8 - 7) \times 10¢ = 25¢ + 10¢ = 35¢$
when $n = 9$, $F = 45¢$: $F = 25¢ + (9 - 7) \times 10¢ = 25¢ + 20¢ = 45¢$
and so on.

Skill 48 Page 109

1. $(^-5,^-5)$

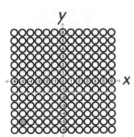

For every point on this line, the x-value is equal to the y-value. This line passes through the origin and has a slope of $+1$.

2. ④ $y = \frac{3}{5}x - 1$
To see which equation is correct, substitute an x-value and y-value of two different points on the line. For each point (value of x and y) the equation is true. For example, if $x = 0$, the point on the graphed line shows a y-value of $^-1$. If you substitute $x = 0$ in the equation you find that the y-value is 1. Try the point $x = 5$, $y = 2$ [the point (5,2)]. This point is on the graphed line and also makes the equation of choice ④ true.

3. ② (2,8)
If $y = 8$, the equation becomes: $8 = 3(x) + 2$, which simplifies to $3x = 6$.
So, $x = 2$ when $y = 8$.
The point is (2,8).

4. $(0,^-4)$

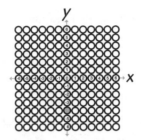

The point where a graphed line crosses the y-axis is called the y-intercept.
The point where a graphed line crosses the x-axis is called the x-intercept.

5. ④ $y = \frac{2}{3}x - 1$
Try substituting $x = 3$ and $y = 1$ in each equation.
Only a true statement results from choice ④:
$1 = \frac{2}{3}(3) - 1 = 2 - 1 = 1$

Skill 49 Page 111

1. ① $x = \frac{1}{2}y + 4$
original equation: $y = 2x - 8$
add 8 to each side: $y + 8 = 2x - 8 + 8$
divide each side by 2: $\frac{y}{2} + \frac{8}{2} = \frac{2x}{2}$
simplify each side: $\frac{1}{2}y + 4 = x$

2. ③ $r = \sqrt{\frac{A}{\pi}}$
original equation: $A = \pi r^2$
divide each side by π: $\frac{A}{\pi} = r^2$
take the square root of each side: $\sqrt{\frac{A}{\pi}} = r$

3. ⑤ $°F = \frac{9}{5}°C + 32°$
original equation: $°C = \frac{5}{9}(°F - 32°)$
multiply each side by $\frac{9}{5}$: $\frac{9}{5}°C = °F - 32°$
add 32° to each side: $\frac{9}{5}°C + 32° = °F$

4. ② between 13 and 14 feet
$s = \sqrt{A} = \sqrt{175} = 13.2$

5. ③ 4%
$i = p \times r \times t$
$r = \frac{i}{p \times t} = \frac{\$210}{\$3,500 \times 1.5} = \frac{\$210}{\$5,250} = 0.04 = 4\%$

6. **②** 3.1

$V = \pi \times r^2 \times h$

$\pi = \dfrac{V}{r^2 h} = \dfrac{124}{2^2 \times 10} = \dfrac{124}{40} = 3.1$

Skill 50 Page 113

1. **①** 2 times the original perimeter
   If each dimension doubles, then the sum of the dimensions also doubles.

2. **①** $\dfrac{6}{5}$

   write the ratio of volumes: $\dfrac{12 \times \cancel{6} \times \cancel{5}}{10 \times \cancel{6} \times \cancel{5}} = \dfrac{12}{10} = \dfrac{6}{5}$

3. **④** $23.00
   payroll increase = total hours worked × $0.25
   92 hours × $0.25 = $23.00

4. **③** 4 times as much
   If the diameter doubles so does the radius.
   If r increases from 1 unit to 2 units, r^2 increases from 1 to 4. The area of a circle quadruples when r doubles.

5. **①** decrease by 60 minutes
   The time changes from 3 hours $\left(\dfrac{120}{40}\right)$ to 2 hours $\left(\dfrac{120}{60}\right)$.
   The time decreases by 1 hour (60 minutes).

6. **②** 95%
   Volume of larger box = $(1.25)^3 \approx 1.95$ yd^3
   Volume of smaller box = $(1)^3 = 1$ yd^3
   95% of 1 = 0.95
   1.95 is 95% larger than 1.

GED Posttest Part 1

1. **①** 0.1
   $1 - (0.4 + 0.125 + 0.125 + 0.25)$
   $= 1 - 0.9 = 0.1$

2. **⑤** 3,100 pounds
   $3 \times (5 - 2)^2 + \sqrt{5^2 + 3^2}$
   $= 3 \times 3^2 + \sqrt{25 - 9}$
   $= 3 \times 9 + \sqrt{16}$
   $= 27 + 4 = 31$
   Answer = 31 hundreds = 3,100

3. **③** $128.70
   $(\$10.40 \times 8) + (1.75 \times \$10.40 \times 2.5)$
   $= \$83.20 + \$45.50$
   $= \$128.70$

4. **④** 50°F
   $35°F - (^-15°F) = 35°F + 15°F = 50°F$

5. **①** $2\frac{2}{3}$ cups
   $8 \times \dfrac{1}{3} = \dfrac{8}{1} \times \dfrac{1}{3} = \dfrac{8}{3} = 2\dfrac{2}{3}$

6. 75%

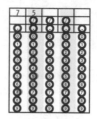

   9 out of 12
   $= \dfrac{9}{12} = \dfrac{9 \div 3}{12 \div 3} = \dfrac{3}{4}$
   $\dfrac{3}{4} \times 100\%$
   $= \dfrac{300\%}{4} = 75\%$

7. **②** $180° - (49° + 43°)$
   The sum of the measures of the three inside angles of a triangle is 180°.

8. **②** decreases 10 beats per minute
   Any 10-year period can be chosen.
   Example: Choose n values of 35 and 45.
   For $n = 35$: $M = 195 - (35 - 25) =$
   $195 - 10 = 185$
   For $n = 45$: $M = 195 - (45 - 25) =$
   $195 - 20 = 175$
   To find the change, subtract: $185 - 175 = 10$

9. $(3, ^-1)$

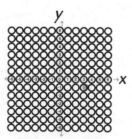

   For a point to be on the line $y = 2x - 7$, the x- and y-values of the point must make the equation a true statement. For an x-value of 3, the y-value is $y = 2(3) - 7 = 6 - 7 = ^-1$ The point is $(3, ^-1)$.

10. **⑤** $\dfrac{\$14.00 - \$11.50}{\$14.50} \times 100\%$

   $\dfrac{\text{difference in price}}{\text{original price}} = \dfrac{\text{original price} - \text{sale price}}{\text{original price}}$

11. ③ $40

The easiest way to solve this problem is to notice that the CD account pays 2% more than the Savings Plus account. In the interest formula, use 2% for the rate and 0.5 year for the time.
$i = \$4{,}000 \times 0.02 \times 0.5 = \$40$
The longer solution is to determine the interest that would be earned by each account and then subtract to find the difference:
CD: $i = \$4{,}000 \times 0.04 \times 0.5 = \$80$
SP: $i = \$4{,}000 \times 0.02 \times 0.5 = \$40$
$\$80 - \$40 = \$40$

12. ④ length = 2.25 ft; width = 2 ft

Try each set of values to see which product equals the given volume: 22.5 cubic feet. $V = l \times w \times h$
Volume = 2.25 ft $\times$ 2 ft $\times$ 5 ft = (4.5×5) ft³ = 22.5 ft³

13. ① $\dfrac{h}{3} = \dfrac{20}{2.5}$

$\dfrac{\text{height of flagpole in feet}}{\text{height of yardstick in feet}} = \dfrac{\text{length of flagpole's shadow in feet}}{\text{length of yardstick's shadow in feet}}$

Remember to write the height of the yardstick in feet.
1 yard = 3 feet

14. $17.64

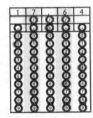

sale price = $24.00 − (30% of $24.00)
= $24.00 − 0.3 × $24.00
= $24.00 − $7.20
= $16.80
total cost = $16.80 + 5% of $16.80
= $16.80 + (0.05 × $16.80)
= $16.80 + $0.84
= $17.64

15. ② 27
$\text{BMI} = \dfrac{703w}{h^2} = \dfrac{703 \times 185}{(70)^2} = \dfrac{130{,}055}{4{,}900} \approx 27$

16. ④ 7

One way to answer this question is to notice that about 55 CDs sell at a price of $16 and about 95 sell at a price of $10. So a $6 price change results in an increase in sales of 40 CDs. You can divide to find the rate of increase:
rate of increase:
$\dfrac{\text{increase in number sold}}{\text{change in price}} = \dfrac{40}{\$6} \approx 7$ per $1,
rounded to the nearest whole number.
[Measuring between two consecutive dollar values gives the same answer, but increases the chance of making an error when reading the graph.]

17. ③ 2 to 1
$\dfrac{\text{number of CDs sold at \$10}}{\text{number of CDs sold at \$16}} = \dfrac{98}{50} \approx \dfrac{2}{1}$

Remember to use the data for the actual number of CDs sold at each price. Do not use the line of best fit for this question.

18. 75

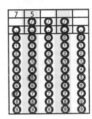

Arrange the sales numbers in order from least to greatest: 50, 60, 72, 75, 80, 90, 98.
The median is the middle value: 75.

19. ③ 16

The path through the park is a hypotenuse of a right triangle. Notice that one side of this triangle has a length of 12 blocks and the other side has a length of 5 blocks. To find the length of the hypotenuse, use the Pythagorean relationship:
hypotenuse = $\sqrt{12^2 + 5^2} = \sqrt{144 + 25} = \sqrt{169} = 13$
Total distance walked = 13 + 3 = 16 blocks

20. ② 22
area of square rug = 10 × 10 = 100 square feet
area of circular rug = π × 5 × 5 ≈ 78.5 square feet
difference in area = 100 − 78.5 = 21.5 ≈ 22 square feet

21.   171

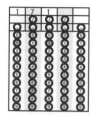

average $= 160 = \dfrac{148 + 161 + 3^{rd}\ score}{3}$

$3 \times 160 = 480$

3rd score $= 480 - 148 - 161 = 332 - 161 = 171$

22.   4%

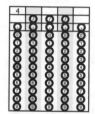

The whole circle graph represents 100%.
less than 5 hours segment equals:
$100\% - (10\% + 27\% + 34\% + 18\% + 7\%)$
$= 100\% - (96\%) = 4\%$

23. ❹   1,105
The 7 hours segment makes up 34% of the whole circle, or 34% of the total number of people responding (3,250).
34% of $3,250 = 0.34 \times 3,250 = 1,105$

24. ❺ $1\frac{3}{8}$ inches
total thickness $= \dfrac{5}{8} + \dfrac{3}{4} = \dfrac{5}{8} + \dfrac{6}{8} = \dfrac{11}{8} = 1\frac{3}{8}$ inches

25.   27

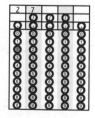

One way to solve this problem is to use a proportion.
$\dfrac{number\ of\ defects}{number\ of\ computers} : \dfrac{6}{265} = \dfrac{n}{1,200}$

Cross multiply: $265 \times n = 6 \times 1,200$
or, $265 \times n = 7,200$.
To solve for n, divide 7,200 by 265.

$n = \dfrac{7,200}{265} \approx 27$

GED Posttest Part 2

26. ❺ $5
savings per can $= \$0.20$
number of cans $= 25$
estimate of savings: $25 \times \$0.20 = \$5.00$

27. ❹   2
0.204 and 0.3 are greater than 0.2.
Comparing decimals is most easily done by giving each the same number of digits to the right of the decimal point:
$0.204 > 0.200$ $0.3 > 0.2$
$0.098 < 0.200$ $0.03 < 0.20$ $0.026 < 0.200$

28. ❸ $\dfrac{9}{16}$
The bits $\dfrac{13''}{32}$, $\dfrac{7''}{16}$, and $\dfrac{1''}{4}$ are each smaller than $\dfrac{1''}{2}$ because in each the numerator is smaller than half of the denominator. The $\dfrac{3''}{4}$ bit $\left(= \dfrac{6''}{8}\right)$ is larger than $\dfrac{5''}{8}$.

29.   12

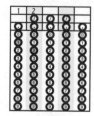

Each chain is 30 inches long.
(1 ft = 12 in.; 2 ft 6 in. = 30 in.)
From each chain, Roberto can make 4 bracelets:
$30 \div 7 = 4$. (2 inches of chain are left over from each piece.)
$4 \times 3 = 12$
Notice that the total leftover chain is 6 inches. This is not enough to make a 13th bracelet.

30. ❷   6,200 meters
Choice ❶ is only 13.7 meters (1 mm = 0.001 m); choice ❸ is greater than 400 miles (1 mi = 1.6 km); choice ❹ is less than one half meter; choice ❺ is 140 meters, the height of a small mountain.

31. ❹ $\dfrac{9}{12 \times 3}$
1 yard = 3 feet = 12 inches $\times$ 3
9 inches is $\dfrac{9}{36}$ yard or $\dfrac{9}{12 \times 3}$ yard.

32. 45

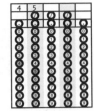

12 tables per hr × 3 hr 45 min

First, write 45 min = $\frac{45}{60}$ hr = $\frac{3}{4}$ hr.

Next, multiply. Note: There are two ways to do this multiplication:

$12 \times 3\frac{3}{4} = 12 \times \frac{15}{4} = \frac{180}{4} = 45$

or, $12 \times 3\frac{3}{4} = (12 \times 3) + \left(12 \times \frac{3}{4}\right) = 36 + 9 = 45$

33. ① 1 inch = 6 feet

1 inch = 6 feet = 2 yards; 7 inches = 14 yards

34. ③ ∠CBE, which has a measure of 140°

Supplementary angles are angles that have a combined measure of 180°. Supplementary angles that are drawn with a common side (an adjacent side) form a straight angle, the same shape as a straight line. In the drawing, ∠ABE is formed by adding ∠ABC and ∠CBE. The measure of ∠ABE is 180°. If ∠ABC is 40°, then ∠CBE is 180° − 40° or 140°.

35. (5,⁻3)

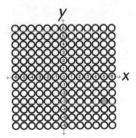

The center of the circle starts at point (2,1). The center point x-value changes by ⁺3; the y-value changes by ⁻4.

(2 + 3, 1 − 4) = (5,⁻3)

36. ② $60

This rate is easily read from the graph. For example, for 2 hours, the charge (solid line) is about $120, which is $60 per hour. The charge for 5 hours is $300, which is $60 per hour.

37. ④ about $50

$300 (Central Auto) − $250 (Auto House) = $50

38. ⑤ Not enough information is given.

The difference in cost depends on the exact time it takes for the work to be done. This time is not given.

39. ① 2,000

Between 1960 and 1980 (a 20-year period), the population of Harney County increased by about 40,000 people: 75,000 − 35,000.

average yearly increase = $\frac{40,000}{20}$ = 2,000 per yr

40. ① $\frac{1}{500}$

The six friends can buy a total of 12 tickets: 2 packs of 5 for $20.00, and 2 individual tickets for $5 each.

Probability of a winning ticket = $\frac{12}{6,000} = \frac{1}{500}$

41. ② Midwest

The circle graph contains this information. The largest segment in the circle represents the greatest population. The Midwest is the largest; the Mountain West is the smallest.

42. ⑤ Mountain West

The bar graph contains this information. The bar graph shows the rate of increase as a percent.

The fraction $\frac{1}{3}$ is equivalent to a percent of $33\frac{1}{3}$%. Mountain West is very close to this value.

43. ③ $\frac{1}{4}$

The probability that Shailan will make her next field goal attempt is assumed to be 18 out of 24 chances, which is written as the probability fraction $\frac{18}{24} = \frac{3}{4}$. The probability she will not make her next field goal attempt is $1 - \frac{3}{4} = \frac{1}{4}$. Or, the probability she will miss is 6 out of 24 chances: $\frac{6}{24} = \frac{1}{4}$.

44. ④ $21.50 + \left(\frac{n}{100} \times \$21.50\right)$

Remember, the sales tax is added to the bill.

total cost = bill + sales tax

= $21.50 + (n% of $21.50)

= $21.50 + $\left(\frac{n}{100} \times \$21.50\right)$

45. ① 2J = $3,280 + $250

Joyce's share (J) + Daffney's share

(J − $250) = $3,280

Write the equation in symbols:

J + J − $250 = $3,280

Combine the Js: 2J − $250 = $3,280

Add $250 to each side: 2J − $250 + $250 = $3,280 + $250

Simplify the left side: 2J = $3,280 + $250

46. **①** 1,500n^2 square inches
Each brick has an area of $2n \times n = 2n^2$ square inches.
There will be 750 bricks used for the patio:
30×25.
total area = $750 \times 2n^2 = 1,500n^2$ square inches

47. **②** $10.50
Notice that as n increases by 1, C increases by $0.60.
Continuing the pattern: $n = 5$, $C = \$7.50$; $n = 6$, $C = \$8.10$; $n = 7$, $C = \$8.70$; $n = 8$, $C = \$9.30$; $n = 9$, $C = \$9.90$; $n = 10$, $C = \$10.50$.

48. **③** $C = \$0.60n + \$4.50$
The table shows that when $n = 0$, $C = \$4.50$.
Each time, n increases by $0.60 plus the cost of C ($4.50).
This equation is a linear equation, the type of equation you are most likely to see on the GED. In a linear equation, each variable is to the 1st power; there are no squared or cubed variables.

49. **③**

The circumference of a circle is given by the formula:
$C = 2 \times \pi \times r$
This formula is another example of a linear equation. The graph of a linear equation is always a straight line. As this formula shows, when $r = 0$, $C = 0$. This means that the graphed line starts at 0. And, as the radius increases, the circumference increases at a constant rate. The slope of the line does not change.
Of the answer choices given, only choice ③ shows a straight-line graph that starts at 0.

50. **⑤** $h = \frac{3V}{s^2}$
The numbers and variables in the formula $V = \frac{1}{3} \times s^2 \times h$ can be rearranged.
First, multiply each side by 3:
$3 \times V = 3 \times \frac{1}{3} \times s^2 \times h$
$3V = s^2 \times h$

Remember, any factor that equals 1 can be dropped. Now divide each side by s^2:
$\frac{3V}{s^2} = \frac{s^2 \times h}{s^2}$
$\frac{3V}{s^2} = h$

Now switch the direction of the rearranged formula:
$h = \frac{3V}{s^2}$

170

Answer Key: Computation Review

Page 133

1. $2\frac{3}{4} = \frac{11}{4}$
2. $5\frac{1}{2} = \frac{11}{2}$
3. $\frac{3}{4} = \frac{12}{16}$
4. $\frac{6}{4} = \frac{12}{8}$
5. $\frac{6}{12} = \frac{1}{2}$
6. $\frac{12}{16} = \frac{3}{4}$
7. $1\frac{8}{16} = 1\frac{1}{2}$
8. $3\frac{6}{8} = 3\frac{3}{4}$

Page 134

1. $\frac{1}{2} + \frac{1}{2} = 1$
2. $\frac{2}{4} - \frac{1}{4} = \frac{1}{4}$
3. $\frac{5}{8} + \frac{1}{8} = \frac{6}{8} = \frac{3}{4}$
4. $\frac{7}{16} - \frac{3}{16} = \frac{4}{16} = \frac{1}{4}$
5. $\frac{1}{4} + \frac{1}{2} = \frac{1}{4} + \frac{2}{4} = \frac{3}{4}$
6. $\frac{1}{9} + \frac{2}{3} = \frac{1}{9} + \frac{6}{9} = \frac{7}{9}$
7. $2\frac{1}{3} + \frac{1}{2} = 2\frac{2}{6} + \frac{3}{6} = 2\frac{5}{6}$
8. $\frac{3}{4} - \frac{1}{2} = \frac{3}{4} - \frac{2}{4} = \frac{1}{4}$
9. $\frac{1}{2} - \frac{3}{16} = \frac{8}{16} - \frac{3}{16} = \frac{5}{16}$
10. $1\frac{1}{2} - \frac{1}{3} = 1\frac{3}{6} - \frac{2}{6} = 1\frac{1}{6}$

Page 135

1. $\frac{2}{3} \times 3 = 2$
2. $\frac{3}{8} \times 2 = \frac{6}{8} = \frac{3}{4}$
3. $\frac{3}{4} \times 2 = \frac{6}{4} = 1\frac{1}{2}$
4. $\frac{2}{3} \times \frac{1}{2} = \frac{2}{6} = \frac{1}{3}$
5. $\frac{1}{8} \times \frac{1}{2} = \frac{1}{16}$
6. $1\frac{1}{3} \times 3 = \frac{4}{3} \times 3 = 4$
7. $2\frac{1}{2} \times 6 = \frac{5}{2} \times 6 = 15$
8. $4\frac{3}{4} \times 4 = \frac{19}{4} \times 4 = 19$
9. $1\frac{1}{3} \times \frac{1}{2} = \frac{4}{3} \times \frac{1}{2} = \frac{2}{3}$
10. $2\frac{1}{2} \times \frac{1}{2} = \frac{5}{2} \times \frac{1}{2} = 1\frac{1}{4}$

Page 136

1. $\frac{5}{8} \div \frac{1}{8} = \frac{5}{8} \times \frac{8}{1} = 5$

2. $\frac{3}{4} \div \frac{1}{4} = \frac{3}{4} \times \frac{4}{1} = 3$

3. $\frac{2}{3} \div \frac{1}{3} = \frac{2}{3} \times \frac{3}{1} = 2$

4. $\frac{1}{2} \div \frac{1}{4} = \frac{1}{2} \times \frac{4}{1} = 2$

5. $\frac{3}{4} \div \frac{1}{16} = \frac{3}{4} \times \frac{16}{1} = 12$

6. $\frac{2}{3} \div \frac{2}{3} = \frac{2}{3} \times \frac{3}{2} = 1$

Page 137

1. $\frac{1}{2} \div \frac{7}{8} = \frac{1}{2} \times \frac{8}{7} = \frac{4}{7}$

2. $\frac{3}{2} \div \frac{3}{4} = \frac{3}{2} \times \frac{4}{3} = 2$

3. $2 \div \frac{1}{2} = \frac{2}{1} \times \frac{2}{1} = 4$

4. $3 \div \frac{1}{3} = \frac{3}{1} \times \frac{3}{1} = 9$

5. $\frac{7}{8} \div 2 = \frac{7}{8} \times \frac{1}{2} = \frac{7}{16}$

6. $\frac{1}{2} \div 4 = \frac{1}{2} \times \frac{1}{4} = \frac{1}{8}$

7. $1\frac{1}{3} \div \frac{1}{3} = \frac{4}{3} \times \frac{3}{1} = 4$

8. $2\frac{1}{2} \div \frac{3}{4} = \frac{5}{2} \times \frac{4}{3} = 3\frac{1}{3}$

Page 138

1. 3 to 5 $= \frac{3}{5}$

2. 1 to 2 $= \frac{1}{2}$

3. 7 to 4 $= \frac{7}{4}$

4. $\frac{4}{8} = \frac{1}{2}$

5. $\frac{16}{4} = \frac{4}{1}$

6. 6 to 9 $= \frac{6}{9} = \frac{2}{3}$

7. 15 to 10 $= \frac{15}{10} = \frac{3}{2}$

8. 5:25 $= \frac{5}{25} = \frac{1}{5}$

9. 32:8 $= \frac{32}{8} = \frac{4}{1}$

Page 139

1. $8n = 48, n = 6$

2. $4x = 60, x = 15$

3. $16n = 16, n = 1$

4. $4m = 100, m = 25$

5. $6y = 180, y = 30$

6. $9p = 180, p = 20$

7. $8r = 24, r = 3$

Page 140

1. $35¢ = 35\%$

2. $8¢ = 8\%$

3. $2¢ = 2\%$

4. $15\% = .15$

5. $6\% = 0.06$

6. $4.5\% = 0.045$

7. $0.61 = 61\%$

8. $0.25 = 25\%$

9. 8%

10. 5.5%

11. $\frac{1}{2} = 50\%$

12. $\frac{3}{4} = 75\%$

13. $\frac{2}{3} = 66\frac{2}{3}\%$

Page 141

1. 4.9

2. 35.6

3. 1.6

4. $3.50

5. 6.4

6. 27.615

7. 6.85

8. $2.11

Page 142

1. 3.72

2. $8.46

3. 3.2

4. 3.22

5. 113.75

6. 6.175

7. $29.75

8. 3.6

9. 3.25

Page 143

1. $12.00

2. 4

3. 12.5

4. $0.28

5. $0.90

Page 144

1. 20%

2. $33\frac{1}{3}\%$

3. 50

4. 64

5. $72

Page 145

1. 5^3

2. 2^4

3. 10^3

4. 6.5^3

5. $\left(\frac{1}{4}\right)^2$

6. $\left(\frac{2}{3}\right)^2$

7. $3 \times 3 \times 3 \times 3$

8. $7 \times 7 \times 7$

9. 2.5×2.5

10. $10 \times 10 \times 10 \times 10 \times 10$

11. 5

12. 7

13. 11

14. 14

Page 146

1. 12

2. 5

3. 5

4. 19

5. $^-15$

6. $^-41$

7. 21

8. $^-4$

9. 20

10. 30

11. $^-4$

12. 33

Page 147

1. 30

2. $^-27$

3. $^-4$

4. $^-24$

5. 50

6. $^-68$

7. $^-5$

8. 4

9. $^-7$

10. $^-2$

11. 3

12. 9

Page 148

1. 5×10^1

2. 1.25×10^2

3. 2.45×10^3

4. 3.5875×10^4

5. 1.64×10^5

6. 2.75×10^6

7. 5×10^{-1}

8. 2.5×10^{-2}

9. 7.5×10^{-4}

10. 400

11. 3,500

12. 5,750

13. 12,500

14. 800,000

15. 0.75

16. 0.09

17. 0.00007

Glossary

acute angle an angle with measure greater than 0° but less than 90°

acute angle

adjacent angles angles that have a side in common and have the same vertex

algebraic expression two or more numbers or variables combined by addition, subtraction, multiplication, or division

angle a figure formed when two rays are joined at a point called the vertex of the angle

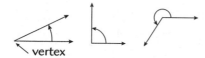
vertex

arc a small curved arrow ⤴ or line ⤸ used to indicate an angle (see *angle*)

area (A) an amount of surface—either within a *two-dimensional figure* or enclosing a *three-dimensional figure* (surface area)

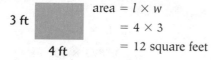

area = $l \times w$
= 4×3
= 12 square feet

- Common area units are square inches, square feet, square yards, square centimeters, and square meters.

associative property grouping does not affect the sum or product of numbers. For example,
$(5 + 6) + 7 = 5 + (6 + 7)$ and
$(2 \times 3) \times 4 = 2 \times (3 \times 4)$

average the arithmetic average (mean), found by adding a set of numbers and then dividing the sum by the number of numbers in the set

- Stacey's scores: 88, 96, 94
- Stacey's average score
$\frac{88 + 96 + 94}{3} = 92\frac{2}{3}$

axes the sides of a graph along which data values or labels are written. In a line graph, the axes are two number lines that intersect at a right angle.

vertical axis
horizontal axis

bar graph a graph that shows data as side-by-side vertical or horizontal bars

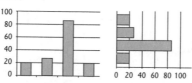
vertical bar graph   horizontal bar graph

base the number that is raised to a power. For example, in 5^2, 5 is the base.

capacity the amount of liquid (such as water) or granular substances (such as flour) that a container can hold

- Common capacity units are fluid ounce, cup, quart, gallon, milliliter, and liter.

Celsius the temperature scale of the metric system of measurement

- 100°C = boiling point of water
- 37°C = normal human body temperature
- 21°C = comfortable room temperature
- 0°C = freezing point of water

circle a plane (2-dimensional) figure, each point of which is an equal distance from the center

center

circle graph a graph that shows data as parts of a divided circle. Each divided part is called a segment or section. The segments add up to one whole or to 100%. A circle graph is also called a pie graph or pie chart.

circle graph

circumference the distance around a circle
Circumference (C) = π × diameter
= π × d
(π ≈ 3.14 or $\frac{22}{7}$)

$C = \pi \times d$ circumference

coefficient a number that multiplies a variable. For example, in the term $3x$, 3 is the coefficient.

column a vertical list of numbers or words that is read from top to bottom

column of numbers	column of words
105	Monday
125	Tuesday
145	Wednesday

common denominator a denominator that is a common multiple of the denominators of two or more fractions. For example, 6 is a common denominator of the fractions $\frac{1}{2}\left(\frac{3}{6}\right)$ and $\frac{1}{3}\left(\frac{2}{6}\right)$.

commutative property the order of numbers does not change the sum or product. For example,
$2 + 3 = 3 + 2$ and $4 \times 5 = 5 \times 4$.

complementary angles angles whose sum has a measure of 90°

∠a and ∠b are complementary angles
∠a + ∠b = 90°

cone a 3-dimensional figure with a circular base and a vertex at a distance (height) above the center of the base

height

congruent having exactly the same shape and size (although the figures may be turned)

congruent rectangles

coordinate plane (also called a *rectangular coordinate system*) a grid made up of perpendicular number lines on which each point is identified by an ordered pair of numbers called *coordinates*

coordinates a set of two numbers that identifies a point on a coordinate plane

- **x-coordinate:** identifies the position of a point along the horizontal axis
- **y-coordinate:** identifies the position of a point along the vertical axis

corresponding angles pairs of matching angles in similar figures. Corresponding angles have equal measure.

Similar Triangles

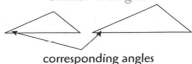
corresponding angles

corresponding sides pairs of matching sides in similar figures. Pairs of corresponding sides are proportional to one another.

Similar Triangles

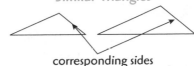
corresponding sides

cross multiply solving a proportion by multiplying the numerator of a ratio times the denominator of the other ratio and setting the *cross products* equal to one another

cross product in a proportion, the product of the numerator of one fraction and the denominator of the other fraction

cube a 3-dimensional shape that contains six square faces. At each vertex, all sides meet at 90° angles.

cube

cylinder a 3-dimensional shape that has both a circular base and a circular top

cylinder

data a group of numbers or words that are related in some way

- **number data:** $1.25, $2.50, $4.00
- **word data:** beef, chicken, fish, pork

decimal a number such as 0.4 or 3.65 that contains a decimal point

degrees (°) a measure of the size of an angle. A circle contains 360 degrees (360°). One-fourth of a circle is a right angle and has a measure of 90°.

denominator the number below the bar in a fraction. In the fraction $\frac{3}{4}$, 4 is the denominator.

diameter the distance from one side of a circle to the other, measured along a line passing through the circle's center.

diameter

distance formula the formula $d = r \times t$ that relates distance (d), rate (r), and time (t). The variables in this formula can be rearranged to write both a *rate formula* and a *time formula*.

rate formula: $r = \frac{d}{t}$

time formula: $t = \frac{d}{r}$

equation a statement that two quantities are equal (have equal value or equal measure)

- **numerical equation:** $25 - 18 = 7$
- **algebra equation:** $x + 12 = 19$
- **geometry equation:** $\angle a + \angle b = 90°$

equilateral triangle a triangle with three equal sides and three angles of equal measure, each 60°

equilateral triangle

equivalent fractions two or more fractions that represent the same number. For example, $\frac{1}{2} = \frac{2}{4} = \frac{3}{6}$

estimate to give an approximate answer by making a reasonable guess based on what you do know

exponent a number that tells how many times the base (of a *power*) is multiplied to find the product

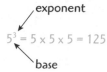

exponent

$$5^3 = 5 \times 5 \times 5 = 125$$

base

extrapolate to estimate a data value that lies outside a given set of values

- **four given data values:** 5, 10, 15, 20
- **extrapolated fifth value:** 25

factor a number that divides evenly into another number, leaving a remainder of 0

Fahrenheit the temperature scale of the U.S. Customary system of measurement

- 212°F = boiling point of water
- 98.6°F = normal human body temperature
- 70°F = comfortable room temperature
- 32°F = freezing point of water

favorable outcome in probability, an event for which you are trying to find the likelihood of occurrence. A favorable outcome may not necessarily be a happy occurrence!

formula a mathematical rule, written as an equation, that tells the relationship between two or more variables. For example, the formula for the area of a circle $A = \pi r^2$ tells the relationship between a circle's area (A) and the circle's radius (r).

fraction part or parts of a whole

- **proper fraction:** a fraction such as $\frac{3}{4}$ in which the numerator is less than the denominator

- **improper fraction:** a fraction such as $\frac{3}{2}$ in which the numerator is greater than the denominator, or a fraction such as $\frac{8}{8}$ in which the numerator equals the denominator

function a relationship in which one value depends on another. Example: $C = 2 \times \pi \times r$ In a circle, the circumference C is a function of the radius r.

histogram a graph that shows the number of times a value or range of values occurs in a set of data

horizontal axis on a graph, the axis running from left to right

horizontal axis

hypotenuse in a right triangle, the side opposite the right angle

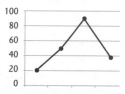

hypotenuse

interpolate to estimate a data value that lies between two given values

inverse operations operations that reverse the effect of each other. For example, addition reverses the effect of subtraction.

isosceles triangle a triangle in which two sides have the same length. The two angles opposite the equal sides have the same measure. The two equal angles are called *base angles*.

isosceles triangle

least common denominator (LCD) the least common multiple of the denominator of two or more fractions (the common denominator for the fractions that has the least value). For example, to compare $\frac{1}{2}$ and $\frac{1}{3}$, the least common denominator is 6: $\frac{1}{2} = \frac{3}{6}$ and $\frac{1}{3} = \frac{2}{6}$

like terms terms that have the same variable raised to the same power. For example, k and $2k$.

linear equation an equation, such as $y = 2x$, that, when graphed, forms a straight line

line graph a graph that displays data as points connected by line segments

line of best fit a line drawn on a graph of data points to show an overall trend in the data. A line of best fit might not pass through any particular data point.

line of symmetry a line that divides a figure into halves that are mirror images of each other

line plot a type of histogram in which data values are represented as dots or Xs placed on or above a number line

mean the *average* of a set of numbers, found by dividing the sum of the set by the number of numbers in the set. (See *average*.)

median the middle number of an odd set of numbers or the mean of the two middle numbers of an even set of numbers

metric system a system of measurement based on the decimal system.

mixed number a whole number together with a proper fraction. Example: $4\frac{1}{2}$

mode the value in a set of data that occurs most often

multiple the product of any number and a whole number. For example, the multiples of 3 are 3, 6, 9, 12, 15, and so on.

negative number a number whose value is less than 0, such as ⁻4, ⁻2.5, and $-\frac{1}{2}$

numerator the number above the bar in a fraction. In the fraction $\frac{3}{4}$, 3 is the numerator.

obtuse angle an angle with measure greater than 90° but less than 180°

obtuse angle

order of operations the order in which expressions are correctly evaluated: numbers within parentheses, powers, multiplication, division, addition, subtraction

ordered pair a pair of numbers, written in parentheses, such as (3,4), that identifies the location of a point on a coordinate plane

- The first number tells the position along the horizontal axis.
- The second number tells the position along the vertical axis.

origin the point at which the x-axis and y-axis intersect in a coordinate system: point (0,0)

outcome in probability, a result or event. When flipping a coin, there are two possible outcomes: heads-up and tails-up.

parallel lines lines that run side by side and never cross

parallel lines

parallelogram a four-sided polygon with two pairs of parallel sides. Opposite sides are equal, and opposite angles have equal measure.

parallelogram

pattern a set of numbers or figures that are in a predictable order, allowing you to determine the next numbers or figures in the set

percent (%) part of 100 equal parts. For example, 5% means 5 parts out of 100 equal parts.

perimeter (P) the distance around a plane (2-dimensional) figure

perpendicular lines lines that intersect at a right angle

perpendicular lines

pi (π) pronounced "pie," the ratio of the circumference of a circle to its diameter

- π is approximately equal to 3.14 or $\frac{22}{7}$

pictograph a graph that displays data as a row or column of symbols

pie chart See *circle graph*

plane figure a two-dimensional figure; a flat figure such as a circle, square, or a triangle. A plane figure has surface but not volume

polygon a two-dimensional closed figure formed by line segments that meet at their endpoints. A *regular polygon* is a polygon in which all sides and all angles are equal. (Equilateral triangles and squares are the two most common regular polygons.)

Polygons

hexagon   regular hexagon

positive number a number whose value is greater than 0, such as $\frac{2}{5}$, 3, and 6.2

power a number raised to an exponent, representing the product of a number multiplied by itself one or more times. For example, 5^3 is "five to the 3rd power."
$5^3 = 5 \times 5 \times 5 = 125$

prime number a whole number greater than 1 that has only two factors, itself and 1

probability the likelihood of something happening or not happening—the ratio of favorable outcomes to total outcomes

proportion two equal ratios. A proportion can be written in words, with colons, or as equal fractions.

- written in words   2 to 3 is equal to 6 to 9
- written with colons   2:3 = 6:9
- written as fractions $\frac{2}{3} = \frac{6}{9}$

protractor a tool for measuring and drawing angles

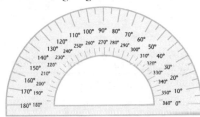

Pythagorean Relationship (theorem) the discovery that in a right triangle the square of the hypotenuse is equal to the sum of the squares of the two remaining sides

Pythagorean Relationship
$c^2 = a^2 + b^2$ $5^2 = 4^2 + 3^2$
or, $\sqrt{25} = \sqrt{16} + \sqrt{9}$

radius the distance from the center of a circle to the circle. The word radius also stands for any line drawn from the center of the circle to any point on the circle.

radius

range for a set of data, the difference between the greatest value and the least value

rate a comparison, using a ratio, of two different units. For example, a speed of 50 miles per hour, a price of $2.89 per pound, a heartbeat rate of 72 beats per minute.

ratio a comparison of two numbers. A ratio can be written in words, with a colon, or as a fraction

- in words   3 to 4
- with a colon   3:4
- as a fraction $\frac{3}{4}$

reciprocal for any nonzero number $\frac{a}{b}$, the reciprocal is the number $\frac{b}{a}$. The reciprocal of $\frac{2}{3}$ is $\frac{3}{2}$.

rectangle a four-sided polygon with two pairs of parallel sides and four right angles. Opposite sides have equal length.

rectangle

rectangular coordinate system See *coordinate plane*

rectangular solid a 3-dimensional figure in which all line segments meet at right angles and all faces are rectangles

rectangular solid

reflex angle an angle with a measure of more than 180° but less than 360°

reflex angle

right angle an angle with a measure of exactly 90°. A right angle is often called a corner angle.

right angle

right triangle a triangle that contains a right angle

right triangle

root the base that corresponds to a given power. For example, the square root of 16 is 4 because $4^2 = 16$; the cube root of 8 is 2 because $2^3 = 8$.

row a horizontal list of numbers or words that is read from left to right across a table

- **row of numbers:** 125, 264, 231
- **row of words:** protein, fat, carbohydrates

scale the ratio of distances on a drawing, map, or model to real-world distances

scale drawing a drawing that is *similar* to the object that it pictures. The dimensions of a scale drawing and the object are proportional.

scientific notation a shorthand way of writing either very small or very large numbers—writing a number as the product of a number between 1 and 10 and a power of 10

- 0.005 is written 5×10^{-3}
- 725,000 is written 7.25×10^5

similar figures figures that have the same shape but not necessarily the same size. Similar polygons have *corresponding angles* and *corresponding sides*.

Similar Rectangles   Similar Triangles

simple interest interest paid on a borrowed or loaned principal, usually expressed as an annual percent rate

simple interest formula formula, $i = p \times r \times t$, used to find the interest (i), earned or paid on a principal (p) after a time (t). The interest rate r is usually written as an annual percent and the time t is given in years.

slope the amount by which a graphed straight line rises or falls in one unit of horizontal distance

solution in algebra, the value of a variable for which an expression has a certain value or for which an equation is true

sphere a 3-dimensional shape, each point of which is an equal distance from the center. A basketball is a sphere.

sphere

square a regular polygon with four equal sides, two pairs of parallel sides, and four right angles

square

square of a number a second number formed by multiplying the first number by itself

$8 \times 8 = \mathbf{64}$ 64 is the square of 8.

square root one of the two equal factors of a number. The symbol for square root is $\sqrt{}$.

$\sqrt{16} = 4$ 4 is the square root of 16.

straight angle an angle that has a measure of exactly 180°, having the shape of a straight line

straight angle

successive events events that happen one after another. Flipping a coin twice in a row is an example of two successive events.

supplementary angles angles whose sum has a measure of 180°

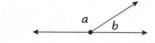
∠a and ∠b are supplementary angles
∠a + ∠b = 180°

table a display of data organized in rows (read from left to right) and columns (read from top to bottom)

three-dimensional figure a figure that has length, width, and height; a figure that has both volume and surface area

cylinder   cube   cone   sphere

trapezoid a four-sided polygon with one pair of parallel sides

trapezoid

triangle a three-sided polygon

triangle

two-dimensional figure a figure that has length, width, and area, but does not have volume. Also called a plane or flat figure.

arrow   square   circle

U.S. Customary system the system of measurement most commonly used in the United States, using such units as inches, feet, pounds, fluid ounces, gallons, and other familiar units not part of the metric system

variable a symbol, often a letter, that is used to represent a number. Examples: x, y, n, r

vertex (plural vertices) the point where two sides of an angle meet or where two sides of a polygon meet

vertical axis on a graph, the axis running up and down

volume the amount of space taken up or enclosed by a three-dimensional object
- **Common volume** units are the cubic foot, cubic yard, cubic centimeter, and cubic meter.

weight a measure of how heavy an object feels when lifted—how much an object weighs
- **Common weight** units are the ounce, pound, ton, milligram, gram, and kilogram.

x-axis the horizontal axis in a coordinate plane, running from left to right

x-coordinate the first number of an ordered pair, telling how far a point is to the right or left on the x-axis

x-intercept the point at which a graphed line intersects the x-axis

y-axis the vertical axis in a coordinate plane, running up and down

y-coordinate the second number of an ordered pair, telling how far a point is above or below on the y-axis

y-intercept the point at which a graphed line intersects the y-axis (the vertical axis)

Index

A
Alternative answer formats, xii–xiii
Algebraic expressions, 96, 98, 100, 110
Angles, 56, 58
Average speed, 78
Area, 62

B
Bar graph, 82, 88
Base, 20, 145, 148

C
Calculator basics, vii–ix
Capacity, 149
Casio *fx-260SOLAR* calculator, viii
Central tendency, 70
Circle graphs, 84, 86, 88
Complementary angles, 56
Coordinate plane, 66
Coordinates, 66
Corresponding angles, 50
Corresponding sides, 50
Cross multiplication, 50, 139
Cross products, 139

D
Decimals
adding, 141
comparing, 16
dividing, 141
estimation with, xi
multiplying, 141
subtracting, 141
word problems, 18, 22
writing as a fraction, 30, 140
writing as a percent, 30, 140
Discount, 32
Drawing, 98, 100

E
Estimation, x, 14, 74
Equations, 98, 104, 106, 108
Equivalent equations, 110
Equilateral triangle, 58
Exponent, 20, 145, 148
Extrapolate, 74

F
Favorable outcome, 90
Formulas, 94, 115
Fractions, 132, 140
adding, 26, 134
comparing, 24
dividing, 28, 135, 136, 137
equivalent fractions, 133, 139
multiplying, 28, 135
simplifying, 133
subtracting, 26, 134
word problems, 26, 28
writing as a decimal, 30
writing as a percent, 30
Functional relationship, 112

G
GED Math Test, iv
Graphing an equation, 104, 108
Grids
coordinate plane grid, xiii
standard grid, xii–xiii

H
Horizontal line, 68
Hypotenuse, 60

I
Improper fractions
as a ratio, 34
Interpolate, 74
Inverse operations, 110
Isosceles triangle, 50

K
Key, 80, 82

L
Length, 149
Least common denominator, 24
Line graph, 78, 80
Line of best fit, 76
Linear equation, 108

M
Median, 70
Mean, 70, 72
Measurement, 44, 54
Metric units, 149
Mixed numbers, 132, 133
computations with, 133–137
estimation with, xi
writing as a decimal, 28
Mode, 70
Mortgage, 82
Multiple line graph, 80
Multiples, 24

N
Number line, 26, 42, 70

O
Outcomes, 90, 92
Order of operations, 20, 94
Ordered pairs, 66, 108

P
Patterns, 102
Percents, 30, 140
percent change, 38
percent statement, 143
writing as a decimal, 140
writing as a fraction, 140
Perfect squares, 145
Powers, 20, 145
Principal, 48
Probability, 90, 92
Proportions, 36, 46, 50, 52, 139
Pythagorean Relationship, 60

R
Range, 70
Rate, 46, 48, 138
Ratio, 34, 138
Root, 20
Rounding, 14

S
Sales tax, 32
Scale, 42, 52
Scale drawings, 52
Scientific notation, 148
Similar figures, 50
Simple interest, 48
Signed numbers, 42, 146–147
Single line graph, 78
Slope, 68
Square roots, 20, 110, 145
Substitution, 104
Supplementary angles, 56

T
Table of Measurements, 149
Table of values, 106
Time, 48, 149
Triangles, 58

U
Unit rates, 46, 138
Units, 40, 44
U.S. Customary units, 149

V
Vertical line, 68
Volume, 64, 112, 149

W
Weight, 149
Whole numbers, xi

X
x-axis, 66
x-coordinate, 66

Y
y-axis, 66
y-coordinate, 66